The Complete Idiot's Command Reference

Files

To	You
Copy a file	Type `cp filename1 filename2`
Delete a file	Type `rm filename`
Identify a file's data type	Type `file filename`
List a file's statistics	Type `ls -l filename`
Move a file	Type `mv filename1 filename2`
View a file	Type `cat filename	more`

Directories

To	You
Change to a directory	Type `cd directory`
Create a directory	Type `mkdir directory`
Delete a directory	Type `rmdir directory`
List a directory's contents	Type `ls -l directory`
Move a directory	Type `mvdir directory`
Print the working directory	Type `pwd`

Getting Help

To	You
Get a manual page	Type `man command`
Get GNU Info pages	Type `info command`
Get manual pages in X	Open an xterm and type `xman` or `man command`
Get quick help	Type `command --help`
Search for manual entries	Type `man -k command`

Searching

To	You
Find commands or binaries	Type `whereis command`
Find files	Type `find . -name "pattern"`
Find patterns in text files	Type `grep pattern file`
Find strings in text files	Type `fgrep string file`
Find text in binary files	Type `strings text file`

Printing

To	You
Cancel a print request	Type `cancel print-job-number`
Get print service status	Type `lpstat`
Paginate and print	Type `pr file`
Send a file to the printer	Type `lp file`

Text Manipulation

To	You
Count lines and words	Type `wc filename`
Cut columns from a file	Type `cut -d delimiter -f list file`
Edit a file with ex	Type `ex filename`
Edit a file with Pico	Type `pico filename`
Edit a file with vi	Type `vi filename`
Find unique lines in a file	Type `uniq filename`
Merge files and fields	Type `join file1 file2 field1 field2`
Sort a file's contents	Type `sort filename`
Spell check a file	Type `spell filename`

Archiving

To	You
Compress a file	Type `compress -fv file`
Create an archive	Type `tar cvf filelist > tarfile`
List compress-file contents	Type `zcat filename`
Uncompress a file	Type `uncompress file`

Shell Metacharacter Reference

Purpose	sh	csh
Command separator	;	;
Execute in background	&	&
Filename metachracters	* ? ~ + - [ ] ! @	* ? ~ [ ]
Group commands	( )	( )
Pipe |	|	
Quoting characters	' " \	' " \
Variable substitution	$	$

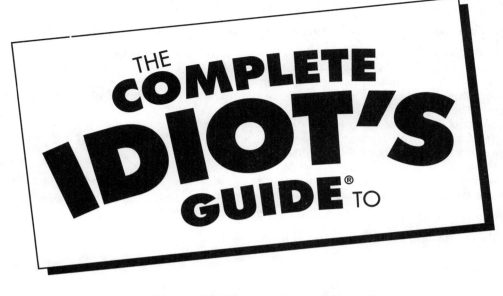

THE COMPLETE IDIOT'S GUIDE® TO

UNIX

Bill Wagner

ALPHA

A Pearson Education Company

The Complete Idiot's Guide to UNIX

Copyright © 1998 by Pearson Education

International Standard Book Number: 0-7897-1805-7

Library of Congress Catalog Card Number: 98-86327

Printed in the United States of America

First Printing: November, 1998

03   02   01   4   3   2

Trademarks

All terms mentioned in this book that are known to be
trademarks or service marks have been appropriately
capitalized. Alpha Books and Pearson Education cannot attest to the accuracy of this information. Use of a
term in this book should not be regarded as affecting
the validity of any trademark or service mark.

Warning and Disclaimer

Every effort has been made to make this book as complete and as accurate as possible, but no warranty or
fitness is implied. The information provided is on an
"as is" basis. The authors and the publisher shall have
neither liability or responsibility to any person or enti-
ty with respect to any loss or damages arising from the
information contained in this book.

Executive Editor
Brad Koch

Acquisitions Editor
Dustin Sullivan

Development Editor
Tom Dinse

Project Editor
Katie Purdum

Copy Editor
Bart Reed

Indexer
Greg Pearson

Proofreader
Jennifer Earhart

Technical Editor
Eric Richardson

Cover Design
Michael Freeland

Layout Technicians
Tim Osborn
Staci Somers
Mark Walchle

Contents at a Glance

Contents

Part III: Working in the UNIX GUI   139

11 Tyrannosaurus X: A Windowing System   141

12 Point and Clique: 151

xiii

Dedication

For Michelle.

Acknowledgements

I would like to acknowledge Dustin Sullivan, Tom Dinse, Eric C. Richardson, and the rest of the Que editing team. Their patience and professionalism far exceeded the call of duty.

Other deserving parties include Marty Rush (system administrator at the MGBS Academic Computing Lab at Pepperdine University), Michael Michaleczko, and the Pacificnet development team.

Finally, I'd like to extend special thanks to David Fugate, my literary agent. There is none better...

Tell Us What You Think!

As the reader of this book, *you* are our most important critic and commentator. We value your opinion and want to know what we're doing right, what we could do better, what areas you'd like to see us publish in, and any other words of wisdom you're willing to pass our way.

We welcome your comments. You can fax, email, or write me directly to let me know what you did or didn't like about this book—as well as what we can do to make our books stronger.

Please note that I cannot help you with technical problems related to the topic of this book, and that due to the high volume of mail I receive, I might not be able to reply to every message.

When you write, please be sure to include this book's title and author as well as your name and phone or fax number. I will carefully review your comments and share them with the author and editors who worked on the book.

E-mail: cigfeedback@pearsoned.com

Mail: Executive Editor
           Alpha Books
           201 West 103rd Street
           Indianapolis, IN 46290 USA

Introduction

Welcome to *The Complete Idiot's Guide to UNIX*! In just a few moments, we'll delve into the inner workings of UNIX. Whether you purchased this book out of sheer curiosity or because your boss foisted UNIX upon you, you'll soon be well on your way to full-fledged UNIX geekdom.

In particular, I've taken pains to demystify UNIX and redeem its undeserved reputation for being difficult to learn. As you'll soon read, UNIX is based on fundamental principles—principles you've probably encountered in Microsoft Windows or Mac OS. (In fact, the technologies on which Windows and Mac OS are based originated with UNIX.)

To get you started, let's look briefly at how this book is constructed.

What's in This Book

This book is broken into seven parts that follow a developmental path. In other words, each part addresses slightly more complex topics than the previous part. The book opens with an explanation of how to boot your system; then it quickly progresses to file manipulation, installation of applications, and finally, system administration.

Let's quickly look at what each section contains.

Part I: Just the Basic Facts

The two chapters in Part I contain the basics, including a description of how UNIX came about, who uses it, and what they use it for. Also included is a special section that covers Linux—the hot, new UNIX-like operating system available for PCs.

Part II: Nuts and Bolts

Part II contains eight chapters that explain how to start a UNIX system and what to expect when you do. UNIX works a little differently than other operating systems because it has more stringent security controls. Beyond this, Part II covers essential topics such as the following:

> ➤ Booting your system
> ➤ Logging in and finding other users
> ➤ Using the various shells
> ➤ Navigating directories and files
> ➤ Searching
> ➤ Opening and editing files

➤ Printing

➤ Installing third-party software

Part III: Working in the UNIX GUI

In the five chapters of Part III, you'll learn about the X Window System (or *X*). X is the standard graphical user interface for UNIX. Topics of interest include the following:

➤ What X is

➤ Manipulating X interface elements

➤ Running applications in X

➤ Cool X programs

➤ Getting help

Part IV: UNIX's Net Worth

Part IV's six chapters examine UNIX and its relation to the Internet. As you may have heard, UNIX has powerful networking capabilities. If you're planning to use UNIX to access the Net, Part IV is for you. It covers all aspects of client networking, including the following:

➤ UNIX and the Net

➤ Email

➤ The World Wide Web

➤ USENET news

➤ Chat systems

➤ Remote terminal sessions and file transfers

Part V: System Administration

Part V provides the minimum information necessary to maintain your UNIX system. Although Part V is by no means exhaustive, it should be enough to get you started. Topics covered in this chapter include the following:

➤ Managing permissions

➤ Adding users

➤ Assigning groups

Part VI: Troubleshooting

Refer to Part VI whenever disaster strikes. (Just kidding.) The chapters in Part VI cover many mistakes you'll make and error messages you'll encounter. This is an important section because UNIX error messages are quite often cryptic. Here you'll find the following items:

➤ A discussion of common mistakes and how to avoid them

➤ An error message table

Part VII: Reference

Finally, the appendixes in Part VII cover a wide range of commands and techniques for getting things done. Points of interest include the following:

➤ A command reference containing 94 common UNIX commands and examples of how to use them

➤ An online resource directory of WWW sites with hundreds of cool utilities and tutorials on maintaining and running a UNIX system

➤ A glossary titled "Speak Like a Geek: The UNIX Bible," which demystifies the many terms you'll encounter in this book (as well as in UNIX in general)

Because of this book's design, you can use it either as a reference (reading isolated sections whenever you're stuck) or as a general UNIX primer.

If this book has any advantage over its competitors, it's this: Many beginner books describe only basic commands and their barest usage. For example, authors explain how to start an editor but not how to use it. This approach is quite ineffective (and it's particularly ineffective when discussing a complex operating system such as UNIX).

In contrast, *The Complete Idiot's Guide to UNIX* provides practical and detailed examples of the commands discussed. This way, when you start a UNIX application, you're not hung out to dry.

What Are You Looking At?

When reading this book, you'll encounter several different fonts. These fonts are used to demonstrate commands, system output, and variables. Here are the fonts and what they mean:

➤ Standard output (output from UNIX) appears in `monospace` font.

➤ Commands appear in **`monospace bold`** font.

➤ Placeholders appear in *`italic monospace`* font.

➤ New terms appear on *italic* font the first time they're used.

➤ The ➥ icon indicates that a code line has wrapped. Certain lines are so long that they won't fit on a printed page. Therefore, when typesetting this book, the printers are forced to wrap the line (that is, extend part of it to the next line).

One More Thing

Every effort has been made to provide the very widest treatment of the UNIX operating system. On that account, the information in this book is largely generic and therefore applicable to nearly all UNIX flavors.

In rare instances, however, I discuss commands that are available only on certain UNIX platforms. Whenever I discuss such commands, I clearly indicate on which platforms the commands will work. (Typically, these commands are Linux centric.)

In closing, I hope you find this book useful and informative. With that said, let's get started. We'll begin with the question a lot of folks have been asking lately: What is UNIX, anyway?

Part 1

Just the Basic Facts

You've picked up this book, so presumably you have a need to know what UNIX is and just what you'll be dealing with. This beginning section is just the place to show you that, while UNIX can seem intimidating to new users, it doesn't have to overwhelm you.

Chapter 1 explains what UNIX is, shares a little of its history, and tells you just what it's good for. Chapter 2 breaks down the different versions of UNIX that are available, lists the kinds of computer equipment you'll need to run them, and finally shows you where (and how) you can get your own copy of UNIX. So if you're ready, take off your coat and let's get started!

I Thought UNIX Lived in Harems

In This Chapter

➤ Learn what UNIX is

➤ A brief history of UNIX

➤ Learn what UNIX is good for

It happens in offices all over the world and has probably happened in yours: Folks gather around the water cooler and share war stories about their operating systems. "Last week, my registry got corrupted and I had to reinstall Windows." "Oh Yeah? That's nothing. I booted my Mac yesterday and the Control Panels disappeared!" The tales get taller and taller and then suddenly, a soft-spoken guy walks up and says he uses UNIX. The room falls silent. Beads of sweat appear on the brows of your coworkers, who scurry away, muttering under their breath. In that moment, even if you never tried UNIX, you feel like a complete idiot.

Rest easy. The truth is, UNIX isn't nearly as difficult to learn as its reputation would suggest. Oh, it has its quirks, like any operating system. However, UNIX is based on fundamental principles. So, let's start with a few of those fundamentals right now.

What Is UNIX?

UNIX can be different things to different people. For example, ask a geek what UNIX is, and you'll get an answer like this:

UNIX is a 32- or 64-bit, highly portable, multiuser, multitasking operating system with a hierarchical file system based on abstract file descriptors, logical partitioning, compatible file, device, and interprocess I/O, asynchronous processing, copious subsystems, a complete suite of TCP/IP clients and servers, and multiple command language interpreters.

That makes perfect sense, right? Sure it does. What the geek is really trying to say is this:

➤ UNIX is fast.

➤ UNIX is powerful.

➤ UNIX can accommodate many users simultaneously.

➤ UNIX can manage many tasks simultaneously.

➤ UNIX is the ideal system for accessing the Internet.

At its most basic, UNIX is an operating system, very much like Mac OS or Microsoft Windows NT. UNIX manages the day-to-day operation of your computer and provides you with a wide range of services, including data storage and data transfer.

To better illustrate what UNIX is (and its various uses), I offer a little UNIX history.

A Brief UNIX History

UNIX has ancient roots. In 1964, MIT, General Electric, and Bell Labs (then a division of AT&T) collaborated to create a new operating system. It was called the Multiplexed Information and Computing System or *MULTICS*. The MULTICS project, I am sorry to say, was a complete disaster. MULTICS was large, unwieldy, and worst of all, buggy.

Despite that early failure, good things emerged from the MULTICS project. Ken Thompson (a programmer from Bell Labs) felt that he could do better. And, with assistance from fellow programmers Dennis Ritchie and Joseph Ossanna, Thompson did just that.

The year was 1969. Marvin Gaye had a hit single (*I Heard it Through the Grapevine*), we were at war, and if you were cool, you were driving a Dodge Charger. It was against this backdrop that Thompson did his work.

Thompson's first version of UNIX was shaky at best, but that quickly changed. UNIX was rewritten in the C programming language a year later. The result was a quicker, more stable operating system.

What happened next was critical. In the early 1970s, UNIX was distributed to universities. There, students and educators alike found UNIX practical, versatile, and easy-to-use. UNIX was therefore incorporated into the basic computer science curriculum. As a result, an entire generation of computer science graduates had UNIX experience. When they took that experience to the marketplace, they brought UNIX into the mainstream.

However, the events that made UNIX the world's most popular networked operating system occurred elsewhere. At the time, the U.S. government was bent on establishing an internetwork for wartime communication. This network was designed to be impervious to a Soviet first nuclear strike.

At the time, the concept was revolutionary. Most networks then being used were centralized. Mainframes housed centralized data that was doled out to terminals here and there. Because of this centralization, if our enemies knocked out a mainframe, they could incapacitate an entire network.

To remedy this, researchers studied ways to create a network where all workstations could communicate with one another. And, through a theory they dubbed *data redundancy*, those

There's Safety (or at Least Popularity) in Numbers

Several other factors contributed to UNIX's popularity, the most important of which was this: UNIX was a network operating system. Thus, several users could access a UNIX system simultaneously. This made it ideal for academic and business environments where folks shared printers and other resources.

workstations each had access to the same information. Hence, if the Soviets knocked out one, ten, or one hundred servers, it still wouldn't matter; the network would continue to operate.

The idea looked good on paper, but there was a problem: Although the government had a conduit for electronic communication (the telephone system), it had no operating system to match. Enter UNIX.

Engineers working on the internetwork chose UNIX as their operating system based on several factors. First, by then, (roughly 1974), UNIX already had powerful networking capabilities. For example, thanks to Ray Tomlinson of Bolt, Beranek, and Newman, UNIX already had an electronic mail system. Other networking services and protocols would soon follow, and by 1978, UNIX was jam-packed full of networking software. So, the U.S. government got its internetwork after all. (In those days, the network was called the Advanced Research Projects Agency Network or ARPAnet. Today, we call it the Internet). From these modest beginnings, then, UNIX became a phenomenon.

Because the Internet was a government project, UNIX had to adhere to certain standards. Hence, throughout its history, UNIX has been standard-based, and this has only increased the operating system's popularity. Between 1978 and 1998, nearly every major computer company developed their own version of UNIX. (Microsoft even gave UNIX a spin, creating Microsoft XENIX. However, the software giant couldn't make a buck. Bill Gates therefore changed his focus to the desktop market. That was 17 years and $50 billion dollars ago.)

Since then, UNIX has gone through many changes. Today, there are millions of UNIX users in dozens of different fields. Let's briefly examine those fields now.

UNIX was the Internet and the Internet was UNIX

Here's a fact: It's estimated that even in 1990, better than 90 percent of all Internet servers were running UNIX. (VAX/VMS, an operating system developed by Digital Equipment Corporation, trailed close behind.) Today, however, Microsoft Windows NT has made substantial inroads in this area. Most information managers find that NT is a suitable Web server platform. Therefore, UNIX's monopoly on Web servers has dwindled considerably, though it still accounts for almost half of all Web servers.

Getting the Bugs Out

How many UNIX boxes does it take to create an alien insect race? Ask Tippett Studio, the company that provided special effects for *Starship Trooper*. They reportedly used 130 Silicon Graphics workstations. (Compare that with the 400 UNIX workstations that Digital Domain used to sink the Titanic. Amazingly, 100 of those machines were running Linux, a free version of UNIX. More on Linux in Chapter 2, "UNIX Flavors.")

What Is UNIX Good For?

You might have heard that UNIX is for super-nerds, and, to a limited degree, that's true. UNIX is often used for scientific research and in highly technical fields. (For example, UNIX sent Pathfinder to Mars.)

However, UNIX is also used for other tasks. For example, UNIX offers precision math and graphics, and therefore, it's a favorite of the film industry. (Here's a little known fact: It wasn't an iceberg that sank James Cameron's *Titanic*; it was UNIX.) In fact, UNIX was used to generate eye-popping special effects in all the following films:

➤ *Starship Trooper*
➤ *Jurassic Park*
➤ *The Mask*
➤ *Toy Story*

George Lucas (the creator of *Star Wars*) is also a big UNIX fan. Interviewers often ask Lucas why he chooses Silicon Graphics UNIX machines over cheaper hardware and software. His answer is simple: He has enjoyed exceptional success with UNIX so why should he switch?

Beyond the film industry, UNIX is used for statistical analysis, aeronautics design, astrophysics, artificial intelligence, war simulation, medical imaging, global positioning, satellite tracking, and even DNA research.

So, does this mean you have to be a geek to use it? No way. In fact, you can also use UNIX to perform many everyday tasks, including the following:

➤ Text and word processing
➤ Accounting and general record keeping
➤ Playing games
➤ Cruising the Net
➤ Establishing your own Web server

UNIX, therefore, is good for any task that demands precision computing. However, UNIX truly excels in one special area: *networking*. No operating system is more suited to this purpose. Whether you're creating a local area network (LAN) or building a Web server, UNIX is an excellent choice. It's exceptionally stable and designed to handle high-speed network traffic flawlessly.

In particular, UNIX is now being used for intranets. (These are small networks that run on Internet protocols. You can use an intranet to create a miniature version of the World Wide Web inside your company.) Intranets save corporations thousands of dollars, and UNIX is largely responsible for that.

So, if all this is true, why does UNIX have such a bad reputation? Why do people insist that UNIX is impossible to learn?

How Did UNIX Get Such a Bad Reputation?

Many people claim that UNIX is simply not user-friendly and until recently, that was true enough; UNIX has traditionally been more difficult to learn than Mac OS or Microsoft Windows. The reason for this disparity lies in UNIX's development history.

Before You Decide to Make Another Jurassic Park

Can you generate those same, awesome special effects? Maybe and maybe not. Not all UNIX workstations or distributions are intended for intense graphics. Primarily, high-power graphics are generated on SGI workstations, machines that ship with special software and hardware specifically designed for the film industry. (These software packages cost thousands of dollars.) However, given the right hardware and software, yes...you too could generate absolutely stunning graphics. To check out Silicon Graphics and its awesome workstations and software, go to its World Wide Web site at `http://www.sgi.com`.

In the past, UNIX developers were concerned solely with functionality. Appearances simply didn't matter. In contrast, Apple and Microsoft spent millions of dollars ascertaining how to make computing a more pleasurable experience. For example, Mac OS is designed so that application menus melt into the general menu bar at the top of your screen. Similarly, Windows applications have a standardized look. The menu bar invariably has choices such as File, Edit, View, Help, and so on. These characteristics make Mac OS and Windows exceptionally easy to learn. Many authors have remarked that if you know one Windows application, you know them all.

In contrast, most tasks in UNIX can be completed in a command-line interface or CLI. In fact, to effectively use UNIX, you must have at least minimal experience with a CLI.

Command-line interfaces differ sharply from graphical user interfaces (GUI, pronounced "gooey".) GUIs display menus with various options. You use your mouse to choose these options. After you choose an option, the GUI articulates the complete command for you and relates that command to the underlying operating system. In

The Command-Line Interface

A *command-line interface* (CLI) is a computing environment where you type your commands (instead of using a mouse). This is also sometimes referred to as a text interface.

Stupid UNIX Pet Tricks

Here's a simple task that would take forever in Microsoft Windows or Mac OS:

1. Open 10 files.

2. Grab the first 20 and last 30 lines of each file.

3. Close the files but keep the 500 lines of text you grabbed.

4. Scan those 500 lines of text for a specific sentence.

5. If your scan finds that sentence, it executes a command.

In a GUI, it would take you a minimum of 40 clicks just to get the 500 lines of text. In UNIX, you can complete this entire task with a single command-line.

contrast, in a command-line interface, you formulate commands on your own and relate these to the operating system using your keyboard.

At first glance, you might conclude that a GUI offers you more flexibility and more power, and for some tasks, that's true. (This is particularly true with respect to desktop publishing.) However, for most general tasks, the UNIX CLI offers you far more power than any GUI. You simply have to know how to use it.

However, you no longer have to sacrifice user-friendliness for UNIX functionality. In the past few years, the general public has gravitated toward UNIX. In response, UNIX developers have incorporated user-friendliness into the operating system. As you'll discover in Chapter 11 "Tyrannosaurus X: A Windowing System," modern UNIX is extremely user-friendly and supports several windowing systems. So, in essence, UNIX is now no more difficult to use than Microsoft Windows.

Can I Run UNIX?

Can you run UNIX? Absolutely. Today, UNIX supports widely diverse hardware. However, this wasn't always the case. Not so long ago, most commercial UNIX distributions ran on *workstations*. Workstations are proprietary computers specifically designed to run UNIX. These machines often contain special hardware that renders exceptionally high performance. (For example, machines used on *Jurassic Park* have a proprietary graphics chip. This chip can perform calculations extremely fast, and therefore, graphics generated with it are smooth and fluid.)

Here are some examples of modern workstations:

➤ **The Indigo product family by SGI.** Indigos are manufactured by Silicon Graphics, Inc. and are most commonly used in the film or graphics industries. Indigos are very stylish and easily distinguished from other computers. Most are deep purple, indigo, or green, and their cases sport sleek, sharp geometric shapes.

➤ **The SPARCstation by Sun Microsystems.** SPARCstations are famous for their "pizza box" design. The main processing unit is housed in a case that has dimensions similar to a pizza box; they are small, sleek, and designed to slip neatly into racks. Many Internet service providers use these racks to house hundreds of "headless" workstation or workstations without monitors.

➤ **The Digital Alpha by Digital Equipment Corporation.** Alphas are compact workstations that pack a wallop, offering 64-bit, 500+MHz performance, and 3D graphics.

➤ **PC-based workstations.** In recent years, PCs have also entered the picture. PCs offer significant bang for your buck in terms of processor speed and memory. Based on these factors, there are now many PC versions of UNIX.

A Window to the Past

Strange but true: Of all the windowing systems ever created, Microsoft Windows is the most popular. However, Microsoft didn't invent windowing systems and neither did Apple. Xerox did. In 1972, researchers at Xerox's famed PARC Place Laboratory created the Xerox Alto. It was the first computer to use a GUI/mouse combination. Both Microsoft and Apple based their windowing systems on Xerox's research, though Apple waited some 10 years before warming up the idea. (In fact, nearly all windowing systems—including UNIX's—are distant descendants of Xerox's system.)

The problem is, workstations have always been cost-prohibitive for the casual user. For example, in 1989, a Sun Microsystems SPARCstation could cost as much as $55,000 and that was just for hardware. UNIX software licensing was also an expensive affair. (Until recently, even development packages for UNIX cost thousands of dollars.) This was a significant deterrent to casual users.

Well, that was then and this is now. Today, UNIX runs on a wide variety of inexpensive chips, including the Intel (X86), Alpha, PowerPC, FIPS, MIPS, and RISC. Furthermore, the expense of software licensing is no longer an issue. Many UNIX distributions are either free or almost free, allowing the mainstream public to enjoy workstation performance at a fraction of the price.

General System Requirements

System requirements for UNIX vary. If you run UNIX in CLI only, you need meager resources. (Technically, you can get along with a 25MHz processor, 2MB of RAM, and a 60MB hard disk.) However, if you intend to use a UNIX GUI, (and avoid pulling out your hair), I recommend a 100MHz processor, 32MB of RAM, and a 500MB hard disk or better.

What Do I Get When I Purchase UNIX?

Most UNIX distributions come with a wide range of programs and resources, including the following

➤ Text processing and editing tools

➤ Programming tools

➤ Internet tools

➤ Tools to manipulate graphics

➤ Help documentation and examples

In this respect, commercial UNIX distributions differ little from Microsoft Windows or Mac OS. Bundled applications include a notepad, a calculator, a personal calendar, a graphics viewer, a CD player, and so on.

Similarly, basic UNIX installations include a help system. Help documentation can generally be accessed in both plain and hypertext text.

What Is Hypertext?

Hypertext is a text display format commonly used on Web pages. Hypertext is distinct from regular text because it's interactive. In a hypertext document, when you click or choose any highlighted word, other associated text appears. This allows powerful cross-referencing and permits you to navigate a document. Help documentation displayed with hypertext is therefore extremely user-friendly. If you ever cruised the World Wide Web, you're probably an expert at navigating hypertext—and you just don't know it. Every time you click a link for a Web page, you're navigating hypertext.

Most proprietary UNIX systems also come with on-board sound and Ethernet. (A good number also include on-board ISDN. However, that's becoming less and less prevalent. When it first emerged, ISDN seemed like a great solution for high-speed Internet access. Since that time, other technologies have emerged that offer much higher transfer rates at much lower prices. One good example is Asynchronous Digital Subscriber Lines or ASDL.)

Finally, as you'll learn in Chapter 11, UNIX windowing systems work much like other windowing systems, with a little extra functionality. In fact, the learning curve in UNIX windowing systems is short if you ever used Mac OS or Microsoft Windows.

Is UNIX Compatible with Other Systems?

UNIX is highly compatible with other systems. In fact, most commercial UNIX distributions have servers for Novell NetWare, Microsoft Windows 95 and NT, and even AppleTalk. In addition, UNIX interfaces seamlessly with a number of commercial and noncommercial database packages including Oracle, Informix, CA Unicenter, and common Ingres.

Additionally, some versions of UNIX can read (or in certain cases, execute) files created on other operating systems. For example, most commercial UNIX distributions support files created in MSDOS, and there is even technology that allows you to run Microsoft Windows applications in UNIX.

What Are Some Advantages of Using UNIX?

One major advantage of using UNIX is that you can reduce your total cost of ownership or **TCO**. TCO is the total amount a computer will cost you in its lifetime. (Machines don't really have lifetimes, of course. At least, not that we know of. We just use that term as a reference. The "lifetime" of a machine ends when the machine blows up, shuts down, or otherwise becomes permanently inoperable.)

If you used computers for any length of time, you're familiar with the upgrade game. This is a game where your software vendors update their software every year or so. When they do, they make certain that previous versions are rendered obsolete (because they can't decode documents or files created by the new version). Therefore, you're forced to purchase the upgrade. The game is good and has made software vendors billions of dollars. (By far, the world heavyweight champion of the upgrade game is Microsoft.)

In the UNIX world, things work a little differently. For the most part, big UNIX customers are the government, Internet service providers, and universities. These folks don't like the upgrade game. When they purchase an operating system, they want that operating system to change as little as possible. Hence, UNIX vendors generally ensure stability and longevity in their product lines. This leads to cost savings for you.

PCs for Under $1,000? Not!

What's the average TCO of a PC? According to Gartner Group (an industry authority), your PC will cost you approximately $9,784 before it dies. This figure encompasses all the following costs: purchase, administration, technical support, upgrades, and repair. (What that figure doesn't account for is lost productivity. Some studies suggest that office productivity drops as much as 200 percent when a PC is introduced.)

UNIX also has other advantages. One is that UNIX can perform most tasks with fewer resources than other operating systems. For example, suppose you want to establish a mail server on your office network. You can throw UNIX on an old 486 with 8MB of RAM and you're good to go. In contrast, Windows NT won't even install on a machine with less than 12MB of RAM.

Finally, UNIX has one last advantage. The UNIX community has always been just a little radical. It has a long-standing history of taking commercial applications and making free clones. Therefore, on the Internet, you can gain access to literally thousands of free programs that perform as well (or sometimes better) than commercial applications.

15

What About Commercial Applications?

Many software vendors develop versions of their commercial applications for UNIX. Thus, many applications common to Windows and Mac OS are also available for UNIX, including the following:

- ➤ Adobe PhotoShop
- ➤ Microsoft Word
- ➤ WordPerfect
- ➤ CorelDraw
- ➤ Microsoft Internet Explorer
- ➤ Netscape Navigator and Communicator

Furthermore, the Java programming language, (a new innovation from Sun Microsystems), is helping to close the operating system gap. Developers are now writing applications in Java that run on all platforms. (This might help to quell the operating system wars currently raging on the net. At present, users bitterly debate which operating system is the best.)

So, What's the UNIX Bottom Line?

The UNIX bottom line can be reduced to this: About two weeks before I started writing this book, I was at a stoplight. The car in front of me had a personalized license plate and this is what it said: UNIXROX.

That says it all.

The Least You Need to Know

The very least you need to know is this:

- ➤ UNIX is powerful, fast, and great for networking.
- ➤ UNIX is now more user-friendly.
- ➤ You can easily learn UNIX.
- ➤ This book will help you learn UNIX quickly and painlessly.

That said, let's quickly examine several UNIX distributions and the differences between them.

## Chapter 2

UNIX Flavors

> **In This Chapter**
>
> ➤ The different versions of UNIX and who makes them
>
> ➤ The chips these versions run on
>
> ➤ Where to get UNIX

It's been almost 30 years since UNIX was invented, and during this time it has undergone many changes. Today, well over a dozen versions (or flavors) of UNIX are available. This chapter briefly addresses the flavors you'll most likely encounter.

Can't We All Just Get Along?

You only need to speak with a few computer users to recognize this: they're very cliquish. Every user thinks that his or her operating system is the best. In fact, on the Internet, this debate has sparked extensive ideological wars. (For many folks, computer use isn't just a hobby—it's a way of life.)

Typically, ideological lines are drawn along system architectures. Eloquent Internet warriors often coin slogans or stock phrases to sum up their feelings about this or that operating system: "Macs rule and PCs drool" and "WinDoze sucks." The derogatory comments are as endless as they are colorful.

In the operating system wars, however, the strangest participants are UNIX users. Here's why: In addition to warring with Mac, Windows, and OS/2 users, UNIX advocates also war with themselves. You see, all the various flavors of UNIX are different. In this chapter, I'll attempt to explain the rather convoluted world of UNIX flavors.

The Great Divide

When engineers at Bell Labs first created UNIX, they had no idea it would become so popular. Hence, AT&T released UNIX (with source code) to the academic community free of charge.

However, in 1978 (or somewhere thereabouts), AT&T took a different view. UNIX was quite popular by then and was worked into computer science curriculums around the country. It was therefore a commercially viable product, and AT&T could see no good reason not to charge for it.

Well, the folks at the University of California at Berkeley had different plans. First, they felt that AT&T's UNIX simply wasn't user friendly. Second, this business of paying licensing fees to AT&T was for the birds. Based on these factors, Berkeley students undertook an ambitious project. They decided to roll their own UNIX, and that's exactly what they did. (Those Berkeley folks were always just a little bit radical.)

Armed with the original AT&T source code, programmers at Berkeley rewrote UNIX from the ground up, replacing more than 90 percent of the original code with their own. They dubbed this new UNIX *Berkeley Software Distribution* (or *BSD*).

From that point on, UNIX was a two-system world. Either you used AT&T or BSD. Or, more accurately, after years of both systems being developed, either you used Sys V (AT&T) or BSD.

Differences Between Sys V and BSD

What are the major differences between Sys V and BSD? Actually, a better question is this: Do you really need to know what these differences are? Not really, but for sake of completeness, I'll briefly describe the differences here.

The chief differences are these:

➤ They use different booting systems.

➤ Accounting is done a bit differently.

➤ The printing systems vary (as do the ports to which printing requests are routed).

➤ In some cases, the file system structures vary slightly.

Also, commands that do essentially the same thing in Sys V as in BSD may have different names (but that's really a minor difference). In all other respects, however, unless you start programming, these UNIX versions work in much the same way. In this book, wherever a task can be done with two commands, I describe both. In other words, this book will prepare you equally for Sys V and BSD systems.

One Last Thing

In the following pages, you'll read that some versions of UNIX are even more unique because they conform to certain standards. I'll briefly mention those standards here.

What's a standard? Well, it's exactly what it sounds like: an agreed-upon system by which all concerned parties conduct their computing. Standards are an important part of the business world and here's why: Without them, large-scale automation cannot be achieved. To understand why, consider this: In Electronic Data Interchange (EDI), machines communicate with one another without human interaction. Through EDI, many billing and procurement tasks are performed automatically.

The reason that such systems work is because all machines engaged in EDI speak the same language. If they didn't, the data would get mangled. In a similar fashion, most Internet applications conform to certain standards. Those standards govern how communication is conducted across TCP/IP-based networks.

Such standards are machine- and network-based, and the rules that govern them are built into applications. However, there are still other standards that are less specific and more sweeping in scope. In the UNIX world, one very important standard (the Portable Operating System Interface or POSIX) measures whether a system is portable or not.

Portable is a term that describes any system or software that can easily be migrated to another architecture. For example, if you can take a program from a SYS V UNIX system and easily rework it to run on a BSD-based system, that program has *portability* (that is, it can be ported from SYS V to BSD).

Portability is important, particularly to government agencies because they don't want to be tied to any particular hardware or software. (For example, you can't take software written for Microsoft Windows and run it on a Mac.) Instead, they want to have the option of terminating any vendor's contract at will. For this reason, government agencies favor POSIX-compliant software. This way, when their programmers write additional code for such systems, it can easily be integrated system wide, no matter what operating system they migrate it to.

Standards don't stop with POSIX, though. Standards exist for everything, including styles of programming. For example, the American National Standards Institute (ANSI) has developed a standard for programming in the C programming language. It's called—you guessed it—ANSI C.

Therefore, in addition to the division of UNIX flavors by SYS V versus BSD, many UNIX flavors also differ in the various standards they support. A good example is the Federal Information Processing Standards (FIPS), which govern the way documents and encryption processes are conducted. (Even international standards exist, making things even more confusing.)

The UNIX family tree is rich in standards, but the bottom line is still this: UNIX systems are based on either Sys V or BSD. Let's take a look at these systems now.

The UNIX Family Tree

This next section covers UNIX flavors you're likely to encounter, the hardware they run on, and their respective place on the UNIX family tree.

A/UX

Apple Computer, Inc.
1 Infinite Loop
Cupertino, CA 95014
http://www.apple.com

Yes, you read this correctly. Apple Computer produced a version of UNIX, and a good one, too. A/UX was publicly launched in February, 1988 and was designed to run on Mac II systems. The system was based largely on AT&T UNIX system V.2.2 (with some BSD extensions) and included the Bourne, Korn, and C shells. (See Chapter 5, "Surviving Shell Shock," to learn about shells.) What's more, A/UX came with a version of MIT's X Window System. In all, it was a very complete release and brought the power of UNIX to the Mac.

Today, more powerful and glamorous versions of UNIX for Mac are available (as you'll see momentarily.) However, A/UX still has many supporters.

AIX

International Business Machines (IBM)
P.O. Box 12195
Research Triangle Park, NC 27709
http://www.ibm.com

AIX runs on both RS/6000 and PowerPC systems and was initially more BSD-based than AT&T-based. That has since changed. Modern AIX is best described as a combination of both BSD and AT&T UNIX, with many standards thrown in. AIX conforms at least marginally—and in many cases, stringently—to Federal Information Processing, POSIX, and ANSI standards.

BSD and Its Variants

Berkeley Software Design, Inc.
5575 Tech Center Drive, #110
Colorado Springs, CO 80918
http://www.bsdi.com

The Computer Systems Research Group (CSRG) at UC Berkeley originally developed BSD, first starting with code from AT&T UNIX and then later rewriting some 90 percent of the operating system. This early BSD was distributed to various sources, and along that road, AT&T ultimately brought suit. (Since that time, pure BSD distributions have emerged that have no AT&T legacy code.)

Berkeley Software Design owns the commercial version of BSD (called BSD/OS), which is optimized for Internet servers. BSDI Internet Server (their flagship product) runs on inexpensive but powerful Intel hardware. For these reasons, Internet Service Providers (ISPs) favor BSDI.

Today, several free versions of BSD are available, including FreeBSD, OpenBSD, and NetBSD. These versions support a wide range of hardware. For example, you can run NetBSD on the following systems:

IBM AIX Makes All the Right Moves

Here's a fact: It was an RS/6000 running AIX (code-named "Deep Blue") that defeated world chess champion Garry Kasparov in May, 1997. This was a major victory for IBM's artificial intelligence researchers. (Of course, Deep Blue cost several million dollars and was beaten by Kasparov several times. Plus, Kasparov is still more cost effective and a far better conversationalist.)

➤ Digital Alpha

➤ Commodore Amiga (is that a kicker or what?)

➤ Atari Systems

➤ Intel (*x86*)

➤ PowerPC

➤ Macintosh 68K

➤ Sparc

➤ Sun3

➤ VAX

Digital UNIX

Digital Equipment Corporation
111 Powdermill Road
Maynard, MA 01754-1418
`http://www.unix.digital.com`

Digital UNIX is a 64-bit UNIX implementation that runs on 64-bit hardware (the Digital Alpha). In respect to its lineage, Digital UNIX conforms to both BSD 4.4 and

System V specifications. It is therefore yet another hybrid of both BSD and AT&T UNIX.

Digital UNIX is most often used in enterprise environments. (That's another way of saying that it's expensive, so only big companies use it.) However, Digital UNIX is well worth the price. It's an extremely stable and powerful version of UNIX, capable of taking a terrible beating. For example, the popular search engine Lycos (http://www.lycos.com) uses Digital Alphas running Digital UNIX to process some 100 million search requests every day.

HP-UX

Hewlett-Packard Company
3000 Hanover Street
Palo Alto, CA 94304
http://www.hp.com

HP-UX runs on Hewlett-Packard workstations, including the HP 9000 series. HP-UX code is based largely on UNIX System V release 2 (but also had substantial features derived from BSD.) Modern HP-UX also comes with HP-VUE, Hewlett-Packard's proprietary version of the X Window System from MIT. (You'll learn more about the X Window System—or *X*, for short—in Chapter 11, "Tyrannosaurus X: A Windowing System.")

IRIX

Silicon Graphics, Inc.
2011 N. Shoreline Blvd.
Mountain View, CA 94043
http://www.sgi.com

IRIX runs on proprietary RISC-based workstations manufactured by SGI (including the Iris, Indigo, Onyx, and Octane product lines.) These are primarily used for high-end graphics in aeronautic, defense, and film modeling. The IRIX operating system is based on UNIX System V release 4 (which is a descendant of both AT&T and BSD UNIX.) Modern IRIX ships with SGI's proprietary version of MIT's X Window System plus OpenGL, a special software programming environment for generating incredible 2D and 3D graphics.

MachTen

Tenon Intersystems
1123 Chapala Street
Santa Barbara, CA 93101
http://www.tenon.com/

MachTen is a powerful version of UNIX for Macintosh. Although MachTen currently supports the latest, super-duper G3 chip, it can also run on older PowerPC and M68K chips. MachTen is based on BSD 4.4 but also has POSIX compliance.

Here's an interesting fact about MachTen: It's actually based on something called a *UNIX Virtual Machine (UVM)*. This extends Mac OS to support a native UNIX environment. Therefore, MachTen coexists with Mac OS, a suitable arrangement for users who need both operating systems. (Mac-based ISPs often use MachTen.)

SunOS and Solaris

Sun Microsystems, Inc.
901 San Antonio Road
Palo Alto, CA 94303
http://www.sun.com

Sun offers two basic versions of UNIX: SunOS (which actually extends into Solaris 1.0) and Solaris. SunOS is Sun's original UNIX implementation and is largely BSD based. In contrast, Solaris (after version 2.0) integrates both BSD and System V.

SunOS runs primarily on RISC-based Sparc processors used to power Sun Microsystems Sparcstations. In contrast, Solaris runs on both Intel chips (this version is called *SolarisX86*) and Sparc processors. (This Intel compatibility will extend into the twenty-first century when Intel releases its Merced chip. Merced will run 64-bit operating systems, offering blazing speed in calculation-intensive tasks.)

A long-time favorite of ISPs, Solaris is optimized for internetworking. In large Internet-based networks, Sun is still a dominant figure, far outweighing Microsoft's Windows NT. This is based on Solaris' ability to handle sustained, resource-intensive network requests. For example, when Microsoft purchased Hotmail—a free-email-for-life enterprise at http://www.hotmail.com—the Hotmail network was originally Solaris based. Microsoft officials migrated that network to Windows NT but found the resource demands too great. (Hotmail gets more than 10 million logins per day.) They therefore migrated back to Solaris.

Sun Products

Sun products are generally given names that relate to summer or the sun (SunScreen, Solstice, and Solaris, for example.) In fact, although it may be coincidence, even Sun audio files have a curious filename extension—.AU. AU is the periodic table name for the element gold, which, in turn, has been associated with the sun for thousands of years.

A Commercial UNIX That's Free

SCO now offers the complete UNIXWare distribution for the price of shipping and handling (which breaks down to about $19). If you're on a tight budget and want to learn a commercial version of UNIX, this is a great choice. (The free distribution comes with all the trimmings, including C, C++, Netscape Navigator, and Netscape FastTrack server).

UNIXWare

SCO (The Santa Cruz Operation)
425 Encinal Street
P.O. Box 1900
Santa Cruz, California 95061-1900
`http://www.sco.com`

UNIXWare is based on UNIX System V release 4 and runs on *x*86 processors and Pentiums. UNIXWare has changed hands many times. Originally, UNIX System Laboratories (USL) owned UNIXWare. In 1993, Novell purchased USL, thus acquiring the operating system. In December, 1995, Novell sold UNIXWare to SCO, the firm that has maintained it ever since.

Linux: Off the Beaten Track

Finally, one UNIX flavor stands in a class by itself: Linux. Linux is more than just an operating system—it's a phenomenon. No other operating system has had such an unusual history. Briefly, the Linux story goes like this:

Some seven years ago, a young man named Linus Torvalds enrolled in some computer science classes in his native Finland. His aim was to study UNIX and the C programming language. During his studies, Torvalds used a tiny UNIX system called Minux. (Minux was a good choice for students because it was small, free, and compatible with inexpensive Intel architecture.)

Torvalds found that Minux had many limitations. Therefore, in his spare time, he began writing his own version of UNIX (hoping to create what he called "a better Minux than Minux.") The result was Linux, but the story doesn't end there. Torvalds released his new operating system to the Internet, offering it to developers and hobbyists free of charge. The events that followed would make computer history.

Initially, very little happened. After all, Linux was merely an operating system core. It certainly wasn't of any practical use. However, programmers from many countries took an interest. Separately and independently, those programmers began expanding

Linux's basic structure. Gradually, Linux supported more and more hardware as developers created a device driver here, a video driver there, and so on.

Likewise, Torvalds continued to improve Linux. Each time the system reached a critical stage of development, Torvalds would issue a new release. In a strange way, Linux developed in much the same manner as commercial operating systems do.

Eventually, Linux generated enough interest that programmers began writing Linux versions of standard UNIX utilities. This, coupled with a massive contribution of programs from the Free Software Foundation, transformed Linux into a viable operating system. By the time Torvalds released Linux 1.1.59, Linux was a full-blown distribution, complete with networking, system utilities, and even a windowing system.

Since that time, Linux has penetrated both the server and desktop markets. Today, many ISPs use Linux as an inexpensive alternative to commercial UNIX. (Some reports state that Linux is now being chosen over Microsoft Windows NT for intranets.) But that's not all. In almost every computing environment, Linux has gained tremendous ground. (For example, Linux was recently used to generate special effects for the immensely successful film *Titanic*.)

So, if all this is true, why hasn't Linux taken the entire world by storm? Simple. Until very recently, if you chose Linux, you were choosing a life without technical support. If something went wrong, you had no one to call. Although that's okay for hobbyists and programmers, the business world simply couldn't take that chance.

This has since changed. Today, commercial Linux vendors (who sell the operating system for a relatively nominal fee) offer technical support.

Noncommercial versions of Linux (without technical support) are listed here:

➤ Slackware—Available at `http://www.cdrom.com/`

➤ Debian—Available at `http://www.debian.org`

➤ MkLinux (for Macs)—Available at `http://www.mklinux.apple.com/`

➤ Yggdrasil—Available at `http://www.yggdrasil.com/`

You can either download these versions from `sunsite.unc.edu` (which costs nothing except 17 hours of modem time), or you can buy them for a nominal fee from the folks just listed.

Commercial versions of Linux include the following:

➤ Caldera OpenLinux

➤ RedHat Linux

➤ LinuxWare

These versions are more expensive, but they typically include commercial applications that greatly enhance Linux's power. (For example, Caldera OpenLinux offers Looking Glass, a desktop manager that has all the functionality of Microsoft Windows NT. This makes Caldera's Linux very easy to use.)

Oh yes, I almost forgot. You're probably wondering whether Linux is Sys V or BSD compatible. With some exceptions, the answer is both. However, Linux compatibility doesn't stop there. In fact, Linux supports more crazy file systems and utilities than any other operating system. (Linux even runs hundreds of DOS programs through the use of a DOS emulator!)

The Least You Need to Know

The least you need to know about UNIX flavors is this: There are lots of them (including some eight or ten I haven't mentioned here.) However, nearly all UNIX systems work in a similar manner.

➤ If you can't immediately identify which UNIX flavor you have (whether Sys V or BSD), check with your system administrator or vendor (they will be delighted to answer that question in far greater detail than you require).

➤ The UNIX family tree is fairly complicated and rich in standards.

➤ UNIX systems are based on either Sys V or BSD.

Part 2

Nuts and Bolts

Now that you've friendlied up to UNIX a bit, what are the first things you need to know? How to get it going and find your way around, of course! There's no need to feel like a stranger in a strange land, though. Part II takes you through the essential tools that you'll use to perform everyday tasks within UNIX.

The chapters in Part II will teach you about starting a UNIX system, printing, navigating directories and files, searching, opening and editing files, installing third-party software, and more.

## Chapter 3

Boot, Lock, and Load

In This Chapter

➤ Different machines that run UNIX

➤ Booting your system

➤ A few words about installation procedures

The first time you approach a UNIX system, you're bound to be nervous. Take me, for example. I migrated to UNIX from MS-DOS, and believe me, there's a world of difference between the two.

I got my first UNIX box from a company auction. (It was a hundred bucks, so I couldn't pass it up.) And, like a complete idiot, I figured I could learn the system without any documentation.

I booted that machine and followed the login procedure I found scribbled on the chassis. After that, things rapidly went downhill. It took me four hours just to figure out how to get help. I kept typing words such as help and dir, only to be confronted with the Not found message.

Finally, I got myself an ancient book on UNIX (circa 1981) and wised up. It was just in time, too, because I was about to hurl my UNIX system out the window.

In this chapter, I'll spare you some initial anxiety by discussing boot procedures and such.

Approaching the Beast

Your first UNIX encounter will happen in one of four ways:

➤ At a workstation or PC

➤ At a dumb terminal

➤ At an X terminal

➤ Over a network connection

Each of these devices work slightly differently (but can be equally baffling), so I'll briefly describe them.

Workstations and PCs

Workstations and PCs look very similar. Their chief characteristics include a chassis, a monitor, a keyboard, and a mouse. (See the following figure.)

A typical workstation or PC layout.

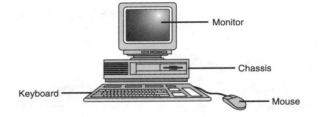

Additionally, most workstations and PCs also have a CD-ROM, a floppy disk drive, and a color screen. (These machines are integrated packages that provide everything you need to do serious computing. If you see an incomprehensible snarl of cables coming from the chassis, you're probably dealing with a workstation or PC.)

Workstations almost always run UNIX flavors designed especially for them. (In other words, the same company that made the workstation also makes the software for it.) Therefore, Sun Microsystems workstations generally run SunOS or Solaris, whereas HP 9000 series workstations (from Hewlett Packard) run HP-UX.

In contrast, PCs can run several different flavors of UNIX, including Solaris, BSD, Linux, UNIXWare, and even XENIX. (In Chapter 4, "Getting In," you'll learn how to identify which UNIX flavor you have.)

Dumb Terminals

Dumb terminals consist of just a monitor (or terminal) and a keyboard. The screen displays simple text, which is typically white, black, or green on a black or amber background. Dumb terminals are designed this way specifically to cause maximum eyestrain. (Just kidding.)

X Terminals

X terminals consist of a monitor, a keyboard, and a mouse. You can easily differentiate an X terminal from a dumb terminal because X terminals provide you with a graphical environment. In this environment, you use the mouse to manipulate windows. Most X terminal screens have a light blue background and the mouse cursor looks like a small X.

The graphical interface used on X terminals is the *X Window System* (or *X*) from MIT. You'll learn more about X in Chapter 11, "Tyrannosaurus X: A Windowing System."

UNIX Network Connections

Still another way you can encounter UNIX is over a network connection. Network connections can be initiated from almost any type of computing device (including workstations, PCs, dumb terminals, and X terminals).

There are two types of network connections. The first type, which occurs over Ethernet, is transparent to you. (That's a fancy way of saying that you won't know it's a network connection. Instead, it looks and behaves precisely as if the local computer were running UNIX.)

Dumb Terminal IQ

Are dumb terminals really dumb? No. However, they *are* designed expressly to connect to UNIX servers, mainframes, or other network servers. In such environments, users seldom need a hard disk of their own because all resources reside on the server. Therefore, dumb terminals aren't dumb at all; they're just cheap, effective networking stations. (Even if you've never used a dumb terminal, you've probably seen one. For example, they're often used in conjunction with cash registers at large retail outlets.)

X Terminals Aren't Always Xclusively Color

Some X terminals—though admittedly few—do not support color. These are typically *grayscale displays*. Grayscale displays support 256 shades of gray. These have very sharp resolution. (Also, there's a small minority of X terminals that support only basic black and white.)

31

About `telnet`

You'll learn more about `telnet` in Chapter 21,"Other Network Services." `telnet` is often used to access UNIX from Windows or Mac OS. For example, if you get involved in Web development, you'll probably log into a remote UNIX server more than once.

When Is a Network Connection Not a Network Connection?

Still a third type of network connection is a connection established over serial lines. This is where a physical cable runs from the UNIX machine to your own. The cable connects to serial ports (like those used for external modems or mice). Serial connections behave almost exactly like `telnet` connections. In fact, serial connections are a popular way to connect dumb terminals to a UNIX system. (Technically, this isn't really a *network* connection but rather a *serial* connection.)

The other type of network connection is often created using a program called `telnet`. You can quickly recognize a `telnet` network session in progress if the screen displays a message like this:

```
Trying 207.171.0.111...
Connected to 207.171.0.111.
Escape character is '^]'.
```

In `telnet` network connections, the local machine may not even be running UNIX. (For example, the local machine may be running Windows 95 and simply be connected to a UNIX server.)

Either way, for the most part, network connections are not very different from "real" UNIX sessions. In network connections, you'll still have access to all the resources that UNIX offers. (The one exception to this is the X Window System. If your network connection is over a `telnet` link, X will generally not be available.)

Giving UNIX the Boot

Whether you use a workstation, PC, or X terminal, you still need to boot UNIX. Usually, this process is as simple as turning on the machine. After the machine checks its memory and disks, you'll hear a horrible grinding sound and dozens of confusing messages will scroll by. Eventually, this clamor will cease and the login prompt will appear.

In rare instances, however, you may need to boot UNIX from a specific device (or worse still, you may have to install UNIX). This chapter provides a little background on these tasks.

Booting UNIX on Different Devices

You can boot UNIX from several different sources, including these:

➤ A floppy disk
➤ A CD-ROM

➤ A network connection

➤ A hard disk drive

However, most often, you'll be booting from the hard disk drive. This procedure differs slightly from machine to machine. Table 3.1 provides some notes on booting UNIX.

Table 3.1. Booting UNIX on workstations, PCs, and X terminals

Machine	Notes

Workstation	Most workstations boot UNIX automatically. Turn on the machine and wait for a login prompt. In most cases, this should do the trick. Exceptions occasionally arise, however, if the machine has multiple disks. If that happens, you'll know it. For example, some Sun SPARCstations will stop at a > prompt. In this case, you must boot the system manually. To do so, issue the b command. If that fails, enter the command n and type `probe-scsi`. This will identify available SCSI disks by number (disk 1, 2, 3, and so on). Once you have this information, boot the system by explicitly specifying the target disk. Here are some commands for booting from different disks and devices:
	
	CD-ROM:
	
	`b(0,6,2), boot(0,6,2), or boot cdrom`
	
	Floppy:
	
	`b floppy, boot floppy, b fd, or boot fd`
	
	Tape:
	
	`b st, boot st, b st(), or boot tape`
	
	Ethernet:
	
	`b le, boot le, b ie, or boot ie`
	
	IPI disk:
	
	`b id or boot id`

PC	Most PC-compatible UNIX distributions automatically boot to a login prompt. However, there are exceptions. SCO UNIX and some versions of Linux will pause at a boot prompt. (The purpose of this pause period is to allow you time to enter special boot parameters. For example, you could specify that the system should boot from a partition other than the default. Similarly, you can call special drivers for odd hardware that may not atch during a normal boot.) To boot from this prompt, hit Enter or simply wait. Within 60 seconds, the system will boot.

continues

Table 3.1.   Booting UNIX on workstations, PCs, and X terminals CONTINUED

Machine	Notes
X terminal	An X terminal requires little prodding. If the X terminal is already running, hit the spacebar, move your mouse, or click the Start icon. Otherwise, if the X terminal pauses at a command prompt, enter the command bt.

Boot Problems

When working with computers (even while performing relatively simple tasks), you can encounter problems. These problems are most frustrating when they occur at boot time. This next section gives hints on various boot problems and their solutions.

Problems Booting from a Floppy Disk

Problems when booting from a floppy are pretty rare. They can happen, though, for several reasons:

➤ The floppy disk drive isn't working.

➤ The floppy disk is corrupted or not bootable.

➤ You specified the wrong directory or disk volume.

First, check to see whether the floppy drive is installed correctly. In particular, you should check for the *flimflam* problem. (Couldn't I have thought up a more technical-sounding term? Probably, but I think this term describes the problem perfectly.) The flimflam problem occurs when the floppy drive cable is inserted upside down into the drive itself. On PCs, this will be pretty obvious, because the floppy drive's light will stay on indefinitely. The solution is to take out the cable, flip it upside down, and reinsert it.

On the other hand, if you've used the box before and the floppy problem suddenly crops up, the disk itself may be corrupted or simply not bootable. If you have another machine nearby, try verifying the disk media. If there are no errors on the disk, the disk might not be bootable. (These conditions are an excellent argument for always having more than one backup boot disk. That way, if your original boot disk is damaged, you can still use your system without having to reinstall or boot from installation media.)

Finally, if the floppy boot procedure requires you to enter boot parameters, you just might fumble these miserably. (Don't take it to heart, though. I do it all the time. It's very easy to make typos, and even the slightest typo can produce catastrophic results.) Check to see that you specified the right directory or target disk volume.

Problems Booting from a CD-ROM

If your system is supposed to boot from a CD-ROM but fails, there could be several reasons, including the following:

➤ You have hardware that's improperly configured or faulty.

➤ You failed to specify the correct boot command.

➤ The CD-ROM drive or CD-ROM media is not bootable.

Let's quickly cover each problem.

Improperly Configured or Faulty Hardware   Many hardware problems are minor and are easy to fix. For example, your problem may be nothing more serious than this: The CD-ROM drive's cable has been knocked loose or disconnected. To eliminate this possibility, check to see that the cable is properly attached.

This procedure is can vary slightly depending on whether you have an internal or external CD-ROM drive. Basically, though, either case involves perseverance. Trace the wires from the CD-ROM drive to its controller and reconnect them (or connect them correctly).

On the other hand, if this is the first time you've tried booting from a CD-ROM (maybe you've just assembled the box), check for termination problems or SCSI ID conflicts. Often, SCSI CD-ROM drives are not self-terminating. To find out, check the CD-ROM vendor's manual. Also, be sure to check whether other devices occupy the same SCSI ID as the CD-ROM. If so, change the SCSI ID of those devices.

Bad Boot Commands or Command Parameters   Still another problem is occurs when the CD-ROM boot procedure is interactive and you've specified the wrong directory, the wrong command, or the wrong command parameters. Check your vendor's documentation to discover exactly which directory to boot from (if any) and the command necessary to do so.

The CD-ROM Drive or CD-ROM Media Isn't Bootable   Lastly, it's possible that either the CD-ROM drive or CD-ROM media is not bootable. In the first case, a simple solution may exist. If the CD-ROM is SCSI, there's a strong chance that it's bootable but the option to boot from the CD-ROM hasn't been enabled. This is a common scenario on PCs with SCSI adapters.

To find out, reboot your machine and engage your SCSI adapter's setup program. (Most PC-compatible SCSI adapters have embedded software tools for configuring, calibrating, and even formatting SCSI drives. For example, if your adapter was manufactured by Adaptec, you can access these tools by entering the Ctrl+a keystroke combination when the machine boots.) There, you can view booting options. It's possible that bootable CD-ROM support has been disabled. If so, enable it.

Finally, if your CD-ROM drive is bootable but your CD-ROM media is not, the only solution is to obtain another CD-ROM that is.

Problems Booting from a Network

When you boot over a network, your machine (running a boot client) contacts another machine (running a boot server). This connection typically occurs over a standard Ethernet connection—a common scenario in corporate or academic environments.

Normally, when you boot from a network, you'll see a series of system messages and then, finally, a login prompt. For example, here's the message output of a clean network boot:

```
Booting from: le(0,0,0)
2bc00 hostname: unixbox
domainname: mydomain.com
root server:
root directory: /export/root/unixbox
SunOS Release 5.4 Version [2.4_FCS] [UNIX(R) System V Release
4.0]
Copyright (c) 1983-1994, Sun Microsystems, Inc.
configuring network interfaces: le0.
Hostname: unixbox
Configuring cache and swap:......done.
The system is coming up. Please wait.
NIS domainname is mydomain.com
starting rpc services: rpcbind keyserv ypbind kerbd done.
Setting netmask of le0 to 255.255.255.0
Setting default interface for multicast: add net 224.0.0.0:
gateway unixbox
syslog service starting.
Print services started.
volume management starting.
The system is ready.

login: root
password:
```

If your network boot fails, however, things will look very different. You'll know it immediately, too, because the system will either hang or repeat the same message over and over again. Here's an example:

```
Booting from le(0,0,0)
Booting from le(0,0,0)
Booting from le(0,0,0)
Booting from le(0,0,0)
Booting from le(0,0,0)
Booting from le(0,0,0)
```

Eventually, the system will generate an error, complaining about the transceiver cable, the boot server, or some other obscure problem. Here's an example:

```
No carrier - transceiver cable problem?
```

There can be several reasons for this. One is that the network cable has been knocked loose or disconnected. Check to see that the network cable is properly attached.

Another common problem with network boots occurs when the boot server is unavailable. Someone may have turned off the machine that runs the boot server or that machine may be down for other reasons. To find out, contact the machine's owner or your system administrator.

Finally, rare instances exist in which the route between you and the boot server is down, or the transport hardware is malfunctioning. (From another angle, the packets from the boot server might be corrupted or have invalid checksum values.) In these cases, contact your network administrator.

The Least You Need to Know

Booting UNIX is usually a pretty simple affair, but it varies, depending on your system's specific configuration. Here are some quick tips on the boot process:

➤ Dumb terminals are usually wired directly to the server. Therefore, to access UNIX, you merely need to turn the terminal on.

➤ To start UNIX on an X terminal, give the terminal a nudge by moving the mouse, clicking the Start button, pressing the spacebar, or entering the command bt.

➤ To start UNIX on a workstation or PC, turn on the machine and wait 60 seconds or so.

## Chapter 4

Getting In

In This Chapter

➤ Logging in

➤ Identifying your hardware and software

➤ Identifying yourself and other users

➤ Logging out

➤ Changing your password

Logging In

If you ever used a computer before, you probably noticed that most operating systems are friendly when approached. (Some even greet you at startup.) UNIX is a little different. The following section illustrates how to log in.

The *login* Prompt: Halt! Who Goes There?

When you first approach a UNIX system, you're confronted by the login prompt. It looks like this:

```
Login:
```

That's a pretty cryptic salutation if you ask me, but it basically says it all. The login prompt is UNIX's way of saying "Halt! Who goes there?" In other words, UNIX is asking you to identify yourself.

You might wonder why UNIX needs to know your name. (After all, that seems a little nosey.) There's a perfectly reasonable explanation: UNIX is a multiuser system. Therefore, many different people can use the same machine simultaneously. To keep track of all those different users (and their files), UNIX requires that each user have a name. In UNIX lingo, this name is called your *username or UserID*.

Obtaining a Username and Password

You receive your username from your system administrator. (Unless of course, you're the system administrator. In that case, you must create your own username, password, and even your own account.) More on system administration in Part 5, System Administration.

Typing Your Login and Password

UNIX is case sensitive. (It differentiates between uppercase and lowercase letters.) Therefore, BWAGNER is interpreted differently than Bwagner or even bwagner. If your username is lowercase and you enter it in uppercase, your login will fail.

Entering Your Username

To log on, you must provide your username followed by a carriage return, like this:

```
Login: bwagner <ENTER>
```

Entering Your Password

After you provide your username, UNIX will respond with the following prompt:

```
Password:
```

Here, you enter your password followed by a carriage return. As you do that, you'll notice that even though you type, the text does not appear on the screen. Don't be alarmed. This is a security feature. In UNIX, passwords are never echoed to the screen. (This prevents busybodies from peering over your shoulder and discovering your password.)

This feature has a major drawback, though: if you mistype your password, you won't know it until it's too late. In that case, UNIX reverts to the login prompt and you have to start over again.

However, when you eventually do provide your correct password, you'll be dropped into the UNIX system. At that point, you'll see the UNIX shell prompt ($) as illustrated here.

The $ prompt signals that UNIX is now ready to accept commands. Congratulations! You are now logged on.

Some UNIX systems display a % prompt instead. That's because they use a different command interpreter or shell. But, I'm getting too far ahead. For at least simple tasks, it doesn't matter whether you have a $ prompt or a % prompt.

The Unix Shell Prompt

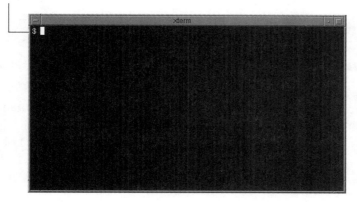

The UNIX shell prompt usually looks like a money symbol: $.

The `whoami` Command: Finding Yourself

After you log on, you'll probably want to do something useful. A good start is to answer that philosophical question that has plagued humans since time began: "Who am I?" Can UNIX help you do this? You bet.

To find yourself on a UNIX system, issue the following command:

```
$ whoami
```

The answer you receive will look like this:

```
bwagner
```

The `whoami` command displays your username. Initially, this doesn't seem very useful. After all, you know who you are (unless you're suffering from amnesia, a problem that's beyond the scope of this book). However, you might sometimes use more than one username. When you do, it's useful to know who you are at any particular moment. (You might also want to know who else is hanging around—the `who` and `finger` commands are great for this, so look for them later in the chapter.)

Who's Hosting This Party, Anyway?

Now that you know who you are, you should get acquainted with your machine. On UNIX networks, it isn't just users that have names. Machines have names, too. (This helps networks to differentiate between them.) UNIX machines are called *hosts* and every machine has a *hostname*.

If you've ever used the Internet, you've seen hostnames before. Most WWW addresses are expressed in hostname form. For example, Macmillan Computer Publishing can be reached at this address:

```
www.mcp.com
```

That address is both a WWW address and a hostname.

To determine your machine's hostname, use the `hostname` command.

The `hostname` *Command: Discovering Your Machine's Hostname*

The `hostname` command is used to either discover or change the current hostname. To learn your machine's hostname, issue the following command:

hostname

My machine is named wagjag. So, when I issue the `hostname` command, my machine responds like this:

wagjag

You can also use the `hostname` command to change your machine's current hostname—providing you have the authority to do so. Only privileged users can do this, so if you're on someone else's box, this command might not be available to you.

For example, suppose I wanted to change my machine's name to que. I would issue the following command:

hostname que

Changing Your Hostname

Be careful about changing your machine's hostname; I wouldn't recommend it until you have more experience. If you change your hostname without updating other information, certain services might fail when you reboot.

Say, What's in the Box?

Next, you'll probably want to know something about your machine. For example, maybe you'd like to know what type of UNIX you're using. That's easy enough. To determine that information, use the uname command.

The uname *Command: Identifying Your Operating System and Hardware*

The uname command collects information about your machine, including its operating system type, operating system release, architecture, number of processors, and name. To identify your operating system, issue the following command:

uname

The machine will respond with its operating system. For example, when I issue the uname command, my SPARCstation responds like this:

    SunOS

From this, I know that I'm using SunOS from Sun Microsystems. But that's just the beginning. The uname command has other uses. For example, try this command:

    uname -a

You'll receive an answer like this:

    SunOS wagjag 5.6 Generic sun4u sparc SUNW,Ultra-1

That's probably more information than you really want. What does it mean? It means that my machine is a Sun SPARCstation Ultra running SunOS 5.6 with a generic kernel.

uname *Options*

uname has a series of command-line options. You can use these options to manipulate uname output. These options are summarized in Table 4.1.

Table 4.1.   Selected uname Command Line Options

What Is a Kernel?

A *kernel* is a special program that constitutes the heart of your operating system. This program gives UNIX access to the file system. (The kernel also controls the creation, management, and deletion of system processes.) Without a kernel, UNIX wouldn't work. All operating systems have a kernel, but in UNIX, you can actually manipulate and modify it.

uname Command	Result
uname	Prints the operating system type
uname -a	Prints the operating system type, the hostname, the operating system version, the operating system release, the machine architecture, the platform, and the kitchen sink
uname -i	Prints the machine platform
uname -n	Prints the machine's name
uname -p	Prints the machine's processor type
uname -r	Prints the operating system release number
uname -s	Prints the operating system name

So, now you know everything about your machine. The next step is to learn about your account. To do so, you should give yourself the finger (not literally of course!).

The `finger` Command: Giving Yourself the Finger

The `finger` utility gathers information about users, including the following:

➤ Their login name

➤ Their real name

➤ Their office telephone (if available)

➤ Their home directory

Using the arch Command Instead

If you just want a report on your machine's architecture, you can also use the arch command. However, arch doesn't offer many of the other features of uname.

To gather finger information on yourself, issue the `finger` command followed by your username. For example, to gather finger information on myself, I issue the following command:

```
finger bwagner
```

This is the resulting output:

```
Login name: bwagner            In real life: Bill Wagner
Directory: /export/home/bwagner    Shell: /sbin/sh
On since Jun  5 02:23:10 on pts/0 from 207.171.0.111
No unread mail
No Plan.
```

This information reveals important facts about my account, including:

➤ My username

➤ My real name

➤ My home directory

➤ My shell (You'll learn about shells in Chapter 5, "Surviving Shell Shock.")

➤ The length of time I've been logged on

➤ Whether I've read my mail

`finger` is a cool utility. You should experiment with it by giving other users the finger.

Giving Others the Finger

To finger a particular user, issue the `finger` command followed by his username. Or if you want to finger all users currently logged on, issue the following command:

```
finger
```

This will result in tabular output, like this:

```
Bwagner   Bill Wagner    pts/4    1:53  Thu 01:29  207.171.0.111
wearp     Wyatt Earp     pts/0    2     Mon 17:42  207.171.38.251
cjarret   Cody Jarret    pts/7    12:   Thu 08:59  knuckleheads.com
```

finger Command-Line Options

`finger` has a series of command-line options. You can use these options to manipulate finger output. These options are summarized in Table 4.2.

Table 4.2.   Selected `finger` Command Line Options

`finger` **Command**	**Result**
`finger`	Fingers all users in short format
`finger -l`	Fingers all users in long format
`finger username`	Fingers a particular user in short format
`finger -l username`	Fingers a particular user in long format
`finger -b username`	Gets everything but the user's home directory
`finger -q username`	Gets the user's name, terminal, and uptime
`finger -s username`	Gets a short, one-line summary

Using `finger` on the Internet

If your UNIX system is connected to the Internet, you can also finger users all over the world. To do so, finger the target's full email address. (This is a combination of their username and their machine's hostname, for example: bwagner@altavista.net) In a good number of cases, you will receive data similar to the previous information. However, in some instances, remote sites might not run `finger` or they might restrict it to on-site use. If so, you might receive a "Connection Refused" message when trying a `finger` query. More on `finger` and the Internet in Chapter 21, "Other Network Services."

The `finger` utility is useful for identifying users. However, it doesn't tell you what those users are doing. To determine that, you use the w command.

The w Command: Finding Out What Users Are Doing

The w command reveals what other users are up to. To find out, issue the w command, like this:

```
w
```

The resulting output identifies each user's username, terminal, login time, idle time, and perhaps most importantly, the last command they used.

Here is a sample w report:

```
4:03am  up 6 day(s), 16:13,  14 users,  load average: 0.00, 0.01, 0.01
User     tty         login@  idle   JCPU   PCPU  what
bwagner  pts/2       2:01am           2           w
wearp    pts/3       3:23am           2           edit letter.txt
cjarret  pts/8       3:43am  5                     finger bwagner
```

As you can see, the last field (what) describes what everyone was doing. For example, at the time I was issuing the w command, user wearp was editing a text file, and user cjarret was busy giving me the finger. (I'll have to have a talk with that guy.)

w *Command-Line Options*

The w program has several command-line options. You can use these to manipulate w output. These options are summarized in Table 4.3.

Table 4.3. Selected Command Line Options for the w Command

w Option	Result
w	See what all users are doing
w *user*	See what a particular user is doing
w -l	See what all users are doing (long format)
w -h	Long format but without a header
w -s	See what all users are doing (short format)
w -u	See a summary of statistics (how many users)

The w command is a good way to keep track of other users, for example, maybe you're the boss and you want to find out who's been goofing off. However, perhaps you don't care what users are doing. Perhaps you just want to know who's logged on, where they logged in from, and how long they've been there. If so, you need the who command.

The who Command: Discovering Who's Using Your Machine

The who program will tell you who is on your system, where they came from, and how long they've been there. To gather who information, issue the who command like this:

    who

Here is a sample who report:

    bwagner   pts/2   Jun 5 02:01   (207.171.0.111)
    cjarret   pts/3   Jun 5 03:23   (knuckleheads.com)
    wearp   pts/8   Jun 5 03:43   (207.171.55.4)

who *Command-Line Options*

The who program has several command-line options. You can use these to manipulate who output. These options are summarized in Table 4.4.

Table 4.4.   Selected Command Line Options for the who Command

who **Options**	**Result**
who	Displays all currently logged users' usernames, terminal, login time, idle time, and so on.
who -a	Displays everything about all users. Warning: On systems with many users, this can take a long time to display results!
who -b	Displays the date and time that the system was last rebooted.
who -d	Displays all dead processes.
who -H	Displays verbose column headings.
who -m	Displays only your own statistics.
who -n *x*	Limits the number of users to include in the w query (where *x* is the number).
who -q	Gets only the number of users and their login names.

Of course, maybe the person you're looking for isn't on the system anymore. If you want to find out when they last logged in, you can use the last command.

The last Command: Finding Out When Users Were Last Logged In

The last command reports when a user last logged in. To find out, issue the last command followed by the user's name, like this:

```
last bwagner
```

The result will look like this:

```
bwagner    pts/6    ppp-208-19-49-18 Mon Jun  8
20:29 - 20:30  (00:01)
bwagner    pts/14   ppp-208-19-49-14 Mon Jun  1
11:16 - 11:28  (00:11)
bwagner    pts/14  ppp-208-19-49-14 Mon Jun  1 11:13 - 11:16  (00:03)
wtmp begins Tue Jan 13 10:35
```

The report above suggests that I last logged in on Monday, June 8, 1998 and that I was on for approximately 20 minutes.

Using the users Command Instead

If you just want a list of currently logged users, you can also use the users command. users is roughly equivalent to the who -q command, except that it doesn't print the number of users.

Limiting the Output of last

If a user logs in frequently, her last report can be many pages long. You probably only want the most recent entries, which are listed first. To limit the number of entries you receive, add a dash (-) and a number after your command, like this:

```
last bwagner -3
```

This will limit the report to the last three times bwagner logged on.

Logging Out

So far, you learned the following tasks:

➤ How to log in

➤ How to identify your hardware and software

➤ How to identify and locate yourself and others

What remains is learning how to log out. You'll be happy to know that logging out is much easier than logging in. You can log out in three ways. One is to issue the logout command:

```
logout
```

Another is to issue the exit command:

```
exit
```

And finally, you can also log out using the key combination **CTRL+D**.

About Your Password

Now it's time to learn how to change your password. You're probably wondering why I waited until now to discuss it. Here's why: the first time you log into UNIX, you're basically getting your bearings. It's strange typing out your password and not being able to see it. On that account, new UNIX users tend to make frequent mistakes while entering their password.

Now that you've done it at least once, you're probably more comfortable with the login-password procedure.

The passwd *Command: Changing Your Password*

To change your password, issue the passwd command, like this:

```
passwd
```

To ensure that you're authorized to make the password change, UNIX will then ask for your current password:

```
Enter login password:
```

Here, you enter your current password. UNIX will respond by verifying your old password and then asking you for a new one:

```
New password:
```

Here, you enter your new password. However, before committing the change, UNIX will ask you to verify it. (This is to ensure that you didn't make a typing mistake.) The verification prompt looks like this:

```
Re-enter new password:
```

After you re-enter your new password (providing you typed it correctly), UNIX will commit the change and notify you:

```
passwd (SYSTEM): passwd successfully
changed.
```

That's it. You changed your password!

The Least You Need to Know

In this chapter, you learned the bare essentials: just enough to get in and look around. In the next chapter ("Surviving Shell Shock"), you'll learn how to manipulate your environment using the UNIX shell.

Be Careful When Typing Your Password

If you make a mistake while entering your new password (and UNIX cannot verify it), the passwd program will stop and report an error. Then, you'll have to try again.

 # Surviving Shell Shock

---

In This Chapter

➤ Learn what a shell is

➤ Learn about different shells

➤ Learn how shells work

Many people think that UNIX is difficult to learn. It's just not user-friendly, they insist, and it never will be. Well, if those folks had seen the first version of UNIX, they'd change their point of view. You see, in 1969, there were no windowing systems, no help files, no file managers, and certainly no install wizards.

Instead, UNIX was an arcane and elusive system, known only to the folks at Bell Labs. Command syntax was primitive, and to be frank, even modern computer wizards would have been intimidated by the UNIX interface.

So, the folks at Bell Labs decided to have pity on the rest of us. To that end, a fellow named Stephen Bourne added the first real amenity to UNIX. By standards of the day, Bourne's contribution was a step toward user-friendliness. He designed a program that would evaluate and execute commands, and he called that program a shell. That's what this chapter is all about: the UNIX shell.

What's a Shell, Anyway?

To understand what a shell is, you need only understand this: computers speak a language all their own. (Of course, you probably already know that, which is why you bought this book.)

Seriously, though. Computers don't speak English; they speak computer language. Therefore, when you enter commands, those commands must be interpreted and translated by an intermediary. In UNIX, that intermediary is the shell.

When you issue a command, the shell interprets it and, if necessary, it passes that command to other programs or to your operating system. For example, when you use the ls command to list your directory's contents, here's what happens:

➤ You type ls and press ENTER.

➤ The shell finds ls (located in /usr/bin).

➤ The shell runs ls.

➤ You receive the output (your directory listing).

Because shells perform this process (a kind of human-to-machine translation), they are called command interpreters.

If you've ever used Microsoft Windows or DOS, you've already had experience with a command interpreter or shell. In DOS, the shell is COMMAND.COM. You use this every time you "shell out" to a MSDOS prompt from Windows.

No matter what version of UNIX you use, you will use at least one (and possibly several) command interpreters or shells. Let's briefly look at those shells now.

Shells

In the UNIX world, developers are constantly improving the system. (They're fastidious folks if nothing else, these UNIX programmers.) As a result, UNIX distributions often have a dozen different programs that perform the same task. Shells are no exception.

There are numerous shells and UNIX advocates often argue furiously about which shell is best. Does it matter? Maybe. As it happens, some shells perform certain tasks better than other shells do. But don't worry; all shells are descendants of either the Bourne Shell (sh) or the C Shell (csh). Hence, whether you learn one, the other, or both, you will be suitably prepared to operate any UNIX system.

Let's take a quick look at the shell family tree.

The Bourne Shell: sh

The original UNIX shell was sh, otherwise known as the Bourne Shell. (sh was named after its inventor, Stephen Bourne, a programmer at Bell Laboratories.) sh is still popular and is available on all UNIX systems, including Linux. You can find sh in the directory /bin.

The C Shell: csh

The C Shell (csh) was created at the University of California at Berkeley. For many years, csh was the only alternative to sh. csh differs from sh in several ways, the most fundamental being that the csh command language is different. (In other words, many commands and programs expressed in csh language are not sh-compatible.)

Big Trouble in Shell Paradise

You're probably wondering why anyone would introduce a new command language for a shell. (Especially since the central goal has always been standardization.) Well, in the C Shell's case, there was good reason: almost all UNIX system utilities are written in the C programming language. In fact, the UNIX operating system is written in C. Since most UNIX developers worked with C on a daily basis, it seemed reasonable to create a shell language that closely resembled C. And that's exactly what csh is.

The problem is, while csh introduced some new concepts that made general tasks easier, it was not as well suited for shell programming. (Shell programming, as you'll soon see, is where many shell commands are stored in text files for later execution.) Therefore, throughout UNIX history, UNIX vendors have shipped either sh, csh, or both.

This created a schism in the UNIX community. Some users stayed with sh, some migrated to csh, and some continued to use both (using csh for general tasks and sh for programming.) Since then, various shells have emerged. All are based on sh, csh, or both. Let's quickly take a look at those shells now.

tcsh

tcsh is a csh-compatible shell with many features not found in csh. You could say that tcsh is csh on steroids. Advantages that tcsh has over csh include

➤ Automated spelling correction. (If you spell a file or directory name incorrectly, tcsh attempts to correct that.)

➤ Scheduling. (You can use tcsh to time command execution.)

➤ Command-line editing. (tcsh allows you to edit your command line.)

tcsh was considered a vast improvement on csh. However, for reasons unknown, commercial UNIX vendors did not adopt tcsh. Hence, for a long time, sh and csh were still the only choices...until the emergence of the Korn Shell.

The Korn Shell: ksh

The Korn Shell was developed by David Korn, yet another Bell Labs/AT&T programmer. (Those folks at Bell Labs stayed busy, didn't they?) The Korn Shell (ksh) is a sh-compatible shell that also has many C Shell features. (Many ksh advocates insist that ksh has the very best features of both sh and csh.) ksh has become increasingly popular in recent years and is now the default shell on several UNIX distributions, including AIX. ksh has advantages over other shells including advanced text manipulation in the spirit of text-scanning languages like awk and PERL. (You'll learn about these languages a bit later.)

The Bourne Again Shell (bash)

Next in line in shell history was bash (or the Bourne Again shell). bash was developed by the Free Software Foundation and the GNU project. bash is entirely sh-compatible. Thus, any sh command or program will work in bash. However, bash goes even further. bash also has many features common to csh. (Are you confused yet?)

ash (A Shell)

ash was developed by Kenneth Almquist, Florian La Roche, Branko Lankester, Sunando Sen, and Arjan de Vet. ash is a lightweight shell that is compatible with both sh and bash. (You can use ash to run most sh and bash programs without editing them.) ash was designed primarily for machines with extremely low memory resources.

The Z Shell (zsh)

The Z Shell was written by Paul Falstad as a college project. Since then, zsh has become popular, particularly in the Linux community. In syntax and functionality, zsh closely resembles both ksh and sh (and is therefore at least marginally compatible with csh.)

Shell We Dance?

Now that I've listed every shell in existence (nearly), we can begin. Before you can become proficient in the shell, you must first learn about your shell environment. Let's start there.

Your Environment

When you first log in, UNIX automatically sets up your working environment. For example, it establishes (among other things) the following parameters:

➤ Your shell
➤ Your shell prompt
➤ Your home directory
➤ Your time zone

These values are stored in variables called environment variables. To view your environment variables, issue the following command:

```
env
```

I use sh, so on my machine UNIX responds like this:

```
HOME=/home/bwagner
LOGNAME=bwagner
MAIL=/var/mail/bwagner
PATH=/bin:/usr/bin:
SHELL=/sbin/sh
TERM=ansi
TZ=US/Pacific
```

That's an awful lot of information. What does it mean? Table 5.1 lists each environment variable and its function.

Table 5.1. sh Environment Variables and What They Mean

Variable	Purpose
HOME	The HOME variable identifies the location of your home directory. This is where you store your files. (HOME is also the directory you first encounter when you log in.) Typically, your home directory will be a subdirectory of /home. For example, my home directory is /home/bwagner.
LOGNAME	The LOGNAME variable stores your username.
MAIL	The MAIL variable stores the location of your mailbox. (From this, the shell knows where to find your mail.)
PATH	The PATH variable stores a list of all directories the shell will search when looking for commands. (This is similar to the PATH variable in DOS. All directories named in the path will be searched when you issue a command. If you issue a command that resides in a directory not included in your path, the shell will respond with an error: not found.)
PS1	The PS1 variable identifies what your system prompt will look like. For example, on my machine, the PS1 variable is set to $.
SHELL	The SHELL variable identifies your default shell.
TERM	The TERM variable identifies the current terminal type. Your terminal type can be very important. UNIX uses this to determine how many characters and lines to display per screen. If you accidentally assign an erroneous terminal type, you'll know it. Displayed data will be completely distorted with text flying every which way.
TZ	The TZ variable identifies the current time zone.

In csh, the same environment variables exist, but some have different names. Table 5.2 lists those characters and their names.

Table 5.2. Important Differences in sh and csh

Value or Variable	sh	csh
Default Root Prompt	#	>
Default Shell Prompt	$	%
Home Variable	$HOME	$home
Path Variable	$PATH	path
Prompt Variable	$PS1	prompt
Shell Variable	$SHELL	shell
Terminal Variable	$TERM	term
User Variable	$LOGNAME	user

In most cases, you'll find the default environment sufficient. However, if need be, you can change your environment by changing your environment variables.

Changing Environment Variables in sh

In sh-compatible shells, you change environment variables with the following syntax:

```
variable=value
```

For example, suppose you wanted your prompt to reflect the current date and time. In sh, you would issue the following command:

```
PS1=`date` ' $ '
```

From then on, your prompt would look like this:

```
Wed Jul  8 16:22:15 PDT 1998 $
```

Changing Environment Variables in csh

In csh-compatible shells, you change your environment variables with the following syntax:

```
set variable=value
```

For example, suppose you wanted your prompt to reflect the current date and time. In csh, you would issue the following command:

```
set prompt=" `date` % "
```

Shell Lingo

No matter which shell you use, you need to learn shell command language and command structure. Let's take a quick look at command structure now.

Command Structure

Simple commands generally consist of several components:

➤ The basic command

➤ Command-line options (or flags)

➤ Command-line arguments

For example, consider this command:

```
ls -l /usr/bin
```

It has three parts:

➤ ls is the *basic command*. This tells the shell that you want a directory listing.

➤ -l is the *command-line option* or *flag*. This tells the shell that the directory listing should be in long format.

➤ Finally, /usr/bin is the *argument*. This tells the shell that your long format directory listing should be performed on the directory /usr/bin.

You're Destroying the Environment!

Until you become more familiar with UNIX, be cautious when changing your environment variables. Even a small typo can produce perplexing results. For example, if you make mistakes when setting your PATH variable, the shell will be unable to find important commands. Similarly, if you fumble the ball while setting your PROMPT variable, output may look distorted. If you ever encounter that situation (or perhaps an even worse one), you can quickly recover: log out and log in again. Presto! The default environment will return pristine, untouched by your shell faux pas. (For information on how to make environment preferences permanent, check Part 5, "System Administration.")

With rare exception, you must articulate your commands in this manner. The typical format is

```
command -> options -> argument
```

Changing this order can produce bizarre results. Let's use the above command as an example. On my machine, I have a directory named cig. In it, there are three files: tom, dick, and harry. To list that directory, I issue the following command:

```
ls -l cig
```

Here's the output:

```
-rw-r--r--   1 bwagner    200        23 Jun 28 12:26 dick
-rw-r--r--   1 bwagner    200        59 Jun 28 12:29 harry
-rw-r--r--   1 bwagner    200        21 Jun 28 12:25 tom
```

That's fine. But suppose I change the order of my command elements. Instead of `ls -l cig` (*command*, *options*, *argument*), I change it to `ls cig -l` (*command*, *argument*, *options*). Now, funky things happen:

```
-1: No such file or directory
cig:
dick    harry   tom
```

UNIX interpreted my `-l` option as an argument, and as a result, disaster struck. I not only failed to get the information I requested, but I also received an error message. To avoid these problems, you should adhere to standard command-line rules.

The Shell's Cast of Characters: Metacharacters

In addition to commands, options, and arguments, the UNIX shell also supports metacharacters. These are characters and symbols that perform special operations on text, filenames, directories, and variables. Metacharacters for both `sh` and `csh` are listed in Table 5.3.

Table 5.3.   Important Metacharacters in `sh` and `csh`

Purpose	sh	csh
Command separator	;	;
Execute in background	&	&
Filename metacharacters	* ? ~ + - [ ] ! @	* ? ~ [ ]
Group commands	( )	( )
Pipe	|	|
Quoting characters	' " \	' " \
Variable substitution	$	$

Let's examine what these metacharacters do.

Filename Metacharacters

Filename metacharacters perform operations on not just one file, but many. This allows you to apply incisive changes to your system (and even automate tasks). Let's take a brief look at shell file metacharacters and what they offer.

Deduces Wild: The Asterisk

Is that an awful pun or what? No matter, it fits in this particular case. The asterisk matches any pattern and therefore works precisely as a wildcard does in a poker game.

For example, suppose you wanted to search your directory for all filenames ending in txt. To do so, you use ls in combination with the asterisk symbol (*), like this:

```
ls *txt
```

Here, the asterisk represents an unknown quantity. This command tells UNIX to get all files that begin with anything but end in txt, for example:

➤ Files.txt

➤ address_book_txt

➤ poem-txt

You can also "nest" asterisks in you search. For example, suppose you issue the following command:

```
ls t*x*
```

This will match any of the following filenames:

➤ mytext

➤ toxic

➤ texan

Use the asterisk to represent any characters that might appear in a filename.

The Question Mark (?)

The question mark is a little more precise. It matches any *single character*. For example, suppose your directory has these files:

➤ mc68000

➤ mc6800

➤ mc680

On a search, the command **ls mc6??** would match only mc680. Likewise, **ls mc6???** would match only mc6800, and **ls mc6????** would match only mc68000.

Therefore, use the ? symbol to restrict your wildcard to matching a finite number of characters. (Use one ? for each character.)

! The Bang Character: Matches? Not!

The bang character (AKA the exclamation point) also serves a special function. In many programming languages (including shell language), the bang character is used to express the word "not". In filename pattern matching, the bang character does just that.

The Big Bang

The bang character is also sometimes still used in email addressing on older systems. For example, my email address in old addressing format would be wagjag!bwagner.

To use the bang symbol to exclude characters, place it before the undesirable character. For example, consider this command:

```
ls [!p]*
```

This command tells UNIX to list only those filenames that do NOT contain p. The brackets are necessary, particularly if you want to match a range of characters. For example, to match all characters between A and M, you would enclose these characters in brackets, like this:

```
[A-M]
```

Or, using the ! symbol, you could exclude all characters between A and M, like this:

```
[!A-M]*
```

Surfing the Pipeline

One of the shell's more interesting and useful features is the ability to assign the output of one command to the input of another. This is called piping. The name is derived from the special shell metacharacter used to perform this task, the pipe: ¦.

Piping Commands: The Pipe Symbol

To pipe the output of one command to another, issue the two commands, separated by the pipe symbol, like this:

```
command ¦ command
```

For example, I have 446 files in my /usr/bin directory. I would like to list those files. However, when I do, the list scrolls by too fast. To remedy that, I issue the following command:

```
ls -l ¦ more
```

This command pipes the output of ls -l to more. This effectively tells UNIX to do two things:

➤ List all regular files and directories in /usr/bin.

➤ Display this information one screen at a time.

UNIX responds by listing the contents of /usr/bin, and pausing each time the screen is full, like this:

```
total 23470
-r-xr-xr-x    1 root   bin        20372 Jul 15  1997 acctcom
-r-xr-xr-x    1 root   bin       123896 Jul 15  1997 adb
-r-xr-xr-x    1 root   bin        10000 Jul 15  1997 addbib
-r-s--x--x    1 root   sys       343164 Jul  2  1997 admintool
-r-xr-xr-x   17 root   bin          131 Jul 15  1997 alias
-r-xr-xr-x    1 root   bin        15736 Jul 15  1997 aliasadm
-rwxr-xr-x    1 root   bin        19292 Jul  2  1997 apm
-r-xr-xr-x    4 root   bin        38504 Jul 15  1997 apropos
-r-xr-xr-x    1 root   bin          944 Jul 15  1997 arch
-r-xr-xr-x    1 root   bin         6200 Jul 15  1997 asa
-rws--x--x    1 root   sys        33800 Jan  5  1998 at
-rws--x--x    1 root   sys        12900 Jul 15  1997 atq
-rws--x--x    1 root   sys        11592 Jul 15  1997 atrm
-rwxr-xr-x    1 root   staff     213048 Jun 25  1997 audioconvert
-rwxr-xr-x    1 root   staff     120712 Jun 25  1997 audioplay
-rwxr-xr-x    1 root   staff      38952 Jun 25  1997 audiorecord
-r-xr-xr-x    2 root   bin        84560 Jul 15  1997 awk
-r-xr-xr-x    1 root   bin         6084 Jul 15  1997 banner
-r-xr-xr-x    1 root   bin          901 Jul 15  1997 basename
--More--
```

Until I hit the spacebar, the current screen remains. This allows me time to view the data.

You can get quite creative with command piping. Table 5.4 lists some interesting piped commands and their results.

Table 5.4. Various Examples of Piping Commands

Command Line	Result
ls ¦ wc -l	Display the total number of regular files in the current directory.
who ¦ wc -l	Display the number of current users.
last bwagner ¦ head	Display the last ten times I logged in.
sort list ¦ pr ¦ lpr	Sort the file list alphabetically, prepare the output for printing, and print it.
who ¦ sort	Display current users, but alphabetize the output.
man sh ¦ mail bwagner	Get the manual page for sh and mail it to Bill Wagner.

Once you get more familiar with various UNIX programs, you'll use the pipe for all sorts of tasks by combining several commands together. For example, suppose you have a directory with several thousand files. All you want to know is the size of the largest file there. Rather than load the windowing system (and use a file manager), you issue the following command:

```
ls -l ¦ awk '{print $5}' ¦ sort -n ¦ tail -1
```

This command line pipes four commands in sequence. The sequence works like this:

➤ `ls -l` grabs a directory list.

➤ `awk '{print $5}'` grabs the file sizes from that list.

➤ `sort -n` sorts this new list numerically.

➤ `tail -1` prints only the last (and largest) file size.

But we're getting too far ahead. The least you need to know about the pipe symbol is this: it can be used to send the output of one command to another.

Pipe Down!

Generally, if you have to use more than three pipes to perform a task, you should probably consider a shell script. Shell scripts are small files that contain multiple shell commands. These files can be executed and can perform multiple tasks at high speed. You'll learn more about shell scripts later in this chapter.

Sequential Execution of Commands

The shell also supports sequential command execution. This is where commands are executed one after the other.

To execute commands sequentially, place a semicolon between them, like this:

```
cd /usr/bin; ls
```

The above command tells the shell to change the directory to /usr/bin and list its contents.

Conditional Execution of Commands

Both sh-style and csh-style shells support conditional execution of commands. There are two conditional command structures: AND and OR:

➤ **AND** specifies that if the first command is successful, the shell should execute the second command.

➤ **OR** specifies that if the first command fails, the shell should execute the second command.

The AND command structure consists of commands separated by double-ampersands, like this:

```
cd /usr/bin && ls
```

This command tells the shell to change the directory to /usr/bin and list its contents. If the cd command fails (/usr/bin does not exist), the ls command is never executed.

The OR structure consists of commands separated by double-pipes, like this:

```
cd /usr/bad-directory || cd /usr/good-directory
```

In the OR scenario, if your first command fails, the second one is executed. (Otherwise, if your first command is successful, your second command is ignored.

Cutting UNIX off at the Pass: Redirection

The shell also allows you to redirect input and output. To understand this process, consider this: From the moment you log in, UNIX opens three files. Each file handles one aspect of your session. The files (and their functions) are

➤ **STDIN.** STDIN is standard input. This is the input you enter at the keyboard.

➤ **STDOUT.** STDOUT is standard output. This is the output you receive when a command completes its job.

➤ **STDERR.** STDERR is standard error output. Error messages are standard error output.

Normally, STDOUT and STDERR are directed to your terminal. For example, when you issue the ls command, UNIX responds by displaying the current directory's contents. That data is STDOUT.

Sometimes, you don't want to see STDOUT. Instead, you simply want to capture the output to a file. That's where redirection comes in handy.

Redirecting Output

Redirection is done using special characters. These characters are listed in Table 5.5.

Table 5.5.   Redirection Characters and What They Do

Metacharacter	Purpose
>	This (redirection character)> character redirects output to a file. During that process, the file is overwritten (any data previously there is destroyed).
>!	This! (redirection character)> character combination redirects output to a file and explicitly overwrites that file. (In other words, the file is overwritten even if the shell was previously told to protect it.)
>>	This> (redirection character)> character combination redirects output to a file. During that process, the output is appended to the file. (In other words, the old data remains, and the new data is appended to it.)

continues

Table 5.5. Redirection Characters and What They Do
CONTINUED

Metacharacter	Purpose
>>!	This character combination will append output to a file (and even create a file if it doesn't already exist) even if the shell was previously instructed not to.
<	This character sends input to a command from a file.
<<	This character combination sends input to a command from standard input until a particular text string is encountered.

Redirection probably seems confusing. Let me clear that up. Suppose you want to store a directory listing in a file called mydirectory. Rather than clipping and pasting the information into mydirectory, you could issue this command:

```
ls -l > mydirectory
```

This tells UNIX to get the directory listing and send the results to mydirectory. (This way, you can view the information later.)

Now suppose that a week goes by. During that time, several hundred more files have been added to mydirectory. You decide to get another directory listing. However, you want to keep the original so you can compare the two. Instead of overwriting the contents of mydirectory, you want to append the new data to it. You do so like this:

```
ls -l >> mydirectory
```

mydirectory will now contain both directory listings.

Redirecting Error Messages

You can also redirect standard error messages. For example, suppose you issue a command that will generate lots of output and error messages. While you may later examine that data, you don't really want it popping up on your terminal. Therefore, you send both output and error messages to a log file, like this:

```
command >& logfile
```

The >& combination specifies that both STOUT and STDERR should be sent to an out file.

Shell Scripts and Programming

Now, it's time to tell you more than you'll ever need to know. Are you ready? As UNIX evolved, shells became very complex. Their command syntax and built-in functions expanded into full-blown programming languages. For example, it's possible to write a spell-checking program in any shell language. However, such programs often consist of several hundred lines of commands. When your shell commands get this complicated, it's silly to enter them at a command prompt. Here's why:

➤ It's easy to make a mistake along the way.

➤ Editing becomes problematic.

➤ Once you write something that complicated, you'd like to save it so you can use it again.

Hence, shell scripts were born. A *shell script* is a plain text file that contains numerous shell commands. These commands are stored for later execution.

For example, here's a shell script that verifies whether a number is more than, equal to, or less than 20:

```
#!/usr/bin/csh
echo "Please enter a number..."

        set i = $<
        if ($i < 20) then
        echo "$i is less than 20"

        else if ($i == 20) then
        echo "$i is equal to 20"

        else
        echo "$i is greater than 20"
        endif
```

If you examine the script, you'll see how it works. The script asks you for a number (which it stores in the variable $i). It then takes that number ($i) and performs two tests:

➤ If $i is less than 20, the script reports it.

➤ If $i is equal to 20, the script reports it.

➤ If $i is neither less than or equal to 20, the script deduces that your number is greater than 20.

Pretty simple stuff. However, when the shell executes this script, the script becomes a functional program. As you gain more experience with UNIX, you'll find scripts like this all over your hard disk. That's because UNIX shell scripts are often used in system administration.

A year from now, long after you've banished this book to your garage, you'll probably be writing your own shell scripts.

The Least You Need To Know

The least you need to know about the shell is this:

➤ It interprets and executes your commands.

➤ It has powerful text and file searching features.

➤ You should almost always structure your command line in this order: command, options, arguments.

➤ Mastering shell command language is one way to become very proficient at UNIX.

Manipulating Files and Directories

When you first log in, UNIX looks pretty desolate. However, under that seemingly boring exterior, UNIX is teeming with life. (Well, that's probably pushing it, but it's a pretty interesting operating system all the same.)

Before you can really benefit from UNIX's power, though, you must understand how UNIX organizes files and directories. Therefore, this chapter begins by answering the most basic question: "What is a directory?"

What's a Directory?

A directory is an area of your hard disk where files are stored. Inside of those files, you keep important data, like addresses and telephone numbers.

In this respect, a directory works much like a Rolodex card file. It stores cards (files) and those cards store your personal data. (See Figure 6.1.)

How a directory works.

In UNIX, there are many directories. These are organized in a simple directory structure. Let's talk about that structure for a moment.

Directory Structure in UNIX

Every operating system uses a directory structure to store and organize files. You can quickly understand the UNIX directory structure by thinking of it as a tree.

A tree's base is made up of roots. From these, the tree grows outward, forming branches. In UNIX, that's exactly how the directory structure works. The root of UNIX's directory structure is called /. All other directories (branches) spring from that point. (See Figure 6.2.)

/ as the top-level directory.

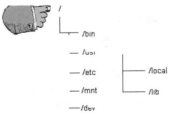

Any directory that branches out from / is a *subdirectory*. Immediate subdirectories of / are /bin, /usr, /etc, /mnt, and /dev. (See Figure 6.3.)

The subdirectories of /.

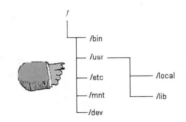

However, the directory tree doesn't stop there. Subdirectories can also have subdirectories of their own. For example, /local and /lib are subdirectories of /usr. (See Figure 6.4.)

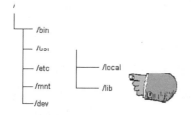

/local and /lib as subdirectories of /user.

/local and /lib as subdirectories of /usr. Files located in /local or /lib are therefore *three directories deep*. (Directory position is referred to in terms of depth.) The full address of a file called mydata located in /lib would look like this:

    /usr/lib/mydata

Here's why: mydata is located in /lib which is a subdirectory of /usr which is a subdirectory of /. This long form address is called the full or absolute path.

The key to navigating UNIX, then, is knowing how to navigate directories. Let's start there.

Where Am I?

All this directory talk is probably very confusing. That's because when you first log in, the only thing you see is the shell prompt, which looks like this:

    $

That's not much help. Your first step, therefore, is to discover what the current directory is. For this, use the pwd command.

Identifying the Current Directory: The pwd *Command*

To identify the current directory, use the pwd command, like this:

    pwd

UNIX will respond by reporting the current directory. For example, when I issue the pwd command, UNIX responds like this:

    /home/bwagner

From this, I know that I'm in /home/bwagner, my home directory. I am therefore three directories deep:

➤ /bwagner is a subdirectory of /home

➤ /home is a subdirectory of /

➤ / is the root directory

So, pwd can tell you where you are at any particular moment. (pwd actually stands for *present working directory*).

I'm Gonna Go Places

Knowing where you are at any particular moment is useful. However, it's much more exciting to go places. In UNIX, you can go to many different directories. All you need to know is how to get there. Let's talk about getting around in UNIX.

Changing From Directory to Directory: the cd Command.

To travel from one directory to another, use the cd command.

For DOS Heads

If you've ever used Microsoft's Disk Operating System, you'll feel right at home with the cd command. cd in UNIX works very much like cd in DOS.

The cd command is nearly always a two-part deal. You issue the cd command plus the directory you want to go to, like this:

cd *directory*

For example, to change to /usr, issue the following command:

cd /usr

Did it work? You can use the pwd command to double-check:

pwd

UNIX responds by telling you where you are:

/usr

So, to change directories, use the cd command. If you do that several times and suddenly realize you're lost, use the pwd command to find out where you are. (cd is an abbreviation for "change directory". You see, UNIX isn't that difficult after all. Most commands have sensible names that are really just shorthand for plain English.)

Finding Out What's in Your Directory

Hopping around from directory to directory can be fun, but it's not very productive. The next step is to find out whether there are any files in your directory. To do that, use the ls command.

Listing Directory Contents: the ls *Command*

The ls command will list a directory's contents. To get a simple directory list, issue the ls command without arguments, like this:

About Your Home Directory

If you want to return to your home directory, you can issue the cd command without arguments, like this:

    cd

This will take you back home, no matter where you are.

    ls

For example, when I list the contents of /home/bwagner, UNIX responds like this:

    dick   harry tom

From this, I know that there are three files in /home/bwagner: dick, harry, and tom. (I sometimes play racquetball with these guys. As you'll soon see, they're pretty weird.)

Unfortunately, the ls command by itself doesn't tell me much about these three files. (All it really tells me is that the files exist.) For example, I'd like to know how big those files are. To find that out, I issue the ls command plus the command-line switch for long format output, like this:

    ls -l

This time, UNIX gives much more information, including the file sizes:

    -rw-r--r--   1 bwagner   200   23 Jun 28 12:26 dick
    -rw-r--r--   1 bwagner   200   59 Jun 28 12:29 harry
    -rw-r--r--   1 bwagner   200   21 Jun 28 12:25 tom

File sizes are reported right before the date. Therefore, from the output above, I know that the file dick is 23 bytes in size. But I also discovered a lot more.

Let's briefly examine the ls long format output.

ls *Output and What it Means*

ls long format prints a wide range of values. Here, we're concerned with only four:

➤ The filename

➤ The time when the file was last modified

➤ The date when the file was last modified

➤ The file size

UNIX displays these values from right to left. (See Figure 6.5.)

ls (long format) displays filename, file time, file date, and file size.

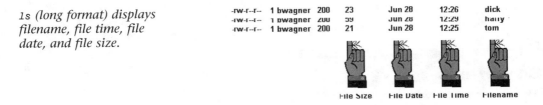

ls can display this and other information in a wide variety of ways. This next section explains how.

ls *Command-Line Switches*

The ls command has endless command-line switches. The more important ones are summarized in Table 6.1.

Table 6.1. Selected ls Command Line Switches

ls Command	Result
ls	A plain file list.
ls -l	A long file list, including filename, file time, file date, file size, file group, file owner, and file data type.
ls -A	A plain file list that also shows hidden files.
ls -F	A plain file list, but files and directories are differentiated. Directories appear with a slash (/) after them.
ls -m	Filenames listed sequentially, separated by commas.
ls -t	A plain file list sorted by date.
ls -1	A plain file list displayed vertically (down the page instead of across).

These options can make output easier to read. For example, I prefer to read files running down the page instead of across, so I use the -1 switch:

    ls -1

This displays the contents of /home/bwagner in column form:

```
dick
harry
tom
```

Listing Other Directories

You can use ls not only to view your own directory's contents, but the contents of other directories. To do so, issue the command ls plus your desired directory. For example, to list the contents of /usr, issue the following command:

```
ls /usr
```

This will list all files in /usr. On my machine, UNIX responds like this:

```
4lib      demo      kvm       old       share     usr
5bin      dict      lib       openwin   snadm     vmsys
GNU       dt        local     platform  spool     xpg4
X         games     mail      preserve  src
adm       include   man       proc      tmp
aset      java      net       pub       ucb
bin       java1.1   news      sadm      ucbinclude
ccs       kernel    oasys     sbin      ucblib
```

/usr has a million files (or at least 43), as you'll see later.

Investigating Tom, Dick, and Harry

So far, you've learned how to list a directory and find the files that reside there. (You even learned how to size a file.) Now it's time to learn something about what those files are made of.

The first thing you want to know is the type of file you're dealing with. For example, is the file text, data, or an executable? It's important to know this. Here's why: If you try to examine the raw contents of a data or executable file, thousands of strange and exotic characters will appear on your screen. They will look like this:

```
G`_NT_T≠_!_\≠__c^L_œ_h_GLOBAL_OFFSET_TABLE_≈Ã∆≈Ã≈
_PROCEDURE_LINKAGE_TABLE__Ã∆Ã_Ú
```

How to Learn More About ls

To learn more about ls (and its endless command-line switches) issue this command:

```
man ls
```

This will display the ls manual page.

Right after you display those characters, your terminal may blow up. (Just kidding. However, on some UNIX systems, if you display crazy characters, your terminal may never recover. Even if you later type regular text, it may still appear scrambled and unreadable. The cure for this is to reboot.)

You're probably wondering why this problem occurs. There's a perfectly reasonable explanation. Terminals weren't made to display certain characters. When you try to print binary file data to the terminal, character translation malfunctions. Since the terminal cannot recognize the characters, it tries to make close matches.

So, before examining the contents of files, you should know what they contain. UNIX has a command made specifically to identify file types. Appropriately enough, it's called `file`.

Identifying the File Type: the `file` Command

To identify a file's type, use the file command:

```
file filename
```

UNIX will respond with a description of the file's type. For example, suppose I want to find out what type of file tom is. I would issue the following command:

```
file tom
```

UNIX responds like this:

```
tom:            ascii text
```

From this, I know that tom is a plain text file (and I can therefore examine tom without fear of blowing up my terminal).

What's cool about `file` though, is this: You can use it to identify almost anything. For example, if I ask UNIX about /home/bwagner:

```
file /home/bwagner
```

UNIX responds like this:

```
/home/bwagner:   directory
```

This tells me that /home/bwagner is a directory. Similarly, if you use `file` to identify a system binary (like /bin/csh), UNIX responds like this:

```
/bin/csh: ELF 32-bit MSB executable SPARC Version 1, dynamically
linked, stripped
```

This tells you that /bin/csh is an executable file.

`file` has many practical uses, which we will examine later.

Master of the Universe

Listing files and discovering their file type is just fine. But maybe you're ready for a more interactive experience. In UNIX, you are the master of your universe. Not only can you list files, but you can also create them, copy them, delete them, display them, and do just about anything you can imagine. In this next section, you'll learn to do all that and more.

Deleting Files: the rm *Command*

Warning: the rm command is very dangerous. Make sure that you completely familiarize yourself with rm before using it. Otherwise, you may accidentally delete important system files!

To delete a file, use the rm command, like this:

```
rm filename
```

For example, in my /home/bwagner directory, I have the files tom, dick, and harry. Suppose I decide that I don't like harry anymore (his racquetball game stinks). I can delete harry like this:

```
rm harry
```

rm *Command-Line Switches*

The rm command has several command-line switches. These are summarized in Table 6.2.

Table 6.2. Selected rm Command Line Switches

rm **Command**	**Result**
rm *filename*	rm removes the specified file.
rm -i *filenames*	rm prompts you before removing each file. (This is called interactive mode. Until you get more familiar with UNIX, you might want to use this option. It can prevent you from accidentally deleting files that you need.)
rm -r	rm removes directory contents recursively. This is where both subdirectories and files are removed from the current directory. Using the -r switch can be dangerous, so use it wisely. (This operation is much like using DELTREE in MSDOS.)

Copying Files: the cp Command

To copy a file, use the cp command (which is the UNIX equivalent of the DOS command COPY). To do so, you must supply two values: the name of the file you want to copy and where you want to copy it to:

    cp filename1 filename2

For example, suppose I wanted to copy the file tom into a file called tom.backup. I would issue the following command:

    cp tom tom.backup

In response, UNIX would create an exact copy of tom. This would be stored in tom.backup in the current directory.

However, you can also use cp to copy files from directory to directory. For example, suppose I wanted to copy tom to /usr. I would issue the following command:

    cp tom /usr

In this instance, UNIX would copy tom to /usr.

A Warning About cp

Be careful about using cp to copy files from one directory to another. Make sure you aren't overwriting another file with the same name. cp doesn't always warn you before it overwrites a file.

Moving Files: the mv Command

To move a file, use the mv command. To do so, you must provide two values: the name of the file you're moving and where you want it to go:

    mv filename destination

In this respect, mv works much like cp. The *destination* is a directory. For example, suppose I wanted to move tom from my current directory to /usr. I would issue the following command:

    mv tom /usr

UNIX would respond by moving tom to /usr.

Displaying File Contents: The cat Command

To display a file's contents, use the cat command, like this:

    cat filename

For example, suppose I wanted see the contents of tom. I would issue the following command:

    cat tom

UNIX would respond by displaying tom's contents, which in this case is a single line of text:

```
Tom has 1 nose ring.
```

The cat command can be used to display the contents of one file or several files. To view the contents of several files at once, issue the cat command followed by the filenames. For example, suppose I wanted to see the contents of tom, dick, and harry. I would issue the following command:

```
cat tom dick harry
```

UNIX responds by printing the contents of each file, in the order specified:

```
Tom has 1 nose ring.
Dick has 2 nose rings.
Harry has 3 nose rings, 1 pair of goggles, and 1 unicycle.
```

The cat command can also be used to identify line numbers in a file. For example, suppose you created a file called poem containing the following text:

```
In days of old
when users were bold
and Windows wasn't invented,
they wrote their code
in plain text mode
and worked away contented.
```

You could have cat display not only poem's contents, but also number each line it finds. You do this by specifying the -n command-line switch, like this:

```
cat -n poem
```

cat will respond like this:

```
1   In days of old
2   when users were bold
3   and Windows wasn't invented,
4   they wrote their code
5   in plain text mode
6   and worked away contented.
```

About Those Darn Directories

On a fresh installation, UNIX has many prefabricated directories. Nearly all of them store important system files (files that are essential to system operation). Whenever possible, you should avoid storing your personal files in these directories. Instead, you should create your own directories and store your personal files there. (In other

words, don't clutter system directories with your own stuff!) You can create your own directories using the `mkdir` command.

Creating Directories: The `mkdir` Command

To create your own directory, use the `mkdir` command, like this:

```
mkdir mydirectory
```

For example, to create a directory called bozos (for storing the email addresses of knuckleheads you meet on the Internet), enter the following command:

```
mkdir bozos
```

Once you create your directory, you should double-check that everything went exactly as you planned.

When cat Runs Amok

Sometimes, files contain more lines than a terminal can display on a single screen. In these instances, using cat to display file contents could get confusing. Here's why: the file's contents will scroll by so fast, you won't get a chance to read it. To remedy that, tell cat to feed you the file one screen at a time using the more command, like this:

```
cat filename ¦ more.
```

To do so, issue the `ls` command plus the directory you created:

```
ls bozos
```

UNIX will verify that your directory was actually created:

```
bozos
```

The `mkdir` command is the UNIX equivalent of `md` in DOS. (Interestingly, DOS also supports `mkdir`, but hardly anyone uses it.)

Moving Directories: The `mv` Command

To move a directory, use the `mv` command, like this:

```
mv directory destination
```

For example, to move /home/bwagner to /home/backup/bwagner, I would issue the following command:

```
mv /home/bwwagner /home/backup/bwagner
```

Removing Directories: The `rmdir` Command

To remove a directory, use the `rmdir` command, like this:

```
rmdir directory
```

For example, to remove /home/bwagner, I would issue the following command:

```
rmdir /home/bwagner
```

Note that the `rmdir` command will not remove a directory (or directory tree) if that directory is not empty. To remove a directory that still has files in it, issue the `rmdir` command plus the `-r` switch, which makes directory removal recursive, like this: `rmdir -r /home/bwagner`. However, be careful about using `rmdir` recursively. It's very easy to accidentally delete directories with valuable files.

The Deadly Asterisk

The commands discussed in this chapter perform pretty basic tasks. And, if you use those commands on one file at a time, your work will go very slowly. You could say, therefore, that until this point in the chapter, you were in the UNIX Stone Age.

To take you out of the Stone Age, I give you fire. Here it is:

```
*
```

It doesn't look like much; it's just an asterisk. However, in UNIX, the asterisk is an extremely powerful tool. It allows you to work strong magic. Here's why: the asterisk symbol is a wildcard.

The asterisk is used as a substitute for generic values. For example, when you issue this command:

```
cat *
```

you are telling UNIX this: "Display the contents of all files in this directory." Or, when you issue this command:

```
file *
```

you are telling UNIX this: "Show me the file types of all files in this directory." Or even worse—which is why you should use the asterisk sparingly—if you issue this command:

```
rm *
```

you are telling UNIX this: "Delete all files in this directory." For this reason, be *extremely* careful when using the asterisk. It can have very sweeping consequences!

The next section demonstrates what will happen when you use an asterisk in combination with the commands previously discussed.

Various Commands and the Asterisk

Table 6.3 details what will happen when you use the asterisk symbol in combination with various commands.

Table 6.3.   The Deadly Asterisk and Various Commands

Command	Result
rm *	All files in the current directory are deleted.
ls *cig	All filenames and directory names that end in cig will be listed.
cat tom*	All files that have names beginning with tom will be displayed.
cp t*m /home	All files with names that begin with t and end with m will be copied to /home.
rmdir h*m?	All directories with names that begin with h and have m as their second-to-last letter will be deleted.

The asterisk can save you a lot of time. We will be looking at the asterisk in Chapter 7, "Regular and Not-So-Regular Expressions."

The Least You Need To Know

➤ In UNIX, there are many directories. Each directory can store either files or other directories.

➤ To navigate between directories, use the cd command. To list files in a directory, use the ls command.

➤ The asterisk is a powerful tool. Don't use it indiscriminately. (For example, if you use the asterisk while deleting files, be sure to use the -i option of rm. This will prevent you from accidentally deleting important files.)

## Chapter 7

Regular and Not-So-Regular Expressions

In This Chapter

➤ Learning regular expressions

➤ Performing text searches

➤ Manipulating text

Many different kinds of expressions exist; I learned that early on. When I was ten or so, my grandfather took me to his golf club where we met a business associate of his named Ralph. Ralph claimed that he'd recently shot a game in the low 60s. (I wasn't sure, but I thought this was probably pretty good). Later, when we were alone, my grandfather told me that Ralph was "full of malarkey." Not wanting to admit that I didn't know what this meant, I simply nodded sternly in agreement.

A week or so went by and I had the occasion to use that same phrase. My mother had thrown a dinner party and someone there was speaking about Ralph. When asked if I knew Ralph, I replied that yes, I knew him, but it didn't matter, because he was full of malarkey. This didn't go over well at all. In fact, my mother told me that this was an *expression* only (one from the turn of the century) and that I should never use it again. (She then went after my grandfather, the obvious culprit.)

So, one kind of regular expression is a figure of speech. There are others. As humans, we generally equate the term *expression* with speech, emotion, or artistic exposition. Alas, UNIX knows little about these things.

Instead, in UNIX, a *regular expression* is a string of text or a series of characters run together in sequential order. For example, these are all regular expressions:

➤ Macmillan Computer Publishing

➤ --++&&**++--

➤ My grandfather never heard the end of it

UNIX has many tools for searching out regular expressions in files, standard output, standard input, or just about anything that contains text. That's what this chapter is all about.

Get a grep on Yourself, for Goodness Sake!

Because UNIX stores accounting, process, and configuration information in plain text, you'll often seek out text patterns (regular expressions) in files. One program designed expressly for this purpose is grep.

Using grep to Search for Regular Expressions

grep searches out regular expression in files and prints all lines that contain a match. (grep is one of the most useful UNIX utilities ever created.)

At a minimum, grep takes two arguments: the regular expression you want and the file you'd like to search. For example, I have a file on my drive named guys. In it, I describe some characteristics about Tom, Dick, and Harry, three guys I play racquetball with. Here's the content of guys:

```
Dick has 2 nose rings.
Tom has 1 nose ring.
Harry has 3 nose rings, 1 pair of goggles, and 1 unicycle.
```

Suppose I wanted to find out which of these guys (if any) wears goggles. I would use grep, like this:

grep goggles guys

Here's the output:

```
Harry has 3 nose rings, 1 pair of goggles, and 1 unicycle.
```

As you can see, grep dutifully grabbed line 3, the only line containing the string "goggles".

Whenever you want to isolate an unbroken string of text, use grep in precisely this manner: grep *string file*.

Using grep *to Search More Than One Word*

To search for two or more words separated by whitespace, enclose your string in quotes, like this:

```
grep "nose ring" guys
```

Here's the output:

```
Dick has 2 nose rings.
Tom has 1 nose ring.
Harry has 3 nose rings, 1 pair of goggles, and 1 unicycle.
```

By using quotes, you're instructing grep to include whitespace between characters. In this way, you can capture one or two words as well as search for entire lines.

grep *Command Line Options*

grep has several command line options that help you control output. These are summarized in Table 7.1.

Table 7.1. Selected grep command line switches

Option	Result
-c string	The -c option tells grep to count how many instances of the string appear in the specified file. For example, to find out how many folks use bash as a shell, issue the following command: **grep -c bash /etc/passwd**.
-h	The -h option prevents file headers from being printed to STDOUT. Normally, when you search multiple files for the same string, for each match, grep prints the name of the file in which the string was found. The -h option prevents that filename from appearing in the report.
-i	The -i option instructs grep to make all searches case insensitive. Therefore, the command **grep -i wagner /etc/passwd** will match wagner, Wagner, and WAGNER.
-l	The -l option instructs grep to print only the filenames in which matches are found. This is valuable if you're trying to locate two files out of a thousand that contain a certain text string. If you only need to know their names (and not actually view their content), use the -l option.

continues

Table 7.1. Selected grep command line switches
CONTINUED

Option	Result
-n	The -n option instructs grep to print the line numbers on which each match is found. (This will work on multiple files as well. For each file that has a match, grep will print the filename plus the line number on which the match appears.)
-v	The -v option reverses your selection criteria. This instructs grep that instead of printing all matching lines, it should print all nonmatching lines.

More Complex Regular Expression Searches

Garden-variety grep queries are useful for quick-and-dirty searches, but sometimes you may require a more industrial-strength approach. To take full advantage of the searching power of grep, you can incorporate several metacharacters into your query.

Let's examine those metacharacters for a moment.

Metacharacters Used in Searching

By coupling special metacharacters with grep, you can refine your searches considerably. Table 7.2 lists some of those metacharacters and what they do.

Table 7.2. Metacharacters for use in pattern matching

Metacharacter	Purpose
*	This is a wildcard. Depending on where you position it, this metacharacter can match several things. For example, [a-z]* will match one or more lowercase characters, whereas [a-z].* will match any lowercase character followed by one (and possibly more) characters.
.	The period metacharacter matches any single character.
^	The caret metacharacter matches lines that begin with any characters that follow it.
[ ]	The brackets are used to indicate a range of characters. For example, [a-z] will match any lowercase character, whereas [A-Z] will match any uppercase character. (From another angle, [0-9] will match any single number).
[^]	When the brackets contain a caret metacharacter, the range or list of characters that follow are excluded from the search. For example, [^abc] specifies that the characters a, b, c should not be matched.

Metacharacter	Purpose
¦	The pipe is used to separate alternate regular expressions. Essentially, this symbol is used as an OR operator. (You can stack pipes, too. For example, to find the words mary, had, little, or lamb, you could "pipe" them together, like this: mary¦had¦little¦lamb.)
+	The plus metacharacter matches any instance of the preceding character.

Not only can you search for strings in files, you can also specify their position. For example, you can specify that you only want matches where the string appears at the beginning or end of a line. Let's briefly take a look at how this works.

Matching Strings at the Beginning of a Line

To find a text string at the beginning of a line, use the ^ (caret) metacharacter. Here's an example:

```
grep '^Harry' *
```

This will match all lines that begin with Harry.

Additionally, you can mix and match with wildcards. For example, suppose you want to search for lines that began with either Harry or Harold. You would issue this command:

```
grep '^Har.' *
```

This will match all lines that begin with Har followed by any characters. Note the use of the period (.) symbol, which will match any character. Furthermore, you can position several wildcards in your search. For example, this command will also match Harry and Harold at the beginning of a line:

```
grep '^.ar.' *
```

Unfortunately, however, grep '^.ar.' is a little too broad, because it will also match many other strings, including these:

➤ Cars

➤ Mars

➤ Bars

Therefore, you should exercise restraint when using wildcard metacharacters. The purpose of regular expression searching is to eliminate all but the most relevant matches. Wildcards can expand your search a little or a lot, depending on how many you use and how you position them.

The End of the Line: The $ Metacharacter

To find a text string at the end of a line, use the $ metacharacter. Here's an example:

```
grep cycle.$ *
```

This will match any line that ends with cycle. Additionally, you can use wildcards in your search, like this:

```
grep 'cy....$' *
```

This will also match cysts.

Egad! It's egrep! Specifying Alternate Searches

In addition to searching for exact (or sometimes vague) matches at the beginning or end of lines, you can also search for several different strings at once. For this, use the egrep program.

The egrep program searches *full regular expressions*. You can therefore think of egrep as a more fastidious grep (egrep will match all alphanumeric and special characters).

You can use egrep (coupled with the pipe symbol) to perform alternate searches (or searches where you're looking for more than just one string). For example, suppose you want to find all files that contain either cycle or cysts. To do so, enclose your terms in quotes and separate them by a pipe symbol, like this:

```
egrep "cycle¦cysts" *
```

This instructs egrep to match all lines where either cycle or cysts appear. However, suppose you only know part of the words you're looking for. Can you still use egrep to search for both? Absolutely. To do so, enclose your terms in quotes and isolate any unique characters in parentheses, separated by a pipe symbol, like this:

```
egrep "cy(cl.¦st.)" *
```

In this case, egrep will only match lines that have either cycl or cyst followed by some other character(s).

egrep and Case Sensitivity

Note that egrep's searches are case sensitive. Additionally, I should mention that while egrep is quite powerful, you'll probably use it less often than plain, old grep. (In most cases, grep will suffice in finding the pattern you seek. Fall back on egrep if grep fails in that regard.)

Hone on the Range: The Bracket Metacharacters ([ ]) and Range Searches

You can also search by range. For example, suppose you had a file named alphabet.txt with the following contents:

```
abc
def
hij
klm
mno
pqr
stu
vwx
yz
```

You can locate lines that contain ranges of letters by using brackets ([ ]) to enclose a range, like this:

grep [v-z] alphabet.txt

This command isolates only those lines that contain the range of letters v through z. Here's the output:

```
vwx
yz
```

Additionally, you can search for several ranges. For this, use the command egrep. For example, suppose you want to search alphabet.txt for ranges a-z and v-z. You would issue the following command:

egrep "[v-z¦a-c]" alphabet.txt

Here's the output:

```
abc
vwx
yz
```

Also, as you might expect, ranges apply to numbers as well. For example, suppose you had a file called numbers.txt with the following contents:

```
123
4567
89
```

You could isolate a particular number range using grep, like this:

grep [4-7] numbers.txt

Here's the output:

4567

Finally, you can mix and match searches. For example, suppose you had a file named `characters.txt` with these contents:

```
There are 52 cards in a deck.
There are 4 suits.
There are thirteen sets.
```

Let's say you wanted to grab lines with numbers as well as text. You could issue the following command:

egrep "[0-4]¦.teen" numbers.txt

This grabs the numbers 52 and 4, as well as the word `thirteen`.

Matches? We Don't Need No Stinkin' Matches! (Exclusionary Searches)

Most often, you'll be searching for a particular text string. However, on rare occasion, you'll want to conduct an *exclusionary search*. This is a search where you're looking for everything *but* the search term.

For example, let's stick with `alphabet.txt`. Here are its contents:

```
abc
def
hij
klm
mno
pqr
stu
vwx
yz
```

Now, suppose you want to find all lines except those that contain the letters a-c. You would use the caret (^) metacharacter, like this:

egrep "[^a-c]" alphabet.txt

Here's the output:

```
def
hij
klm
mno
pqr
stu
```

```
vwx
yz
```

You can also compound your exclusionary criteria by adding additional ranges, like this:

```
egrep "[^a-c¦^v-z]" alphabet.txt
```

This command tells egrep to find all lines *except* those that contain a-c or y-z. Here's the output:

```
def
hij
klm
mno
pqr
stu
```

The Big Guns: awk

On occasion, you'll encounter a problem that requires an even more aggressive approach. In these cases, one program can help you tremendously: awk. Let's take a brief look at awk now.

Looking "awkward"

awk is a pretty strange name unless you know its origins—it's named after the programmers who invented it: Alfred V. Aho, Peter J. Weinberger, and Brian W. Kernighan.

awk was introduced some time in 1977 and has been a pretty standard utility on nearly all UNIX systems since 1985. If I could sum up awk in one sentence, it would be this: awk is a powerful text-scanning language.

awk comes in handy when you need to extract values from a file without knowing what they are beforehand. Here's an example: Suppose you want to keep track of employee hours. To do so, you could create a file called hours.txt that looks like this:

```
Jack, Programming Department, 43
Susan, Marketing Department, 20
Jonathan, Vice President, 5
```

In hours.txt, you have three fields, separated by commas:

➤ Employee name

➤ Employee department or function

➤ The number of hours the employee worked this week

89

Now, you could use grep to find out how many hours an employee worked, like this:

```
grep Jack hours.txt
```

Here's the output:

```
Jack, Programming Department, 43
```

That's great. However, suppose you need different information. For example, suppose you want to extract only the hours worked. In this case, grep wouldn't be very useful. You'd be better off using awk.

awk splits lines of input or output into fields automatically, provided those fields are separated by some common denominator. For example, suppose you want to pull all current processes. You might issue this command:

```
ps -a
```

Here's the output:

```
PID TTY      TIME CMD
15529 pts/26  0:00 sz
19013 pts/1   0:00 telnet
19249 pts/3   0:00 pine
19264 pts/0   0:00 ps
17804 pts/4   0:06 pine
```

In this output, four fields are separated by whitespace. This whitespace consistently separates all fields and is therefore your common denominator.

Suppose you only want the last field. You could use awk to extract it, like this:

```
ps -a ¦ awk '{print $4}'
```

Now, instead of a full listing, you would get this:

```
CMD
sz
telnet
pine
ps
mv
sh
pine
```

In fact, you could even trim the CMD header by issuing the following command:

```
ps -a ¦ awk '{print $4}' ¦ grep -v CMD
```

Here's the output:

```
sz
telnet
pine
vi
ps
sh
pine
```

So, awk automatically breaks words separated by whitespace into fields—but that's just the beginning. awk doesn't necessarily have to read whitespace as a field delimiter. You can tell awk to use *any* character as a delimiter by using the -F flag.

Let's go back to the employee hour database. Here's what it looks like:

```
Jack, Programming Department, 43
Susan, Marketing Department, 20
Jonathan, Vice President, 5
```

Note that the file has a uniform structure—it contains three fields and a comma separates each. To extract those fields, you must take three steps.

First, you tell awk to use commas as field delimiters, like this:

awk -F,

Next, you specify the field you want to print (in this case, the hours), like this:

'{print $3}'

Lastly, you specify the filename:

hours.txt

The entire command line looks like this:

awk -F, '{print $3}' hours.txt

Here's the output:

```
43
20
5
```

Also, you can choose different fields. For example, to extract employee names, you'd switch to field 1:

awk -F, '{print $1}' hours.txt

In response, awk prints the first field:

```
Jack
Susan
Jonathan
```

Finally, you could isolate employee departments by choosing field 2 instead:

awk -F, '{print $2}' hours.txt

awk would respond with the requested data:

```
Programming Department
Marketing Department
Vice President
```

Advanced awk

Simple awk commands are useful when you want a quick view of static data. However, suppose you want to actually derive reports from that data. For this, you should learn the fundamentals of awk scripting. Although this might sound very intimidating, you'll be pleasantly surprised to discover that no magic is involved (at least, not when scripting simple tasks).

Suppose you had a file called records.txt in which you kept track of four values:

➤ Each department in your company

➤ How many workstations each department has

➤ How many employees each department has

➤ How many hours a week the workstations are used

Assume that records.txt has the following contents:

```
Accounting      5       5       30
Development     17      20      40
Marketing       5       3       10
```

To extract a report from records.txt, you create an awk script. This is a plain text file that holds multiple awk commands. For example, let's suppose you want to extract a report from records.txt in tabular form. You want the data to be formatted in nice, clean tables, like this:

```
Department:     Accounting
Workstations:   5
Employees:      5
Hours:          30
```

You begin by editing a new file. (In this case, we'll call it `tables`.) The first line of
tables calls awk, like this:

```
#!/usr/bin/awk
```

This tells the shell where it can find awk. Next, you open your procedure by inserting
a { symbol. So, `tables` should now look like this:

```
#!/usr/bin/awk


{
```

Next, you describe the procedure. In this case, you want to label each line and insert
the value. Therefore, you insert the following text:

```
print ""
print "Department: \t", $1
print "Workstations: \t", $2
print "Employees: \t",  $3
print "Hours: \t\t", $4
```

Now, let's break this down. The first line (`print ""`) tells awk to print a blank line
between records, which will make your tables easier to read. The remaining lines
print a label (for example, "Department:"), a field value (for example, $1, which rep-
resents field 1), and a tab (\t). Therefore, the contents of `tables` now looks like this:

```
!/usr/bin/awk


   {

   print ""
   print "Department: \t", $1
   print "Workstations: \t", $2
   print "Employees: \t",  $3
   print "Hours: \t\t", $4
```

Finally, you close your procedure with the } symbol. The entire `tables` script should
now look like this:

```
#!/usr/bin/awk


   {

   print ""
   print "Department: \t", $1
   print "Workstations: \t", $2
   print "Employees: \t",  $3
   print "Hours: \t\t", $4


}
```

93

From here, you perform two tasks: You save your script and then make it executable, like this:

```
chmod +x tables
```

Finally, you run the script with this command:

awk -f tables records.txt

Here's the output:

```
Department:        Accounting
Workstations:      5
Employees:         5
Hours:             30

Department:        Development
Workstations:      17
Employees:         20
Hours:             40

Department:        Marketing
Workstations:      5
Employees:         3
Hours:             10
```

Talking awk

Regular expression searches in awk work very much like those in egrep, except awk is more powerful. For example, not only can awk locate regular expressions, it can also execute commands based on what it finds.

Also, xe "awk utility" the awk man page has some good examples and a brief summary of awk commands.

The Least You Need to Know

UNIX is a largely text-based operating system and therefore has many power tools for searching and manipulating text. Here are some simple points to remember:

➤ When searching for simple text in a file, use grep.

➤ If the pattern for which you're searching is more complex, try egrep.

➤ If you need industrial-strength text manipulation, try awk, which can save you many hours of heartache, especially when you're searching through large files with mountains of data.

➤ To widen or narrow your search, use wildcards and metacharacters as needed.

## Chapter 8

Opening, Editing, and Saving Files

In This Chapter

➤ Processing text in UNIX

➤ Learning about different UNIX text editors

Back when Bell Labs engineers were designing UNIX, word processors didn't exist. In fact, the closest thing to a word processor probably wore a suit and tie (or a skirt and stockings) and packed a mean set of typing fingers. (Have Smith-Corona, will travel.) Seriously, though. In those days, even tasks such as formatting and printing a book were done largely by human hands.

Similarly, windowing systems didn't exist, so users had to interface with their computers in a command-line, plain text environment. It was in this climate that UNIX flourished; hence, many UNIX utilities still rely on plain text databases, log files, and configuration files. Therefore, as you use UNIX, you'll find yourself dealing with plain text more and more.

In this chapter, you'll learn about tools that can help you process that plain text effectively.

Text Support

UNIX has very extensive support for text processing. So extensive, in fact, that modern distributions of UNIX still include a line editor. (A *line editor* is a text-editing tool that can operate on one line at a time from the command line.) Such tools have faded from existence on most platforms, having been replaced by powerful word processors packaged in user-friendly windowing systems. So, initially, it seems silly that UNIX folks keep such ancient tools around. However, as you'll soon see, these tools offer you great speed and flexibility.

Sending a Single Line of Text to Disk: The echo Command

For very simple tasks, you may not even require a text editor. Here's an example: Suppose you have a plain text database of department telephone numbers (we'll call it phone.txt). Each line is a record, and fields are separated by commas, like this:

```
Susan, Marketing, Room 200, 555-5555
John, Production, Room 204, 555-5556
```

The fields are for name, department, room, and telephone number. To add a single record, you don't need a text editor. Instead, you can use the echo command to save time, like this:

```
echo "Bill, Programming, Room 210, 555-5557" >> phone.txt
```

This command appends the quoted text to phone.txt. The result is that phone.txt now looks like this:

```
Susan, Marketing, Room 200, 555-5555
John, Production, Room 204, 555-5556
Bill, Programming, Room 210, 555-5557
```

Pretty nifty, but not practical for large tasks. In this next section, we'll look a whole slew of editors (ranging from primitive to sophisticated) and what they can do for you.

Big ed

The most primitive text-editing tool in UNIX is called ed. ed is most useful when you need to add just a few lines of text to a file. (In other words, you're really busy with other things and need an instant solution.) To start ed, enter his name at the prompt, followed by the filename you intend to create, like this:

```
ed textfile
```

ed will respond by opening textfile and waiting for your command:

```
?textfile
```

At this point, you want to enter some text. To do so, you first tell ed that you'll be appending text to textfile. You do this by entering the letter a (short for *append mode*) on the command line:

```
a
```

In response, ed enters append mode and prepares to receive your text. From here, you type your desired text:

This line of text will test ed.

When you're finished typing, add a period by itself on a blank line, like this:

```
.
```

This tells ed that you're done typing. (In response, ed exits append mode). Next, you tell ed to write your text to textfile. To do so, you enter the letter w on a blank line, like this:

```
w
```

Finally, to exit ed, enter the letter q on an empty line, like this:

```
q
```

That's it. ed will return you to the shell. To check whether your file was actually written, use the cat command:

```
$ cat textfile
This line of text will test ed.
```

ed has some pretty interesting features, which are summarized in Table 8.1.

Table 8.1. ed commands and what they do

Command	Purpose
$p	This will take you to the file's last line.
.	The period tells ed that you're done typing.
.+Xp	Where *x* is a number that allows you to skip ahead. For example, suppose you were currently on line 18 and you wanted to go to line 20. You could avoid viewing line 19 by issuing the command .+2p.
.-Xp	In this case, *x* is a number that allows you to move backwards. For example, if you were on line 20 and wanted to go to line 18, you would issue the command .-2p.
a	The letter a throws ed into append mode so you can begin typing your desired text.
d	This signals ed to delete the current line. For example, say you wanted to go to line 3 and delete it. You would enter the following commands in succession: 3p d.

continues

Table 8.1.   ed commands and what they do CONTINUED

Command	Purpose
ed *filename*	This starts ed and creates or opens the desired file.
i	This signals ed to enter *insert mode*. In insert mode, you can go to a particular line and add text.
q	The letter q signals ed that you're exiting the program.
s/*text1*/*text2*/	This performs text substitution. For example, suppose your file contained the phrase "Ronald Reagan is President of the United States." Well, that would be a little dated. To fix this, you would issue the following command: **s/Ronald Reagan/Bill Clinton/**.
w	The letter w (short for *write*) tells ed to commit your text to disk in the file you specified.
Xp	Here, *x* is a number that will take you to the specified line. For example, suppose your file has 20 lines and you want to go to line 19. You would enter the following command in ed: **19p**.

ed has a lot of functionality for a line editor. Of course, in practice, you'll rarely use ed. However, it's good to know a little ed in case something goes wrong. (If your windowing system fails, for example, you'll still be able to edit configuration files.)

Well, enough about ed. Let's check out vi.

The vi Editor

As I explained in Chapter 2, "UNIX Flavors," the folks at Berkeley found that AT&T UNIX wasn't very user friendly. (Gee, I can't imagine why.) As part of their campaign to remedy this, they created vi (or the *visual editor*).

vi had several advantages over line editors, the most important of which was visualization. Using vi, users could see an entire page of text at one time. This reduced the likelihood of error, increased efficiency, and generally made the user experience more enjoyable.

Starting vi and Opening Files

To start vi, enter the vi command (preferably followed by name of the file you're about to edit.) Let's stick with phone.txt for a moment. To edit phone.txt with vi, enter the following command:

```
vi phone.txt
```

The vi environment will start, and vi will load the requested file, as shown in the following figure.

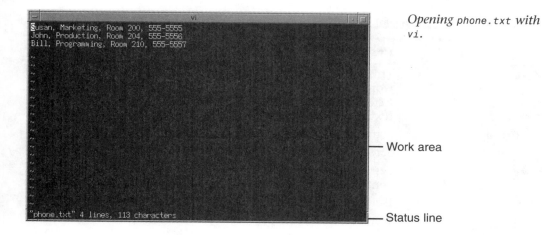

```
Susan, Marketing, Room 200, 555-5555
John, Production, Room 204, 555-5556
Bill, Programming, Room 210, 555-5557
```

```
"phone.txt" 4 lines, 113 characters
```

Opening phone.txt *with* vi.

— Work area

— Status line

The vi Editing Environment

The vi screen is divided into two sections. The work area (where you enter and edit text) occupies over 90 percent of the screen. In contrast, the status line (where statistics are reported and your commands are echoed) is a single line at the bottom of the screen.

When vi first loads, it begins in command mode. While in command mode, vi recognizes a wide range of commands that perform searching, cutting, pasting, deleting, and inserting. You'll learn those commands momentarily. However, to immediately start typing, enter the letter a, like this:

a

As a result, vi will exit command mode, and you can begin editing your file. When you finish editing your file, issue the :wq command, like this:

:wq

vi will respond by saving your changes and returning you to a prompt.

The Power of vi

Initially, you might think that the only advantage of vi (over ed, for example) is that you can see your file's contents (which doesn't seem like too much to ask.) However, under the hood, vi is extremely powerful.

At any point, you can enter command mode (by pressing the Esc key) and perform a wide range of operations on your file. Table 8.2 lists some important vi commands and what they do.

Table 8.2. Important commands in vi

Command	Result
a	This tells vi to begin appending text after the cursor. (In other words, as you type, characters appear to the cursor's right.) Issue this command when you first start vi. (If you don't, no text will appear until you strike the "a" key).
Ctrl+b	Scrolls up one page at a time.
Ctrl+f	Scrolls down one page at a time.
d	Sent once, this command will delete a character or operator. Sent twice, this command will delete an entire line.
Shift+d	Deletes an entire line.
i	Initializes insert mode (much as it does in ed.)
x	Notifies vi to delete the current character.
Shift+x	Notifies vi to delete the character immediately preceding the cursor.
w	Allows you to jump from word to word.
w:	Writes changes to the current file.
Shift+p	Pastes text.
Shift+h	Places the cursor at the beginning of the file. (This works much like the Home button in many word processors.)
Shift+l	Takes you to the last line of the current file.
w: *filename*	Saves changes to a new file.
:wq	This is the save and exit command. After you finish appending text to your file, hit the Esc key and issue this command. vi will save your work and return you to the shell.

Performing Searches in vi

Additionally, vi supports searching, matching, and replacing. To search, use one of the following four commands:

➤ */search term*—Searches from the cursor to the file's end

➤ *?search term*—Searches all text that precedes the cursor

➤ n—Repeats a forward search

➤ Shift+n—Repeats a backward search

For example, we've been using phone.txt as our sample file. It contains the following lines:

```
Susan, Marketing, Room 200, 555-5555
John, Production, Room 204, 555-5556
Bill, Programming, Room 210, 555-5557
```

Let's say you opened this file in vi (and, hence, your cursor's at the first line). To find the string "Room 210", you would enter vi's command mode (hit ESC) and issue the following command:

    /Room 210

vi would then find "Room 210" (on the third line) and position your cursor at the letter *R* (when vi finds a match, it places your cursor at the first character of the matched text).

However, if you were already on line 3 and wanted to find the string "Room 200", you would issue the following command for a backward search:

    ?Room 210

Summary on vi

vi is one text editor you should learn to use at least marginally well. No matter what version of UNIX you use, it's sure to have vi. (Even a very stripped-down configuration with no windowing system, networking, or language compiler is likely to have it.)

The pico Editor

Where do they get these names? What on earth is a pico? No matter. pico is an excellent alternative to vi, particularly if you're migrating from the Microsoft platform. Although pico isn't a windowed text editor, its interface is quite user-friendly, as shown in the following figure.

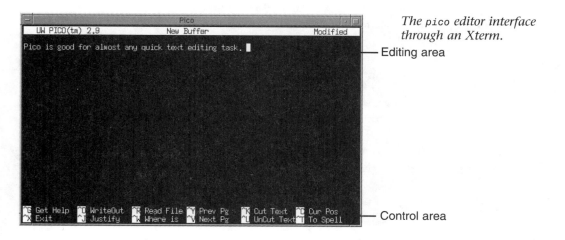

The pico *editor interface through an Xterm.*

— Editing area

— Control area

101

The pico interface is broken into two parts: the editing area and the control area. You do your work in the editing area (with pico responding much like a DOS editor) and enter your commands (explained in the control area) with keystroke combinations.

Text Manipulation in pico

pico supports all the basic functions you'd expect in a text editor, including clipping, pasting, searching, and so forth. To accomplish these tasks, use the keystroke combinations described in Table 8.3.

Table 8.3. Basic pico keystroke commands

Command	Result
Ctrl+c	Reports the current cursor position by line number. (This is a particularly useful feature if you decide to write shell scripts, because they can often be several hundred lines long.)
Ctrl+g	Displays the pico help documentation.
Ctrl+j	Justifies the selected text, region, or line.
Ctrl+k	Cuts the current line. (Used in conjunction with Ctrl+u, this function allows easy clipping-and-pasting of text throughout a document.)
Ctrl+r	Reads in a file from the hard disk drive. (This is a paste-like procedure where you specify a filename and pico pastes that file's contents into the current document.(During this procedure, you should place your cursor in the exact position you want the pasted text to begin; the read-in function inserts the pasted text at the cursor.)
Ctrl+t	Checks spelling.
Ctrl+u	"Uncuts" the current line. (Used in conjunction with Ctrl+k, this works much like Paste in Microsoft Windows.)
Ctrl+w	This is the "whereis" or search function. Roughly equivalent to Search in Microsoft Windows. pico prompts you for a search string and scans the current file for matches. You can move forward through those matches by successively hitting Ctrl+w until pico reaches the last match.
Ctrl+x	Exit (pico will prompt to save if you've made edits).

Navigating pico

Additionally, although you can use the traditional arrow keys to get around, pico allows you to navigate your documents using various quick key combinations. These key combinations are described in Table 8.4.

Table 8.4.   Commands for navigating documents in `pico`

Command	Result
Ctrl+^	Starts a selection block. Once that block is started, you can use the arrow keys to highlight your desired text.
Ctrl+a	Jumps to the beginning of the current line.
Ctrl+b	Moves back one character.
Ctrl+d	Deletes the selected character.
Ctrl+e	Jumps to the end of the current line.
Ctrl+f	Moves forward one character.
Ctrl+n	Jumps to the next line.
Ctrl+p	Jumps to the previous line.
Ctrl+v	Jumps to the next page.
Ctrl+y	Jumps to the previous page.

Unfortunately, `pico` is not a standard utility on most UNIX systems. Therefore, you may have to cajole your system administrator into getting `pico` (it's worth it, though). Out of all the UNIX text-based plain text editors, `pico` is by far the easiest to use.

Egad! It's emacs!

The GNU Project
Free Software Foundation, Inc.
59 Temple Place, Suite 330
Boston, MA 02111
`http://www.gnu.org`

Yet another editor with a bizarre name, right? Not quite. The name `emacs` comes from the term *editing macros*. However, `emacs` isn't just an editor—it's a phenomenon. Originally developed by Richard Stallman for the PDP-10 (ancient history), `emacs` is probably the most complete text editor ever created. (Perhaps that's because `emacs` has had so many years to mature. After all, the `emacs` project was started in 1975.)

`emacs` is not for the faint-of-heart. In fact, if you tell other users that you're an `emacs` user, they'll instantly label you a super-geek. Here's why: Nearly all operations in `emacs` are accomplished using keystroke combinations.

However, modern `emacs` also runs in X (this version is appropriately called Xemacs). If you have X, I recommend getting Xemacs.

Xemacs

Xemacs has come a long way. Today, it's an extremely user-friendly application and closely resembles editors you may have used in Mac OS or Microsoft Windows. (See the following figure.)

The XEmacs opening screen.

Menu bar

Work area

Status bar

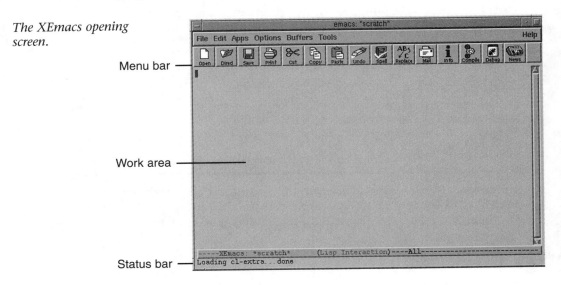

In Xemacs, you use the menu to perform text manipulation, the work area to type, and the status bar to enter commands or receive status reports. (Curiously, Xemacs will actually run the output of system commands into a window within the work area. When this happens, the screen splits.)

If you read the documentation on Xemacs, you'll be flabbergasted at all the tasks Xemacs performs. You could say that Xemacs is the ultimate text editor. In addition to editing, copying, pasting, and saving text files, Xemacs performs all the following functions:

Xplaining X

X is a commonly used windowing system and is UNIX's equivalent of Microsoft Windows. We'll be looking at X in Chapter 11, "Tyrannosaurus X: A Windowing System."

➤ It doubles as a plain text WWW browser.

➤ It doubles as a programming and debugging environment.

➤ It doubles as a personal calendar and checks the phases of the moon. (No, I'm not kidding. I'm not sure why the developers included this feature, but it's there, just the same.)

➤ It runs spell checks and syntax checks on code.

emacs *Keystroke Combinations*

emacs supports a wide range of keystroke combinations, most of which you'll never use. However, the good news is this: Any keystroke combination in regular emacs will also work in Xemacs. Therefore, you only need to learn emacs once. In Table 8.5, I list the more important functions you can perform with keystroke combinations.

Table 8.5. Important emacs keystroke combinations and what they do

Keystroke Combination	Result
Ctrl+x + Ctrl+c	Exits emacs. This is an important one! When you first start emacs, it gives you no clue how to exit.
Ctrl+u + Esc+!	Starts a shell process. This allows you access to the UNIX shell without leaving emacs.
Alt+function key	Switches between emacs windows. Alt followed by any function key (F2, u) will switch you from one emacs window to another. This allows you to maintain different terminal sessions.
Ctrl+x + Ctrl+w	Saves a new file. emacs will ask you to name the file and then save that file to disk.
Ctrl+x + Ctrl+s	Saves the current file. If you're editing a file that already exists, this keystroke combination will cause emacs to save your changes up to this point.

Navigating *emacs*

Like most functions in emacs, to move around your document, you must use keystroke combinations. Navigation keystroke combinations are described in Table 8.6.

Table 8.6. Keystroke combinations for navigating emacs

Keystroke Combination	Result
Ctrl+b	Moves back one character
Ctrl+d	Deletes the character positioned immediately after the cursor
Ctrl+f	Moves forward one character
Ctrl+k	Deletes the current line
Ctrl+n	Moves down one line
Ctrl+p	Moves back one line

continues

Table 8.6.   Keystroke combinations for navigating emacs
CONTINUED

Keystroke Combination	Result
Ctrl+v	Moves forward one screen
Esc+d	Deletes the word positioned immediately after the cursor
Esc+v	Moves back one screen

Searching and Replacing in emacs

Finally, emacs supports a wide range of search and replace functions. These are summarized in Table 8.7.

Table 8.7.   Search and replace commands in emacs

Task	How to Get It Done
Search	To search for text, issue the command Ctrl+s. emacs will prompt you (in the command line window at the bottom of the screen) for the desired text string.
Cancel a search	To cancel a search, issue the command Ctrl+g.
Search in reverse	To change the direction of your search, issue the command Ctrl+r. (Reverse is relative to your current position.)
Repeat a search	To repeat a search, issue the command Ctrl+x+s (repeat forward search) or Ctrl+x+r (repeat a reverse search).
Replace text	The replace function is an extension of the search function. To replace text, start a search (Ctrl+s). emacs will prompt you for a search term on the command line. Here, issue two arguments: your search term followed by the text to replace it with. Example: Ctrl+s, **Reagan Clinton**. (This will replace Reagan with Clinton.)
Replace all	To globally replace one word with another, issue the command Esc+r. Then, enter the search term and press Enter. emacs will ask you for the replacement text. Enter the replacement text and press Enter.

emacs is a very powerful and extensible editor. To get further guidance on how to use emacs, query emacs help (Ctrl+h) or view the emacs man page.

textedit

Finally, an editor that has a simple, understandable name! Sun Microsystems first introduced textedit in SunOS 4.1. At that time, it was bundled with a graphical environment called SunView. textedit supports most functions that are common to word processors, including copying, clipping, pasting, and so on. (It also has search and replace functions.)

textedit is available mainly on SunOS, Solaris, and Linux systems (although free versions are available for most UNIX systems).

Starting textedit

To start textedit, issue the textedit command in a shell window, like this:

```
textedit
```

This will load the textedit application, as shown in the following figure.

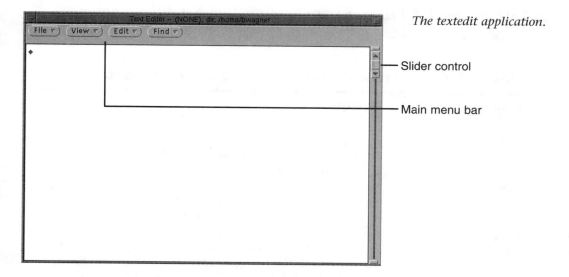

The textedit application.

You can move though screens (or scroll down the page) by using the slide control at the far right side of textedit.

Using textedit Menus

textedit is very "point and click" oriented. The main menu bar (refer to the previous figure) closely resembles menu bars you've seen in Mac OS or Microsoft Windows. From these, you can choose various options (such as Find). However, all such options are also available from a *text pane window*, which you can summon by right-clicking any empty portion of the textedit screen. (See the following figure.)

107

The textedit text pane window.

```
     Text Pane
  File        ▸
 ( View       ▸ )
  Edit        ▸
  Find        ▸
  Extras      ▸
```

To use any menu operation, perform these steps:

1. Place your mouse cursor at the beginning or end of the desired block of text.
2. Hold down the left mouse button and drag the selection shading over the text you want to change.
3. Release the left mouse button
4. Grab a menu (either from the main menu bar or by right-clicking the screen).
5. Choose the desired operation.

Other textedit Functions

Table 8.8 describes some more common textedit functions and how to perform them.

Table 8.8. textedit functions and how to perform them

Function	Procedure
Open a file	Choose File from the menu bar. textedit will display a file selection window. You choose files in one of two ways. Either use your mouse to double-click the desired file or type the filename in the File field.
Search for text	Position your cursor at line 1, choose Find (from the menu bar) and enter your search term. Then, click Find. Warning: Be careful to choose Find, not Replace.
Paste foreign text	Sometimes you'll need to paste text into textedit from another application or an Xterm. To do so, highlight the desired text in the foreign application. Then, return to textedit and click the middle mouse button. (If you have a two-button mouse, choose Edit|Paste instead.)
Close textedit	You close textedit by clicking the window control in the upper-left corner and choosing Quit. At that time, textedit will prompt you to save any changes.

For further guidance on how to use textedit, please see the textedit man page.

Visual SlickEdit

MicroEdge, Inc.
PO Box 988
Apex, NC 27502-0988
http://www.slickedit.com/

A commercial product, Visual SlickEdit is by far the most user-friendly UNIX text editor available. In both appearance and functionality, it closely resembles well-known editor packages from the Microsoft world. Perhaps that's because Visual SlickEdit was developed for Windows 95 and Windows NT. (If you're wondering what's so "slick" about Visual SlickEdit, it's this: Visual SlickEdit is simple, fast, and easy to learn.)

Even Visual SlickEdit's interface resembles a Windows application, as shown in the following figure.

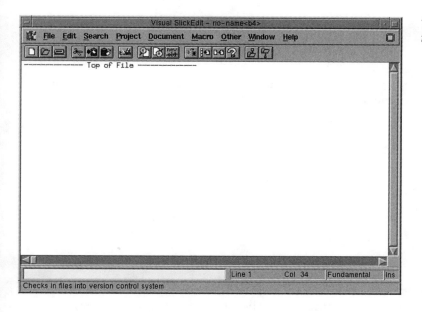

The Visual SlickEdit editor for UNIX.

Nearly all supported functions can be accessed through Windows-style drop-down menus, like the one shown in the next figure.

You can manipulate text with your mouse—copying, cutting, pasting, deleting, and replacing it with a click of a button. Furthermore, Visual SlickEdit records keystroke and menu-based macros, so automating tasks is a snap.

Finally (and here's the rub), Visual SlickEdit has a native programming language. Therefore, you can extend its capabilities. The programming language closely resembles C, but the visual application builder works more like Microsoft Visual Basic. (You can visually build forms such as windows, dialog boxes, and frames. To these objects, you can attach complex code to build mini-applications within the Visual SlickEdit environment.)

The main Visual SlickEdit menu.

Quick Search
Open...
Save
Close
Copy Word
Undo
List Clipboards...
Find...
Replace...
Go to Error/Include File
Check Out...
Check In...
Spell Check...   ➤
File Comment
Function Comment...

In all, Visual SlickEdit is a very complete text-processing package, and it works on many UNIX platforms, including these:

➤ AIX

➤ HP-UX

➤ Irix

➤ Linux

➤ SCO

➤ Solaris

➤ SunOS

➤ UNIXWare

Visual SlickEdit is of special interest to programmers, because it automatically color-codes functions, variables, subroutines, and other structures common to programming. This feature supports multiple languages, including C, C++, HTML, Java, BASIC, Fortran, Pascal, and Perl. If you work in a commercial or production environment and plan to do heavy text editing in UNIX, I would highly recommend Visual SlickEdit.

The Least You Need to Know

Different flavors of UNIX have different text editors, including the following:

➤ ed

➤ vi

➤ pico

➤ emacs

➤ Xemacs

➤ textedit

➤ Visual SlickEdit

➤ Proprietary text editors

You can find out which editors your system has by querying the whatis database, like this:

```
man -k editor
```

At a minimum, you should learn the basics of ed and vi, because nearly all systems have them. However, as a free, general-purpose editor, I would recommend pico.

## Chapter 9

CHUGA
CHUGA
CHUGA

Printing

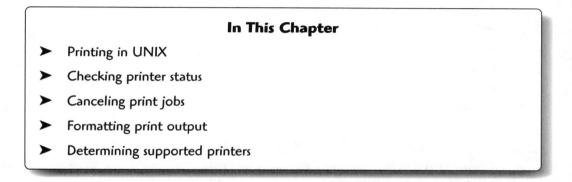

In This Chapter

➤ Printing in UNIX

➤ Checking printer status

➤ Canceling print jobs

➤ Formatting print output

➤ Determining supported printers

Printing seems like such an easy task; you're probably wondering why we need a chapter about it. Here's the scoop: Printing from UNIX is different than printing from other operating systems. There are a wide range of options and, as you might expect, many little programs are involved. (UNIX is teeming with little programs that do big jobs. This is just one of the advantages of using an operating system that was designed while Bill Gates was still in high school. UNIX geeks demanded low overhead, and that's exactly what they get.)

Therefore, this chapter addresses all those little points, such as how to stop a printer when it runs amok, how to find out what happened to your print job, and so on.

Printing from X

Printing from applications in X is pretty straightforward, especially if those applications are commercial. For example, to print a Web page from Netscape Navigator or Communicator, simply choose File|Print. Navigator will do the rest. (Nearly all applications in X either have their own printer drivers or utilize standard printing commands. Either way, these applications require little tweaking.)

In contrast, printing from a command line involves several different commands. That's what this chapter is all about.

Command-Line Printing

In UNIX, the printing commands you'll most often use are as follows:

➤ lp

➤ lpr

➤ cancel

➤ lprm

➤ pr

➤ lpstat

➤ lpq

Let's look at how each command is used and what it does.

Using lp to Send a Print Request

For many UNIX flavors, lp is the favored print command. (lp stands for line printer.) Using lp, you can send files to the local printer, like this:

```
lp myfile.txt
```

This sends myfile.txt to the printer to be processed. (How long this takes will depend on how many other print jobs are currently queued as well as their priority over your own. Printer job priority—or *rank*—is discussed a bit later in this chapter, in the sections on lpstat and lpq.)

Note that lp is an AT&T/System V command. On BSD-based systems, you may need to use lpr instead. (Some UNIX distributions have lp, some have lpr, and some have both.) lpr is also discussed later in this chapter.

Using lp to Print Data Not Contained in Files

You can also use lp to print data that's normally directed to standard output. For example, suppose you want to print a list of all GIF files in your directories and subdirectories. You could issue the following command:

```
find . -name "*gif" ¦ lp
```

To print the contents of the current directory, you could issue this command:

```
ls -l ¦ lp
```

A quick warning about redirecting data to the printer: Watch your syntax! If you accidentally make a typo, you could inadvertently send many megabytes of data to your printer. Always carefully examine your command line before you press Enter.

For Simple Tasks, Simply Redirect Output

To print output from a command, you don't need to use lp. Often, you can simply redirect output to a printer, like this:

```
ls -l > /dev/lp0
```

This redirects the output of ls -l to the first printer device. This works well on Linux and many other systems. However, if you receive the error No such device, you should revert to using lp or lpr.

The lp command has many command-line switches through which to manipulate printed output. The more important ones are summarized in Table 9.1.

Table 9.1. Some lp command-line switches

lp Switch	Purpose
-#	The number switch specifies how many copies to print. For example, **lp -3 myfile.txt** will print three copies of myfile.txt.
-c	The -c option specifies that the file should be copied prior to printing. This adds a link to the file. This way, if you make changes to the file before the print request is actually executed, those changes will be reflected in the final printed product. (This is good when the printed material is derived from logs or other files that are constantly being updated.)

continues

115

Table 9.1.   Some `lp` command-line switches CONTINUED

`lp` Switch	Purpose
`-d [destination]`	Use the `-d` option when you want to direct your print request to a particular printer or device. For example, **`lp -dMondo myfile.txt`** sends `myfile.txt` to be printed on the printer Mondo. (This is useful when the default printer is unsuitable for your needs. For example, suppose the default printer is a LaserJet and you want to print a spreadsheet. You'll probably want to redirect that print job to an IBM ProPrinter or some other contact/dot-matrix printer suited for wide-format pages.)
`-m`	The `-m` option tells `lp` to send mail after the print job has been completed.
`-P [range]`	Use the `-P` option to print a range or series of pages. For example, **`lp -P 2-4 myfile.txt`** will print pages 2 through 4 of `myfile.txt`.
`-q [number]`	Use the `-q` switch to specify a priority for the print job. Values range from 0 (the very highest priority) to 39 (the lowest). Note that depending on your system configuration, your mileage may vary. For example, your system administrator may have set limits on how high a priority you can set on your jobs.
`-t [title]`	Use the `-t` switch to add a title to your pages. (Note that if the title contains whitespace, you must enclose the title in quotes. Otherwise, `lp` will interpret additional words as command-line arguments.)
`-w`	Use the `-w` option to write a message to the terminal when the print job is finally printed. (This is much like the `-m` switch in that it provides a way to notify you that the job was successfully completed.)

lpr: Printing with BSD Commands

On many systems, you have to use `lpr` instead. If this is your case, don't worry: `lpr` works much like `lp`. To print a file using `lpr`, issue the `lpr` command plus the name of the file you want to print, like this:

```
lpr myfile.txt
```

`lpr` has several command-line switches through which to manipulate print output. The more important ones are summarized in Table 9.2.

116

Table 9.2.   Some `lpr` command-line switches

lpr Switch	Purpose
-#	The number switch specifies how many copies to print. For example, **lp -3 myfile.txt** will print three copies of myfile.txt.
-c	The -c option specifies that the file should be copied prior to printing. This adds a link to the file. This way, if you make changes to the file before the print request is actually executed, those changes will be reflected in the final printed product.
-m	The -m option tells lpr to send mail after the print job has been completed.
-P [*destination*]	Use the -P option when you want to direct your print request to a particular printer or device. For example, **lpr -PMondo myfile.txt** sends myfile.txt to be printed on the printer Mondo.
-r	Use the -r switch when you want to remove the file after printing it. For example, **lpr -r myfile.txt** tells lpr to print myfile.txt and then delete it. (Be careful with this switch. If something goes wrong and you lose your printout, the data will be gone. Unless the data is of the throwaway variety, you shouldn't use the -r switch.)
-T [*title*]	Use the -T switch to add a title to your pages. (Note that if the title contains whitespace, you must enclose the title in quotes. Otherwise, lpr will attempt to interpret the words as arguments.)

Finally, note that you can also print to a file if you want. This is done using the lpr command with the -v switch, like this:

```
lpr -v myfile
```

This will produce a PostScript file named myfile.

Canceling Print Jobs with the `cancel` Command

So, you accidentally sent a 25MB file to the printer, eh? It happens to me all the time. Don't sweat it; UNIX has excellent print job control.

To cancel a printer job, issue the cancel command plus the job number of the job you want to cancel, like this:

```
cancel print-request-id
```

Check This Out

Except in rare cases, you can only cancel your own print requests (and then only on the local host). If you have accounts on several machines and plan to print from more than one, tell your system administrator. He or she can configure the system to allow you to cancel your print requests on any host on the network.

To cancel a job that was sent to a specific printer, add the destination:

```
cancel print-request-id destination
```

More Canceling: The lprm Command

Still another canceling command (common to all BSD variants) is lprm. To kill a print job using this command, issue the lprm command plus the print job number, like this:

```
lprm 312
```

To cancel a job on a particular printer, use the lprm command and the -P switch to identify the printer:

```
lprm -PMondo 312
```

This kills print job 312 on the printer Mondo.

Formatting Display Output with the pr command

Sometimes, simply printing a file can produce strange results. For example, the text may not be justified or, worse, it may print in odd positions on the page. Therefore, you may occasionally need to format the information. For this, the pr command is very useful.

The pr command is for formatting output. pr formats pages neatly, paginates them, and prints a header on each page. Use the pr command to clean up output before printing it, like this:

```
pr myfile.txt ¦ lp
```

pr has several command-line switches. The more important ones are summarized in Table 9.3.

Table 9.3.   Some pr command-line switches

pr Switch	Purpose
-d	Use the -d switch to force double-spaced output. This will add an extra newline for every newline found. (This can make output easier to read. For example, log files often have thousands of lines that look very similar. Sometimes, these are easier to read when they're double-spaced.)

pr Switch	Purpose
-h [*header-text*]	Use the -h switch to customize your header.
-l [*number-of-lines*]	Use the -l switch to change the number of lines displayed per page. (The default value is 66.)
-m [*file1 file2*]	The -m option tells pr to merge the output of *file1* and *file2*. Their contents will be displayed in columns, side by side. (This is good primarily for examining word lists or other files that have only one or two words per line.)
-s [*character*]	Use the -s option when you want to specify a particular delimiter for columns. For example, to separate columns by colons, enter the command **pr -s:** *filename*.
-t	Use the -r switch to suppress headers and footers.

Using lpstat to See What Happened to a Print Job

On occasion, you may want to check the status of the print service. For example, maybe your print job hasn't finished yet and you're wondering why. To check the printer service status, use the lpstat command, like this:

    lpstat

lpstat has several command-line switches. The more important ones are summarized in Table 9.4.

Table 9.4. Some lpstat command-line switches

lpstat Switch	Purpose
-R	Use the -R switch to find out where your print job is in the process queue. (This tells you whose jobs are ahead of yours. From this information, you can ascertain how long you have to wait.)
-s	Use the -s switch to get a summary of all print service information, including available printers, their names, and their default settings. Here's some sample output:

```
scheduler is running
system default destination: myprinter
device for myprinter: /dev/tty00
system for myprinter: myprinter-system
character set ascii
character set iso-88591
character set iso-88592
character set iso-88597
```

continues

119

Table 9.4.   Some lpstat command-line switches
CONTINUED

lpstat Switch	Purpose
-m	The -m option tells lpr to send mail after the print job has been completed.
-P [*destination*]	Use the -P option when you want to direct your print request to a particular printer or device. For example, **lpr -PMondo myfile.txt** sends myfile.txt to be printed on the printer Mondo.
-r	Use the -r switch when you want to remove the file after printing it. For example, **lpr -r myfile.txt** tells lpr to print myfile.txt and then delete it.
-T [*title*]	Use the -T switch to add a title to your pages. (Note that if the title contains whitespace, you must enclose the title in quotes. Otherwise, lpr will attempt to interpret the words as arguments.)

Getting Print Job Status Using lpq

Still another tool you can use to check your print job status (especially on Linux and BSD-type systems) is lpq. To determine the status of all print jobs, issue the lpq command without arguments, like this:

```
lpq
```

lpq reports the following values:

➤ **The rank of the print request**—This tells you the current progress of the job.

➤ **The owner**—This identifies the user who issued the request.

➤ **The job number**—This reports the job number.

➤ **The files being printed**—This could be a filename (or filenames) or standard input or output.

➤ **The job's size**—This reports the size of the current print job.

Here's some sample lpq output from a Sparc system:

```
Rank      Owner    Job      Files            Total Size
active    bwagner  312      standard input   5940 bytes
```

On different systems, lpq output might look slightly different. For example, here's a lpq report from a Linux box:

```
Printer: ps@linuxbox1
Queue:    2 printable jobs
Server:   pid 398 active, Unspooler: pid 399 active
```

```
Status:     printed all 511 bytes at Sun Aug 9 17:43:21 1998
  Rank  Owner/ID        Class  Job Files    Size  Time
active bwagner@linuxbox1+396 A 396 (stdin)   511 17:43:21
```

lpq supports very few command-line switches. The important ones are summarized in Table 9.5.

Table 9.5.   Some lpq command-line switches

lpq Switch	Purpose
+ [*seconds*]	Use the + switch to get up-to-the-minute reports on the printer queue status. The time you specify (expressed in seconds) is the time between report intervals. For example, the command **lpq +5000** will pull printer queue status reports every 5,000 seconds.
-1	Use the -1 switch to force lpq to print output in long format. (This is more detailed and is often easier to read.)
-P [printer]	Use the -P switch to pull a lpq report on a particular printer. For example, **lpq -Pmondo** will pull a status report on the printer Mondo.

About Supported Printers

To determine the local machine's supported printers, check the /etc/printcap file, like this:

cat /etc/printcap

Here's some sample output:

```
# /etc/printcap

# Please don't edit this file directly unless you know what you are
doing.'
# Be warned that the control-panel print tool requires a very strict
format!
# Look at the printcap(5) man page for more info.

# This file can be edited with the print tool in the control-panel.

##PRINTTOOL## LOCAL laserjet 300x300 letter {}
ps:\
    sd=/var/spool/lpd/ps:\
    :mx#0:\
```

```
    :lp=/dev/lp1:\
    :if=/var/spool/lpd/ps/filter:\
    :sh:

##PRINTTOOL## LOCAL
lp:\
    :sd=/varlspool/lpd/lp:\
    :mx#0:\
    :lp=/dev/lp1:\
    :sh:
```

Do you really need to know what all this means? No. Instead, just check for printer names. These are usually on the first line of each definition. For example, in the /etc/printcap file, you can see a Hewlett-Packard LaserJet whose print resolution is set to 300×300:

```
##PRINTTOOL## LOCAL laserjet 300x300 letter {}
```

Unfortunately, not all printer names are fully articulated. Therefore, you may often see abbreviated names. Table 9.6 summarizes some of those abbreviations and the printers they refer to.

Table 9.6.   Printer names in /etc/printcap

Name	Printer
bj10e	Canon BubbleJet
deskjet	Hewlett-Packard DeskJet 500
epson	Epson dot-matrix printer
ibmpro	IBM ProPrinter (contact printer)
laserjet	Hewlett-Packard LaserJet
lbp8	Canon LBP-811 laser printer
ljetplus	Hewlett-Packard LaserJet Plus
okil 82	Okidata MicroLine 182
paintjet	Hewlett Packard PaintJet
sparc	Sparc printer

Troubleshooting Your Print Jobs

You may occasionally encounter problems with your print jobs. Here are a few possible reasons:

➤ **The printer is not available**—If you send a print job but it never prints, check to see whether the printer is on. If so, perhaps the cable was knocked loose.

➤ **You chose a printer that doesn't exist**—If you receive an error reporting that the specified printer is unavailable, check /etc/printcap. Are you sure you specified the right printer? (You might have misspelled the printer name.)

➤ **You don't have the necessary privileges**—You might be sending print jobs to a printer for which you have no access privileges. Try the local printer instead.

➤ **UNIX reports that it cannot print the file and refers to stdin**— Sometimes, certain files simply won't print because their format is mangled. For example, when you redirect man page output to a file, it may sometimes retain nonprintable characters. If so, it won't print. Check the file by opening it in an editor. If it contains nonprintable characters, you may have to regenerate the file.

➤ **The printer is looking for PostScript, not text**—On rare occasion, you may encounter this problem. If so, you have two options: You can have your system administrator install a text filter or the appropriate ASCII-to-PostScript filter.

However, by far, the most common problem is that your print job is last in line. Remember that UNIX is a networked operating system. Many folks may have printing privileges on your printer. Therefore, before you go tracing down the printer wires, always check the print queue with lpstat or lpq first. In all probability, some users are ahead of you. For this, the only cure is patience.

The Least You Need to Know

When printing in UNIX, the least you need to know is this:

➤ To print, use lp or lpr.

➤ To cancel a print job, use cancel or lprm.

➤ To check the status of a print job, use lpstat or lpq.

➤ To identify supported printers, check /etc/printcap.

## Chapter 10

Working with Applications

In This Chapter

➤ Unpacking files

➤ Installing software

It happens to the best of us. Sooner or later, you're bound to get "download happy." This condition usually sets in shortly after you discover that there are thousands of free programs available for UNIX. (Sunsite at University of North Chapel Hill is enough to keep you busy for decades. Sunsite can be reached at `http://sunsite.unc.edu`.)

The problem is, once you download all that good stuff, you need to know how to unpack it, install it, and run it. That's what this chapter is all about.

Before You Start: Is It Really Your Cup of Tea?

When you first stumble across a UNIX software archive, you'll be shocked to see the amazing range of free programs available. However, before you actually download any, you must first ascertain a few things:

➤ Whether the software will run on your UNIX flavor

➤ Whether the software is in binary or source form

➤ Whether you have the necessary tools to run it

Software Compatibility Issues

You can tell whether downloadable software is compatible with your machine in one of three ways:

➤ Check the directory it's in
➤ Check the filename for clues
➤ Check the README file

For example, most software archives break up their sites so that goodies for Solaris are stored in different directories than goodies for Linux. Here's a sample listing of one directory at Sunsite:

```
ftp> ls
200 PORT command successful.
150 Opening ASCII mode data connection for file list.
lost+found
X11
packages
academic
multimedia
sun-info
gnu
docs
micro
electronic-publications
languages
archives
UNC-info
talk-radio
patches
solaris
Linux
226 Transfer complete.
170 bytes received in 0.05 seconds (3.40 Kbytes/sec)
```

Notice the solaris and Linux directories? By creating separate directories for each operating system, many sites make your job of choosing software easier. Netscape does this. Check out their directory for Communicator 4.5:

```
drwxr-xr-x  20 888      999         4096 Aug 24 22:50 .
drwxr-xr-x   5 888      999           50 Jul 15 03:22 ..
-rw-r--r--   1 888      999        16379 Jul 14 21:04 README.txt
drwxr-xr-x   2 888      999          116 Aug 24 22:50 aix4
drwxr-xr-x   2 888      999          116 Aug 24 22:50 freebsd2
drwxr-xr-x   2 888      999          114 Aug 24 22:50 hpux10
```

```
drwxr-xr-x    2 888       999        114 Aug 24 22:50 hpux10_pro
drwxr-xr-x    2 888       999        113 Aug 24 22:50 hpux9
drwxr-xr-x    2 888       999        113 Aug 24 22:50 irix62
drwxr-xr-x    2 888       999        113 Aug 24 22:50 irix62_pro
drwxr-xr-x    2 888       999        117 Aug 24 22:50 linux12
drwxr-xr-x    2 888       999        117 Aug 24 22:50 linux20
drwxr-xr-x    2 888       999        117 Aug 24 22:50 linux20_pro
drwxr-xr-x    2 888       999        117 Aug 24 22:50 linux20glibc2
drwxr-xr-x    2 888       999        117 Aug 24 22:50 mklinux
drwxr-xr-x    2 888       999        110 Aug 24 22:50 ncr40
drwxr-xr-x    2 888       999        111 Aug 24 22:50 sinix54
drwxr-xr-x    2 888       999        117 Aug 24 22:50 sunos54
drwxr-xr-x    2 888       999        115 Aug 24 22:50 sunos54_x86
drwxr-xr-x    2 888       999        119 Aug 24 22:50 sunos551
drwxr-xr-x    2 888       999        119 Aug 24 22:50 sunos551_pro
```

A directory exists for almost every UNIX flavor, and even several versions of the same flavor (such as early Linux releases).

Unfortunately, however, not all sites do this. In fact, you'll often find software dumped in a single directory. For example, take a quick look at the NCSA Mosaic FTP site located at `ftp://ftp.ncsa.uiuc.edu/Mosaic/Unix/binaries/2.6/`:

```
total 22596
drwx------    2 101     10      2048 Jul  7  1995 .
drwxr-xr-x    6 12873 wheel   2048 Oct 25  1995 ..
-rw-r--r--    1 101     10    936964 Jul  7  1995 Mosaic-alpha-2.6.Z
-rw-r--r--    1 101     10   1111311 Jul  7  1995 Mosaic-dec-2.6.Z
-rw-r--r--    1 101     10    853351 Jul  7  1995 Mosaic-hp-2.6.Z
-rw-r--r--    1 101     10    797705 Jul  7  1995 Mosaic-ibm-2.6.Z
-rw-r--r--    1 101     10    915718 Jul  7  1995 Mosaic-indy-2.6.Z
-rw-r--r--    1 101     10    903973 Jul  7  1995 Mosaic-linux-2.6.Z
-rw-r--r--    1 101     10    648431 Jul  7  1995 Mosaic-sgi-2.6.Z
-rw-r--r--    1 101     10   1708074 Jul  7  1995 Mosaic-solaris-23-2.6.
-rw-r--r--    1 101     10    809343 Jul  7  1995 Mosaic-solaris-24-2.6.Z
-rw-r--r--    1 101     10   1427238 Jul  7  1995 Mosaic-sun-2.6.Z
-rw-r--r--    1 101     10   1442713 Jul  7  1995 Mosaic-sun-lresolv-
2.6.Z
-rw-r--r--    1 101     10      1835 Jul  7  1995 README-2.6
-rw-------    1 101     10       845 Jul  7  1995 README.solaris
```

In this case, the filenames themselves indicate what UNIX flavor the software is compatible with. This is yet another way of discovering which file to download: examine the filename.

In rare cases, you may actually have to download and read the README file, because neither the directory name nor the filename reflects platform compatibility.

Binary or Source?

UNIX software comes in two formats:

➤ Binary

➤ Source

There's a big difference between the two—a difference that can greatly influence whether you can run a particular software package.

Binary distributions are prepackaged executables already prepared to run on your system. In this respect, binary packages closely resemble the software you download for Windows or Mac OS. To use them, you simply unpack them and run them. In most cases, you'll have no problems. (Provided, of course, that the binary was designed to run on your particular UNIX flavor.)

In contrast, *source distributions* come with source code. Source code is what a program consists of before it has been packaged into machine language. I realize this doesn't make much sense, so I'll illustrate the difference.

Source Code

On more than one occasion, you've probably wondered how programmers create programs. (After all, it can't be that difficult. There's a lot of software floating around.) In this section, I'll give you an inside look at this process.

At its inception, the process starts with the programmer's notion of what the program will do. Once he knows that, he can begin writing the program in a computer programming language. (A *computer programming language* is a collection of instructions and functions that can be expressed in plain English).

In UNIX, most programs are written in the C programming language. (In fact, UNIX itself is written in C.) Here's a typical C program in source form:

```
#include <stdio.h>

void main() {
    printf("This is a typical C program in source form.\n");
}
```

What does this program do? It displays the following message:

```
This is a typical C program in source form.
```

This is a pretty lame program, but it serves our purposes here. Take a look at the source code. Notice that you can read it. Also, if you needed to change something, you can open the file and edit it. That's great. Unfortunately, however, a computer can't read source code, so programmers have to convert it into another language called *machine language*. To do that, they use a tool called a *compiler*.

Compilers create binaries from raw source code. For example, when the previous sample code is run through a compiler, it comes out the other end as machine code, suitable for execution. At this point, the program is no longer in source form. Instead, it's in binary form. (Therefore, although you can't read it, your machine can.)

On the Internet, many UNIX programs are distributed in source code, and there are several reasons for this. One is that this allows you to change the program if you want. (You'll probably never modify source code in your life, but many people do. Those that do appreciate the convenience of having the source code handy.)

Another reason is this: Some programs are written to compile on multiple UNIX flavors. In such a case, the software's author provides generic source code. This source code will dynamically compile into a functional binary only after ascertaining on which operating system it's compiling. Therefore, the same source code can compile cleanly on Solaris, SunOS, Linux, HP-UX, and so on.

Either way, programs are often distributed in source form. You can easily determine whether the program you've downloaded was distributed in binary or source form by using either of the following methods:

➤ Take another look at the Web page or FTP site where you got the file. Was there any accompanying text? Usually software authors include a description file or comments that relay this information. For example, software authors often offer you the option of downloading binary or source files.

➤ Examine the filename. Often, the file's structure is described in the filename. For example, `llxdir2.0.bin.tar.gz` is a binary file (notice the `bin` in the filename?), whereas `llnlxdir2.0.src.tar.gz` is a source file (note the `src` in the filename). In fact, software authors may be even more explicit by naming the file something like `llnxdir2.0.source.tar.Z`.

Whenever a software program comes in both binary and source form, you should always seek out the binary. Here's why: You may not have the right tools to compile raw source. However, if the program sounds just too cool to pass up and only comes in source form, get it anyway.

In the next section, I'll describe the steps you need to follow in order to take downloaded software and install it.

Zips

If you look at the previous filenames, you'll notice that they end in `.gz` or `.Z`. You'll see these endings a lot on the Internet. What do they mean? They mean that these files are zipped or compressed.

Most downloadable files have been zipped or compressed. The purpose of doing this is pretty basic: In the old days, UNIX users had 300-baud modems. Therefore, developers sought a way to make transfers go faster. They settled on compression.

Compression is the process of packing a file's contents tight in order to reduce the file size. (The smaller the file, the faster it will transfer.) You would think that today, because modems are pretty fast, people no longer need to compress files. Think again! As time progressed, program file size grew at a much faster rate than modem speed. So, even today, users still compress their files. (UNIX compressed files are nearly identical in behavior and purpose to *.SIT files on the Macintosh and *.ZIP files on the PC.)

Almost all the downloadable UNIX software you encounter will be compressed. Your job is to decompress (or *unzip*) that software once you've downloaded it. You'll know immediately if you're downloading a compressed file because it will have a .Z, .gz, or .tgz extension. Here are some examples:

    Ftptool4.6.bin.tar.Z

    Ftptool4.6.bin.tar.gz

    Ftptool4.6.bin.tar.tgz

Many UNIX compression programs are available, but the most popular are compress, uncompress, gzip, and gunzip. Depending on your UNIX system, you have at least two (and possibly all four) of these programs.

Let's briefly cover these programs now.

Compressing Files with the compress Command

compress is probably the most popular commercial UNIX compression utility. You'll find it on almost any UNIX system. To use compress to compress a file, issue the compress command plus the name of the file you want to zip up, like this:

    compress myfile.txt

In response, compress will pack down myfile.txt and give it a .Z extension, like this:

    myfile.txt.Z

Uncompressing Files with the uncompress Command

Files that are compressed with compress (that is, those that have a .Z extension) can be uncompressed with the uncompress utility. To uncompress such a file, issue the uncompress command plus the name of the file, like this:

    uncompress myfile.txt.Z

In response, uncompress will uncompress `myfile.txt.Z` and return it to its original state, with a regular filename:

> `myfile.txt`

gzip *and* gunzip

gzip and gunzip are distributed by the Free Software Foundation. These programs are free alternatives to traditional "zip" and "unzip" programs (such as compress and uncompress.) As you might expect, gzip zips files and gunzip unzips zipped files.

Gee, Zip!

You can get gzip and gunzip (and dozens of other useful programs) at the Free Software Foundation's home page, located at
`http://www.fsf.org`.

Zipping Files *with* gzip

To zip a file using gzip, issue the gzip command followed by the name of the file you're zipping, like this:

> `gzip myfile.txt`

In response, gzip will zip `myfile.txt` and give it a `.gz` extension, like this:

> `myfile.txt.gz`

Unzipping Files *with* gunzip

Using gunzip is pretty simple. In most cases, you'll issue the gunzip command plus the filename, like this:

> `gunzip Ftptool4.6.bin.tar.gz`

This will unzip the file into the current directory.

gzip and gunzip also support several command-line switches. Using these switches, you can control how your files are zipped or unzipped. Table 10.1 summarizes these switches.

Table 10.1. Some `gzip` and `gunzip` command-line switches

Switch	Result
1	Optimizes compression for speed. (This results in larger files that uncompress more quickly.)
9	Optimizes compression for size. (This results in small files that take longer to unzip.)
c	Tells `gunzip` to preserve the original files but simply display the results. (It basically writes the archive's contents to STDOUT.)
d	Used to decompress files. For example: **gunzip -d Ftptool4.6bin.tar.gz**.
h	Provides quick help on `gunzip`. (**gunzip -h** calls the usage summary.)
l	Provides a test run. This is where `gunzip` does not actually unzip the files. Instead, it shows you the contents of the zip file.
N	Preserves the original timestamp and filenames.
n	Ignores the original timestamps. (Timestamps will be set to the current time.)
q	Tells `gunzip` to suppress any warning messages. The q option is for seasoned zippers only!
r	Tells `gunzip` to operate recursively on directories. (This means that your zip or unzip reaches into subdirectories and either packs the files into or from these subdirectories.)
S *suffix*	Imposes the specified suffix on compressed files.
v	Forces verbose messages. (Use verbose messages when you're not sure what's about to happen. This way, you get the complete report on what happens with your archive. I always use verbose messaging so I can track errors and identify the reason for them.)

Does all this compressing, uncompressing, zipping, and unzipping really do any good? It depends. Compressing or zipping files can save a little space or a lot. Some files have a greater compression ratio (meaning they shrink quite a bit when compressed), whereas others don't. I personally think that compression is most beneficial when you're moving large files (a megabyte or more).

Unpacking Archives with the `tar` Command

Once you unzip a file, you may find that it has also been archived. Many zipped files are archived with a command called `tar`, which is short for *tape archive*. (`tar` dates back to the days when UNIX file archives were stored on tape.)

tar is a very special command; it packages entire software distributions for later use. For example, when a UNIX developer creates a powerful and useful program, that program is usually comprised of many files spread across several directories. To get that directory structure from his hard disk to your own, he uses tar.

tar takes the programmer's directory structure (and all the files in it) and packages them in a single file with a .tar extension (for example, ftptool.tar). This file can later be unpacked; when it is, all the files and directories will expand to their original locations. (Why would anyone want to do that? Simple: At startup, the program probably looks for certain files to be in certain directories. If those files are absent—or if they aren't in the directories they're supposed to be in—the program exits on error.)

Extracting a tar Archive

To extract a tar archive, use the tar command, your desired command-line options, and the filename you want to extract. Here's an example:

```
tar xvf Ftptool4.6.tar
```

Here's what that command does:

➤ The tar command starts tar.

➤ The x switch tells tar to extract the file.

➤ The v switch tells tar to print verbose output.

➤ The f switch tells tar to use the file Ftptool4.6.tar as the target.

Depending on the size of the archive, you'll then see several filenames and directory names scroll by. This is tar's way of telling you where it's extracting the files.

Ninety percent of the time, you'll use the tar xvf command to extract tar archives. However, tar supports many other command-line switches. These switches are summarized in Table 10.2.

Table 10.2. Selected tar command-line switches

Switch	Result
C *archive-file files*	Tells tar to create a tar archive file from the specified files or directories.
f *archive-filename*	Tells tar to use the specified archive filename to pack or unpack files.
F *filename*	Tells tar to take additional archive parameters from the specified filename.

continues

Table 10.2. **Selected tar command-line switches**
CONTINUED

Switch	Result
m	Tells tar to ignore the original creation dates of the files and instead update them to the current time.
o	Tells tar to change the ownership of the extracted files to the UID of the current user. (This is the opposite of the p switch.)
p	Tells tar to preserve original permissions on all files in the archive.
q	Tells tar to quit after the archive has been unpacked.
v	Tells tar to generate verbose output. This way, when you "untar" a package, tar prints all the directories to which the archive has been unpacked. (Generally, you should redirect this information to an output file in case you later need to find isolated files from the archive.)
w	Tells tar to request confirmation for its actions. This is useful when you think that you might overwrite data when creating a tar archive.

Creating a tar Archive

So, you've decided to distribute your files to the world—tar can help with this task, as well. For example, suppose you want to create a tar archive of the directory /home/bwagner/companies. You would issue the following command:

```
tar cvf Companies.tar /home/bwagner/companies
```

From another angle, you could archive your entire directory structure by issuing this command from the root directory:

```
tar cvf - `find . -print` > my_system.tar
```

In this example, find generates a massive list of all files and directories, and these are used in making the tar archive my_system.tar.

Installing Your New Program

Let's recap a bit. You were surfing the Net when suddenly you found an interesting UNIX program. After checking whether it will run on your UNIX flavor, you downloaded it. You found that it was zipped up, so you unzipped it. Then, finally, you found that it was "tarred" so you "untarred" it. During this last step, the files were extracted to some directory or other. Now the question is, what do you do next?

The answer varies. Most binary distributions pose no problem at all. Usually, they extract to a single, executable file. If you encounter this situation, rejoice! To run the program, you simply have to issue it as a command. For example, xdir binary distributions contain a file called xdir. To launch it, you simply type xdir while in X and, bingo, the xdir program appears on your screen.

Unfortunately, not all distributions are that simple. Some require you to move one or more files to a specific directory. Others require you to configure the program before executing it. Finally, some require you to actually compile the program. To find out, you need to examine the distribution carefully.

Examining the Distribution

By now, you're probably thinking that these UNIX folks are pretty tough. After all, they make you download, unzip, and untar their software. As if that wasn't bad enough, they also make you set up the software on your own, without any instructions, right? Not quite.

If the software distribution requires additional hacking, you'll know it, and here's how: Software authors include instructions (often very detailed instructions) in one or more text files included with the software. It has been a long-standing rule that these files must be named something reasonably familiar. For that reason, 99 percent of all such distributions will come with files named either README or INSTALL.

A good example is the wonderful FTP client for UNIX called MoxFTP. MoxFTP's distribution comes with a file named mftp.readme. Here are the contents of that file:

```
This is a static version of moxftp compiled with Motif 1.1.

To install:

# cp mftp /usr/bin/X11
# cp ftp_for_xftp /usr/bin/X11
# cp Mftp /usr/lib/X11/app-defaults

To run:

# mftp

Enjoy,
rocco@perseus.maschinenbau.TU-Ilmenau.DE
```

As you can see, the author gives pretty clear instructions on how to install and run the program. In this case, the author explains that you need to copy certain files to various directories and then execute the program. In most cases, by following the software author's simple instructions, you'll be running your new program in no time.

Real Trouble: You Downloaded Source Code

On the other hand, perhaps you downloaded source code instead. This might not be a problem—it depends on your specific configuration, as you'll see later. However, one thing you *will* need regardless of what version of UNIX you use is a C compiler.

Do You Have C?

As noted earlier, most UNIX programs are written in the C programming language. To compile such programs, you must have a C compiler installed on your local network (preferably your local disk drive.) To find out whether you have a C compiler, you can take several steps. One is to ask your system administrator. However, because system administration folks are generally busy, you should probably conduct your own investigation first. To do so, issue the following commands:

➤ **cc**—This attempts to run the generic C compiler.

➤ **gcc**—This attempts to run the Free Software Foundation's C compiler.

➤ **whereis cc**—This attempts to find the C compiler.

C 4 Free!

If you don't have C, you can get a free version at the Free Software Foundation, located here at http://www.fsf.org.

If none of these commands produce results, you might not have a C compiler. How can this be? Well, there could be several reasons. One is that your particular UNIX distribution may be a commercial version. Many UNIX vendors sell their C compiler software separately at premium prices. (Some charge as much as several thousand dollars for a full development package.) However, today, this practice is becoming less and less prevalent. Instead, it's more probable that whoever installed the system simply didn't install the compiler option. To remedy that, you can either install the compiler yourself (check your manuals) or have your system administrator do it.

Finding the Magic Words

On the other hand, if you find that C (the compiler) has been installed, you're well on your way. The next step, then, is to determine what commands are needed to install the software. For this, you must check the README or INSTALL file.

For example, there's a good chat client for UNIX called to-talk. to-talk comes in source form and needs to be compiled. When you first unpack the to-talk distribution, the file to-talk-1.4.README is written to your drive. Here's an excerpt from to-talk-1.4.README:

```
INSTALLATION FROM SOURCE CODE


Under Linux, follow these steps:

unpack:      tar xvfz to-talk-1.3.src.tar.gz
compile:     cd to-talk-1.3 ; make
install:     su root -c "make install"
```

In this example, the author shows how to install the program for Linux. (The distribution also has similar instructions for generic UNIX.) As you can see, the procedure is pretty simple. In most cases, source distributions will contain similar instructions. So, what happens when you issue these commands? It depends. In general, however, you'll see many hundreds of lines of code scroll by. Your hard disk will sound like it's been sent through a meat grinder. If this happens, don't panic! The program is simply being compiled. When the process is over, you'll see a message like this:

```
make: done
```

At that point, the UNIX shell prompt will be released back into your control. Unless you see error messages accompanying this message, the program has now been installed.

Troubleshooting Installations

Finally, what happens if you try compiling the program and the compile fails? Well, this situation is a bit beyond the scope of a *Complete Idiot's Guide* book. However, I feel I should offer a least a few encouraging words on the subject.

You'll rarely encounter a bad compile because developers make every effort to prevent that from happening. For them, this is a very boring process of testing compiles on various architectures. Usually, when they're done, the process is error free. Therefore, if you encounter a compile error, it's almost certain that the problem is at your end. (Sounds like something a tech support person would say, right? In this case, though, it's actually true.)

In my experience, the greatest potential for error is when you're compiling a program that will run in X. Here's why: Software developers have a wide range of graphics libraries to choose from when they write an X program. Some folks like the look of Sun's OpenWindows, so they use Xview libraries. Other folks dig Motif, but perhaps they can't afford it, so they use more offbeat libraries, such as Lesstif (a free Motif clone).

Assorted Facts about Libraries

You're probably wondering just what these libraries are all about. Let me remedy that. Libraries are prefabricated software modules or snippets of code that, when woven into a program, influence the way that program appears or behaves. For example, graphics libraries greatly influence the look of windows. Some graphics libraries create windows that resemble the windows in Windows 95. Others create windows that look like those found in Mac OS. Additionally, graphics libraries aren't the only kind of libraries available. Others influence how math, graphing, charting, typesetting, or communication is done. Finally, some libraries are commercial (and therefore expensive), whereas others are free. What does all this mean to you? It means this: When you compile a new program, you must have the required libraries. If you don't, the program might not work properly. Unfortunately, even if you have C, you may be lacking the necessary libraries for certain applications (and, conversely, it's quite possible to have the libraries but no C).

Some developers erroneously assume that you have all the necessary include and library files to compile their applications. If you don't actually have these files, the compile is bound to fail. You'll know instantly, too, because the compiler will exit and give an error saying it cannot find a particular file.

If this happens, jot down the name of the file the compiler cannot find. Then, take a closer look at the documentation accompanying the software. If you can't find any reference there to the missing file, try searching for the file on the Internet. When you find the file, it will be accompanied by a description of its function. (For example, perhaps it's a graphics library.)

All in all, you'll probably encounter this situation very rarely.

The Least You Need to Know

The range of software available for UNIX on the Web is amazing. To take advantage of that treasure trove, here's the least you need to know:

➤ Software distributions can come in two forms: binary and source. Whenever possible, try to find the binary version.

➤ Most files available for download are zipped. To unzip them, use uncompress (**uncompress filename.Z**) or gunzip (**gunzip filename.gz**).

➤ Most zipped files are also tarred. After you unzip the file, untar it, like this: **tar xvf filename.tar**.

➤ After unzipping and untarring a software distribution, always check the README or INSTALL file. It will contain instructions on how to install the program.

➤ Source distributions require a C compiler. To check whether you have one, try the following commands: **cc**, **gcc**, **whereis cc**.

➤ To compile a source distribution, follow the instructions in the README or INSTALL file.

Part 3
Working in the UNIX GUI

UNIX isn't all text and command line prompts. In fact, UNIX has it's own Graphical User Interface, the X Window System, or X. X opens up UNIX to a whole new world of usability and power features, and Part III uncovers the capabilities made possible by X.

Within the chapters of Part III, you'll learn how to create, destroy, and manipulate windows; how to choose a window manager; how to navigate in a mouse-driven world; how to customize menus; and how to launch applications in X.

## Chapter 11

Tyrannosaurus X: A Windowing System

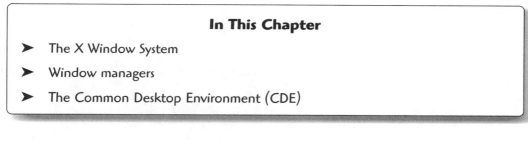

In This Chapter

➤ The X Window System

➤ Window managers

➤ The Common Desktop Environment (CDE)

Up until now, this book has probably confirmed your worst fears—namely that UNIX is a largely text-based operating system. In this chapter, you'll get a reprieve from that rather intimidating world and discover that UNIX, too, has a windowing system.

Indeed, contrary to what you may have heard, UNIX can be extremely user-friendly. In this chapter, we'll examine the windowing system for UNIX and how it developed.

About Window Systems in General

As I mentioned in Chapter 1, "I Thought UNIX Lived in Harems," windowing systems have been with us a relatively short time—since 1972, in fact. (Xerox tested the first real prototype of a windowing system in 1972.) Since then, windowing systems have done more to bring computing to the average public than any other single innovation. There's no secret as to why: Windowing systems make computing easy and fun.

Moreover, windowing systems allow users to perform several tasks at once. For example, you can open several word processors at the same time. If one doesn't do the type of formatting you're looking for, you can transfer your text to another that does.

Even more important, windowing systems make it possible for you to understand the data you're working with. This is possible through the *visualization* of data. To appreciate the power of visualization, check out this table of meaningless data:

Table of Meaningless and Difficult to Understand Information

	1985	1990	1995	1998
UNIX	30	35	40	50
Vax	25	30	35	45
Windows	20	25	30	40
Mac	15	20	25	35

Imagine going through this stuff, column after column, page after page. After a while, your eyes would ache. On the other hand, if you use a visualization tool (in this case, a charting program), the data is easier to understand and far more visually inviting. Take a look at the same data illustrated visually in the following figure.

A chart of equally meaningless data.

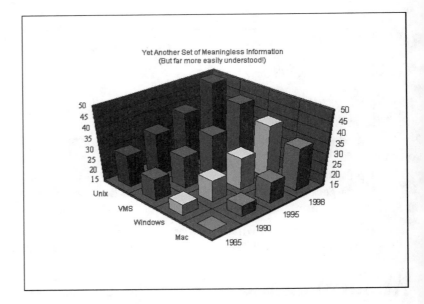

Quite a difference, right? Most windowing systems are all about visualization. For example, in Microsoft Windows and Mac OS, drives and other devices are represented by icons that resemble the actual tools you're working with (in other words, CD-ROM devices are represented by CD-ROM icons, and so forth).

By designing their windowing systems this way, software manufacturers hope to make their systems *intuitive* (that's another way of saying that complete idiots can easily guess how to perform a task, simply by looking at the icons on their desktop).

In UNIX, the standard windowing system is the *X Window System*, developed at the Massachusetts Institute of Technology (MIT). (Hip UNIX users tend to refer to the X Window System as *X*, so we'll do the same.) X, too, allows you to visualize data and your system devices. However, X goes beyond simple visualization.

Windows That Can Talk: The X Protocol

X isn't just a windowing system—it's a network protocol. In fact, X was originally designed more for networking than for visualization. To understand X networking, you just need to understand remote application deployment. (Oh, is that all?)

Here it is in a nutshell: With X, you can run a program on your own system, even though that program resides somewhere else. (That "somewhere else" could be in the next office or 10,000 miles away.) You can do this even though the specified program isn't installed on your machine. But wait, there's more. Using X, you can run UNIX programs on a Mac (or even run Microsoft Windows programs on UNIX).

UNIX-Windows Compatibility

You have several ways available to you to run Microsoft applications on UNIX. One is to use standard X functionality. In this scenario, you can run a Microsoft application within your favorite Web browser. Conversely, you can also use suites such as WABI (from Sun Microsystems) that will actually run Windows applications locally. (There's also a terminal that will now run Windows NT and UNIX on the same box.) In short, the gap between Microsoft applications and UNIX is closing every day.

How is this possible? It's possible through the X protocol, which is built on the client/server model. Traditionally, a *server application* is any program that distributes data to clients from a centralized point. A *client application* is any program designed to interact with (and receive information from) a server. A perfect example is the relationship between a Web server and your Web browser (the client). In X, however, the client/server relationship is a little more complex.

In X, your system is both a client and a server. The client interacts with other servers over the network, getting various data. Meanwhile, your local server displays that data graphically. If that sounds confusing, don't worry about it. It all basically breaks down to this: Using X, you can run remote applications from anywhere on just about any machine.

As you can see, X developers have traditionally been more concerned with moving data over networks than the visualization of that data. For them, the graphical user interface could look relatively generic as long as it could reliably network data and present it in graphical form. For this reason, as you'll soon discover, X applications are often simplistic in appearance. Don't let that fool you, though. X is a complex and powerful windowing system.

The Windowing System That Launched a Thousand Chips

In addition to networking capabilities, X developers were also concerned with platform and hardware constraints. For example, many windowing systems (such as Microsoft Windows, OS/2, and Mac OS) run only on a handful of chips and systems.

To avoid such limitations, X developers made their design as "architecture neutral" as possible. Therefore, X servers and clients run on all the following systems:

➤ Microsoft Windows 95 and NT

➤ Mac OS

➤ UNIX

➤ VMS

This means that X runs on almost every available processor chip, including Intel, Alpha, PowerPC, and garden-variety RISC. Indeed, X could conceivably run on other systems as well, because X is highly portable (the core of X is written in the C programming language, and official X development follows fairly strict standards and guidelines).

The Windowing System with a Thousand Faces

With all the work that X developers put into making X a malleable, portable system, they admittedly neglected X's appearance (that is, until recently). In fact, until recently, no real standards had been developed in this regard. Therefore, X can look very different on different systems.

This is in sharp contrast to Mac OS and Microsoft Windows, which both conform to very rigid (though perhaps proprietary) standards in terms of appearance. These standards reach to the very core of their respective graphical user interfaces.

X's appearance depends solely on the window manager you're using. Let's talk about window managers for a moment.

Window Managers

Window managers govern every aspect of X's appearance, including menus, windows, borders, mouse cursors, and so forth. Like many issues in the UNIX community, window managers have attained cult status. (When conversing with other UNIX users about their window manager, watch your step! These folks are serious about computing, and even more serious about window managers. UNIX folks often hotly debate the issue of which window manager is the best.)

Let's take a look at several now.

twm

By far, the most generic window manager is twm (or *Tab Window Manager*). Rumor has it that the term originated with its creator, Tom LaStrange. Therefore, some people refer to it as *Tom's Window Manager*.

twm is quite basic, as you can see in the following figure.

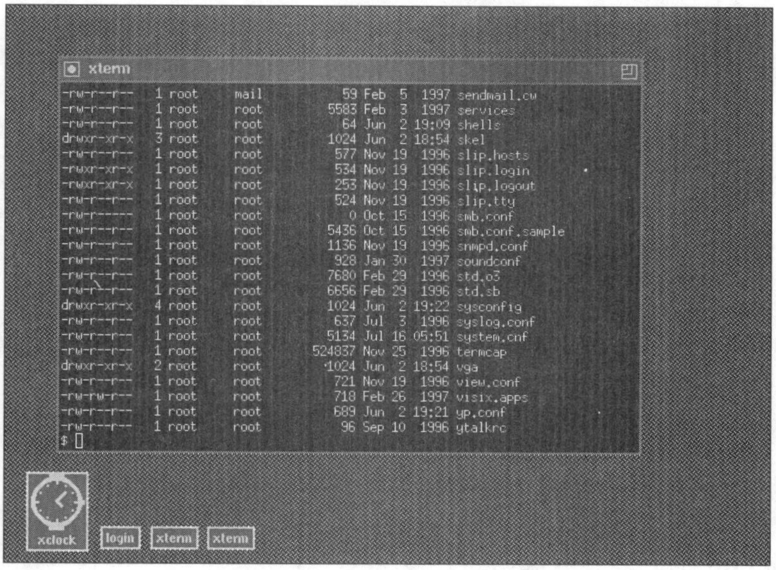

The Tab Window Manager at startup.

Initially, you might be turned off by twm's rather Spartan appearance. However, twm makes up for this in many other ways. One way, in particular, is that twm absolutely smokes. It's indisputably the fastest window manager available due to its lightweight design. For this reason, twm is a favorite of folks working with limited memory resources.

twm is included in most UNIX distributions now, including Solaris. However, it's rarely configured as the default window manager, so you'll have to look for it. (A good place to start would be the twm man page.)

OpenWindows and olwm

Another popular window manager, olwm, grew from Sun's OpenWindows windowing system. olwm has a look and feel very different than twm, sporting a more panel-oriented appearance, as you can see in the following figure.

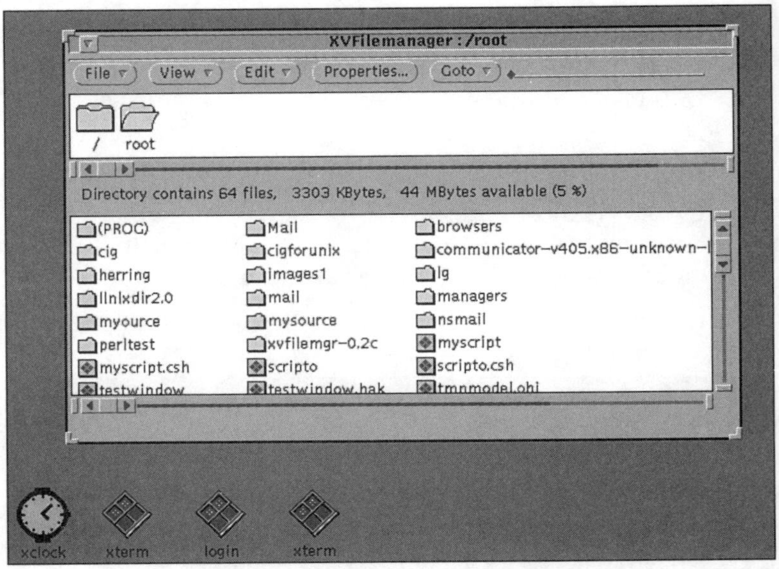

The olwm window manager at startup.

One valuable feature of olwm is that it comes with tools that allow you to easily manipulate text within terminal windows. Clipping, copying, cutting, and pasting text are all achieved with a click of the mouse. (You'll learn about this feature in Chapter 12, "Point and Clique".)

On SunOS and Solaris, olwm comes with a wide range of desktop tools, including a calculator, mail tool, file manager, audio player, and PostScript interpreter. On other systems (such Linux), olwm comes alone, accompanied only by a shell tool and a terminal emulator called cmdtool. However, nearly all X applications will function smoothly when run through olwm.

olwm is a standard window manager on both SunOS and Solaris. However, to obtain olwm for other platforms, try `ftp://ftp.x.org/R5contrib/olvwm4.tar.Z`

mwm and fvwm

By far, the most popular window managers of all are mwm (Motif Window Manager) and its free clone, fvwm. Both provide a very attractive interface, as shown in the following figure.

In appearance, there's little real difference between mwm and fvwm. (In fact, fvwm can be made to emulate almost any windowing system, although in its native state, it most closely resembles mwm.) In other ways, however, mwm and fvwm differ considerably.

The fvwm window manager at startup.

mwm (the industry standard for several years now) is based on Motif graphics libraries. Obtaining a development license for Motif is an expensive affair. In fact, a full distribution license is about $17,000. (This allows you to write and distribute applications developed in Motif.) For this reason alone, mwm is out of reach of students and other folks short on cash.

A fellow named Robert Nation changed all that, however. He took the source code of twm and fashioned a mwm clone called fvwm. (It's never been clear what fvwm really stands for. The generally accepted view is that the letters *vwm* stand for *Virtual Window Manager*. The meaning of the *f*, however, is something that has never been settled.)

fvwm is available at `http://www.hpc.uh.edu/fvwm/`.

So, by now, you've probably surmised that while X conforms to rigid networking and portability standards, X window manager development is a raucous free-for-all. Until recently, this was very true. However, in the last several years, the X community wised up. Having dozens of different window managers, they realized, meant that users might have to learn the X interface several times instead of once. That wasn't suitable, so they sought to develop a common standard across all UNIX platforms.

That effort produced the Common Desktop Environment.

147

Getting More for Less

As an interesting side note, the Linux community (known to be radical and revolutionary) got quite worked up about the high-priced Motif. In response, (as they have done so many times before), Linux developers created a free alternative. What did they call it? *Lesstif.*

The Common Desktop Environment (CDE)

The Common Desktop Environment has become an industry standard on many commercial UNIX distributions. Based largely on Motif, CDE provides a desktop environment that looks and operates identically on all supported UNIX flavors.

The look and feel of CDE is also very clean, as you can see in the following figure.

A typical CDE window.

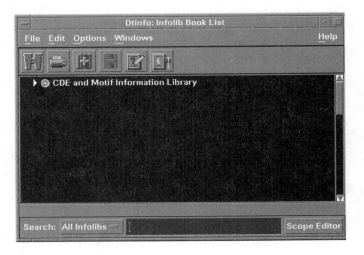

Additionally, CDE-based systems are more user-friendly. They generally have very powerful and easy-to-use help applications that are based on hyperlinked documents. This allows you to navigate help systems in a more-or-less aimless manner without regard for where you start or stop.

The downside to CDE is that it's a commercial product and quite expensive. To learn more about CDE, check out the OpenGroup's Web site, located at
`http://www.camb.opengroup.org/tech/desktop/cde/`.

The Last Word on Window Managers

Over two dozen other window managers are available for UNIX. Some are free and some are commercial. Table 11.1 provides a little background on some of the more popular ones.

Table 11.1.   Some alternative UNIX window managers

Window Manager	Description
AfterStep	AfterStep (formerly the BowMan Window Manager) is a NeXTStep emulator (NeXTStep was the windowing system for NeXT computers). This is probably one of the most stylish window managers. AfterStep is available at `http://www.afterstep.org/`.
amiwm	amiwm (Amiga Window Manager) emulates the look and feel of the Amiga Workbench. amiwm can be obtained at `http://www.lysator.liu.se/~marcus/amiwm.html`.
gwm	gwm (Generic Window Manager) is a bare-bones window manager suitable for systems with limited resources. (This window manager doesn't have much flash, by default, but it can be made to emulate many other window managers.) gwm is available at `http://www.inria.fr/koala/gwm/`.
KDE	The K Desktop Environment is a commercial window manager that resembles a cross between the Common Desktop Environment (CDE) and Microsoft Windows 95. In fact, many of the management applets in KDE closely resemble those in Windows 95, including the Display Properties tab window. KDE is available at `http://www.kde.org/`.

Where X Is Going

For many years, X's development went unnoticed by all but serious UNIX users. Certainly, no one ever expected X to compete with more consumer-oriented windowing systems such as Microsoft Windows or Mac OS. However, today, that climate has changed.

Today, everything is about networking, and especially networking over the Internet. Finally, the long, hard-earned research done by X developers is paying off big time. X is now experiencing a renaissance, because companies large and small are finding it a superb choice for running embedded applications over high-speed Internet links.

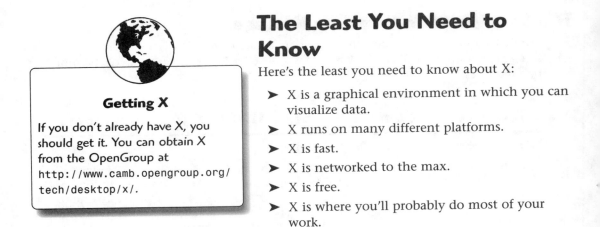

Getting X

If you don't already have X, you should get it. You can obtain X from the OpenGroup at http://www.camb.opengroup.org/tech/desktop/x/.

The Least You Need to Know

Here's the least you need to know about X:

➤ X is a graphical environment in which you can visualize data.

➤ X runs on many different platforms.

➤ X is fast.

➤ X is networked to the max.

➤ X is free.

➤ X is where you'll probably do most of your work.

In the next chapter, we'll look at how X works, how you start it, and what it can do for you.

## Chapter 12

Point and Clique:

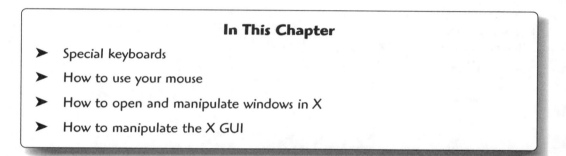

In This Chapter

➤ Special keyboards

➤ How to use your mouse

➤ How to open and manipulate windows in X

➤ How to manipulate the X GUI

Windowing systems are supposed to make computing easier. At least, that's the theory. Industry professionals work hard to standardize the behavior and appearance of their windowing systems. Such standardization provides you with convenience and helps you learn how to use your system. Certainly, if most windows on your system behave similarly, the learning curve on each new application should be less dramatic.

X is a little different than other windowing systems, though. Until recently, there was not a lot of standardization in third-party X applications (or even various implementation of X.). Therefore, one X application might work one way and another would work completely different. This seems to be especially so when it comes to Function key combinations. To a lesser extent, this extends to menu behavior. There are several reasons for this.

One reason is that not all X applications are written using the same development package. (As I indicated earlier, Motif licenses are quite expensive.) Programmers often use new graphics libraries, experimental window toolkits, or homegrown menu code. This can lead to unorthodox (or even bizarre) menu and window behavior. Therefore, X can be very confusing at first.

What's Up with X Programmers, Anyway?

X programmers can be very eccentric folks. This is especially so of Linux developers. If you start an application and its menu and Function keys don't respond as you expect them to, check the man page. There, you'll find clues about key bindings and menu structure. (For example, perhaps you have to type ALT+CTRL+SHIFT+F7+P to print a document. Silly of you not to figure that out on your own, right?)

Nevertheless, once you become acclimated to this rather quirky environment, you'll realize that X rocks. Because X was specifically designed for networking, you can network almost any application. (You might say that the X development community has gone hog-wild with the client/server model. Everything from CD players to scratch pads are networked.)

This chapter will get you on the fast track to using X comfortably.

Your Keyboard

Most modern UNIX systems support keyboards and keyboard layouts that are similar (if not identical) to PC-style keyboards. For the most part, these keyboards will behave much like PC keyboards. Exceptions to this rule are Sparcstation keyboards from Sun Microsystems.

You can immediately tell if you have a Sparc by looking at the box or by examining the keyboard. Generally, the Sun logo appears either on the keyboard or the main unit.

Sun Microsystems keyboards have special Function keys that run down the keyboard's left side. In newer models (late Type 4 and all Type 5 keyboards), these Function keys are marked with words that describe their purpose. Table 12.1 gives a few examples of these function keys and what they do.

Table 12.1.   Some Sun function keys

Key	Result
Stop	This halts the workstation. (On some models, this will halt all activity and present you with the interactive command prompt. From here, you can boot or perform diagnostics.)
Props	This summons the Properties window. From Properties, you can change the way OpenWindows looks and acts (including changing fonts, color, mouse behavior, and so forth).
Help	This launches either the help tool (if no window is currently open) or the help file on the current window or operation.
Undo	This will undo your last command.
Copy	This will copy the currently highlighted text.
Cut	This will cut the currently highlighted text.
Paste	This will paste the contents of the Clipboard into the current document.

Additionally, some Sun keyboards have sound controls located in the upper-right corner. (These are easily recognizable from their icons. They look like speakers.)

In all other respects, you'll find that your keyboard behaves no differently than a PC keyboard.

Different Mouse Types

If you've ever used a mouse before, you'll have little trouble using one in X. Most UNIX systems support standard mechanical mice. These are similar (and in certain cases, identical) to PC mice. However, there's one exception: the optical mouse.

Optical mice are different from standard mechanical mice in several ways. First, they're constructed differently. Optical mice, for example, don't rely on balls to track their position. Instead, optical mice read patterns from the mouse pad using infrared light. (Mouse pads for optical mice are generally made of metal. This metal surface has fine patterns in it that the mouse can interpret and translate into mathematical coordinates to reflect its position. This is why optical mice don't use track balls.)

Particularly on older optical mice models, you may find that the mouse is not as sensitive as a PC mouse. (In other words, you may have to exert more effort to move the cursor across the screen. This can sometimes lead to peculiar medical conditions, such as "optical mouse elbow.") There are solutions to this problem:

➤ Replace the optical mouse with a mechanical mouse

➤ Get a mouse pad with finer patterns

You can also manipulate your mouse settings. Upping your mouse's acceleration and speed will help tremendously.

The Mouse and X

For the most part, your mouse will behave the same in X as it does in other GUIs. As you move your mouse across the mouse pad, your mouse cursor moves across the screen. You select items by moving your mouse cursor over them and clicking one of the mouse buttons. In this respect, using a mouse in X differs little from using a mouse in Microsoft Windows or Mac OS.

However, there are some subtle differences in X mouse functionality. For example, in X, you can use a three-button mouse, and each button can have a different function. In most X window managers, for example, you can resize a window by grabbing a border with the left mouse button and dragging it. However, if you perform precisely the same action with the right mouse button, the window will move instead.

Additionally, some window managers allow you to summon menus by clicking empty portions of the screen. (In other words, if you click an area that doesn't contain a window, a menu will appear.) Different menus will appear depending on which button you click. For example, if you click the main desktop with your right mouse button, an application menu will appear. If you click the middle button, a window manipulation menu will appear. Finally, if you click the left mouse button, a tool menu will appear.

Different Strokes for Different Folks

I'd like to tell you that all X window managers behave the same, but that's simply not true. To find out which menus are available to you, try clicking the empty desktop with all three mouse buttons (or two, if that's what you have). By doing this, you can immediately determine what menus are available.

Mouse Buttons

All window managers support three-button mice. However, not all systems ship with three-button mice. If you have a two-button mouse, don't feel left out. In most cases, functions that are available from the middle button are also available through other means.

On Linux systems, developers have an interesting approach to the two-button mouse. They have developed three-button mouse functionality for two-button mice through a technique they call *chording*. In chording, you can simulate a three-button mouse event by clicking the right and left mouse buttons simultaneously. (The effectiveness of this technique is debatable. Some folks find chording difficult because it demands fairly precise coordination. If you see a coworker using X and he's smashing his mouse against the table, he may be trying to master this subtle technique.)

Doing Windows: How Windows Work in X

Windows in X perform exactly the same tasks as windows in other GUIs. However, you wouldn't know it by looking at them. For the most part, X windows just sit there, waiting for you to do something. For example, take a look at the Xterm window in the following figure.

From its appearance, the Xterm window tells you little (although there's at least one familiar face: the $ shell prompt. From this, you know that you can enter commands in the window.) So, let's look at the composition of the Xterm window. Here are the two things we're concerned with in this window:

➤ The work area

➤ The window controls

Now, let's examine each.

A typical window in X.

The X Window Work Area

The main area of a window in X is the work area. This area almost always spans from the window's center all the way to the borders. (See the following figure.)

The X window work area

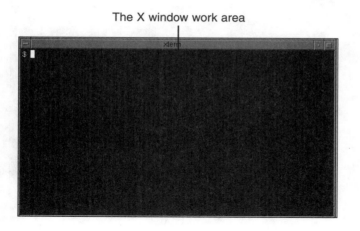

The work area of an X window.

The work area is where you do your work. In this area, you can interact with applications or the underlying operating system. For instance, when you use the window to gain shell access, the work area behaves precisely as the shell does. The next figure illustrates what happens when you use a Xterm window as a shell and then list a directory.

As you can see, you type text, enter commands, and basically perform your work in the work area.

Window Controls in X

Outside of the work area, windows in X have various controls. These are tools that help you control the window's behavior and appearance. The following figure points out these controls.

*Using an Xterm window
to list directory contents.*

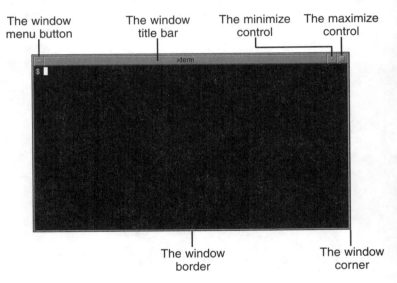

```
$ ls -l
total 4
-rw-r--r--    1 root      root            3 Jul  4 17:42 Hayden
-rw-r--r--    1 root      root            3 Jul  4 17:42 Macmillan
-rw-r--r--    1 root      root            3 Jul  4 17:42 Que
-rw-r--r--    1 root      root            3 Jul  4 17:42 SAMS
$ ▮
```

Window controls in X.

The window   The window   The minimize   The maximize
menu button   title bar   control   control

The window
border

The window
corner

There are six controls in all:

➤ The title bar

➤ The border

➤ The corner

➤ The maximize control

➤ The minimize control

➤ The window menu button

You can use each of these controls to manipulate your windows. Let's take a look at
what each control does.

156

Moving a Window: The Title Bar

The title bar serves three purposes:

➤ It reports the name of the current application.

➤ It allows you to grab focus (something we'll discuss momentarily).

➤ It allows you to move the window.

You can use the title bar to move a window around the screen. To move a window, perform these steps:

1. Place your mouse over the window's title bar.

2. Hold down the left mouse button.

3. Drag the window to your desired location.

4. Release the left mouse button.

While you're moving the window, it will disappear. The only thing you'll see is the border as it moves across the screen. Don't be alarmed; that's exactly what it's supposed to do.

In many window managers, as you move the window, a tiny window will appear at the bottom of the screen. This tiny window reports the coordinates of the window you're moving. Personally, I've never figured out the advantage of this (other than to demonstrate that the programmer can track the movement of a window). However, it's moderately amusing.

When Size Really Does Matter: The Border Control

You'll undoubtedly be faced with many instances when the current window is either too big or too small. To remedy this, you can resize the window.

You resize a window by grabbing its border and either stretching or shrinking the window to suit your needs. To resize a window's height, perform the following steps:

1. Place your mouse over the window's top or bottom border.

2. Grab the border by holding down the left mouse button.

Warning: Don't Become a Fashion Victim

Maybe you're thinking about sprucing up your desktop. Perhaps you'd like a black background. If you're new to UNIX, don't do it! Until you learn how to manipulate window border colors, having a black desktop can be fatal. Here's why: While a window is moving, its border is black. If you change your desktop to black, the borders will be invisible. Therefore, when you move a window, you'll have no way of knowing where it will end up (because you can't see it.)

3. Drag the window to the desired height.

4. Release the left mouse button.

To resize both a window's height and width, perform the following steps:

1. Place your mouse over any corner on the window.

2. Grab the corner by holding down the left mouse button.

3. Drag the window to the desired size.

4. Release the left mouse button.

How you drag the window will influence how the window is resized. For example, to obtain uniform sizing of both height and width, drag your mouse in a diagonal motion to or from the center of the screen (*inward* to shrink the window and *outward* to expand it). This retains the window's aspect ratio of height to width. Therefore, a window that's 200×400 will become 400×800, and so on.

Secrets of a Sharpshooter

Resizing a window can be frustrating if you're new to X. Here's why: To grab a corner, you need to be pretty accurate. To make this easier, you should slow the velocity of your mouse as your cursor nears the window's corner. If you move slowly enough, you'll see that your mouse cursor changes into a vertical bar when you are precisely over the border. Only then should you hold down your mouse button and start dragging. (As a general rule, until you get acclimated to using X, you should grab the window by its corners, not its borders. Grabbing the corner requires less accuracy.)

Blowing Up Your Windows: The Maximize Control

Maximizing a window is where you blow it up so that it fills your entire screen. (While a window is maximized, it blocks your view of all other windows.)

You may occasionally need to maximize a window. In fact, some applications actually require it—if you don't maximize the window, various menu items or other important components of the application might be hidden from view because they extend beyond the border of the current window. This sometimes happens because the window was in a maximized state when the application was created.

The maximize control can save you the time of resizing the window to full screen. To maximize a window, simply click the maximize control button. You'll find this button in the window's upper-right corner. (See the following figure.)

While a window is maximized, the maximize control button will take on a slightly different appearance. This is to notify you that the current window is maximized. To return the window to normal size, simply click the maximize control button again.

The window will pop right back to its original size.

—The maximize control

The maximize control button.

Some applications shouldn't be run in a maximized window. If you try to maximize the window and get strange results, it's probably best to revert to a normal window. (Strange results can be many things: for example, the application's interface may stretch out of proportion, pictures and text may become completely distorted, or the application interface may not change at all. Instead, you'll be left with a large window in which the application only occupies a small portion of it.)

Lastly, if you're going to maximize a window, you should generally do so prior to working in it. Here's why: Sometimes when you maximize a window, the position of text within that window will change. Text that was previously visible won't be, and vice versa.

The Incredible Shrinking Window: The Minimize Control

The problem with windows is that they can get in the way (in other words, one window may block your view of another). Whenever you have more than two windows on the screen, it's often easier to minimize the obstructive window than to move it. By taking this approach, you effectively make the obstructive window temporarily disappear without actually killing it. You should kill windows as seldom as possible; otherwise, you may get a visit from the ASPCW (the American Society for the Prevention of Cruelty to Windows). Believe me, you don't want to tangle with them.

To minimize (or *iconize*) a window, click the minimize control button, located in the upper-right corner of the window. (See the following figure.)

When you minimize a window, its icon is placed on the desktop and will remain there until you click the icon. Clicking the icon will return the window to its original state. (Some window managers demand that you double-click the icon to restore it. The easiest way to find out which method is used is to try it out.)

Why Is My Window Cut in Half?

Some applications—such as Netscape Navigator—will open in odd positions. Often, much of the window is hidden because it expands beyond the borders of your viewable screen. (This happens frequently when you use 640×480 resolution on a desktop or application that was originally designed in 800×600 or higher.) In such cases, the maximize control button comes in very handy. Instead of trying to capture the window and resize it, just use the maximize button. When you do, the application will automatically snap to attention, filling up only the entire screen's viewable area.

The minimize control
button.

The minimize control

Controlling Windows with the Window Menu

In previous sections, you learned how to move, resize, and position a window using single-click methods. However, you can also perform any of these tasks by using the window menu.

You invoke the window menu by clicking the window menu button located in the upper-right corner of the window. (See the following figure.)

The window menu
button.

The window menu
control button

When you click the window menu button, a drop-down menu appears. This menu will look very similar to the menu shown in the next figure.

The window menu.

```
Move
Resize
Front
Back
Iconify
(Un)Stick
Quit
Delete
```

Your window menu may look slightly different, depending on your window manager. However, all window managers present at least these choices on their window menu:

➤ Move

➤ Size or Resize

➤ Iconify or Minimize

➤ Delete or Close

To use the window menu, follow these steps:

1. Click the window menu control button.
2. Hold down the mouse button until the menu appears.
3. Drag the mouse down to the desired action (for example, Move).
4. Release the mouse button.

At this point, your mouse icon will change, and any movement you make will affect the window. (For example, if you choose Move and subsequently move your mouse, the window will move with it.)

Breaking Windows

Whenever a window outgrows its usefulness, you'll want to get rid of it. To do so, you can take several measures:

➤ Exit the application

➤ Use the window menu to close or delete the window

➤ Kill the application or window

Let's take a look at each method.

Exiting the Application

In most cases, application windows will willingly leave without much resistance. To banish them from your site, simply terminate the application. (For example, you can destroy an Xterm window by typing exit at the prompt. Also, many X applications have a File menu with Exit or Close as an option. Use your mouse to pull down that menu to choose the appropriate action.)

Using the Window Menu

Some windows are more stubborn. (They just don't know when to quit.) In this case, you must forcibly remove them from the premises. To do so, pull down the window menu and choose either Close or Delete. This will send the stubborn window packing.

Killing the Application or Window

In rare instances, a window will persist even after you try exiting the application by using the window menu. If you encounter this situation, make no mistake, you're being stalked by a belligerent window. (The FBI estimates that two out of every five X users are likely to fall victim to a window-stalking attack during their lifetime.) The solution is to sneak up behind the offending window and smash it on the head with a rubber mallet. To do so, follow these steps:

➤ Open an Xterm window to get a shell.

➤ Get a process listing using ps.

➤ Find the offending window's process ID number.

➤ Type kill *process_id_number*.

For example, suppose you get a process entry like this:

```
PID    TTY      TIME CMD
9638   pts/7    0:00 xterm
```

You can kill it by typing the following:

```
kill 9638
```

Killing Can Be Costly

You should kill processes very sparingly. Sometimes, killing a process can mean losing your work. Moreover, some processes (such as your window manager, for example) are essential to certain operations. If you kill a vital process, your system could fail. Then, you would be forced to restart.

Focal Chords: Managing Multiple Windows

Once you get down to business with UNIX, you'll undoubtedly run several windows at once. For example, you might open an Xterm window, an instance of Netscape Communicator, a file manager, and a text editor simultaneously. Managing all those windows can be confusing. That's what this next section is all about.

The Current Window

No matter how many windows you open, only one can be the current window. When a window is current, it is said to have *focus*. While a window has focus, you can access objects inside of it using your mouse or keyboard. However, when a window loses focus, even though you can see objects inside of it, you'll not be able to use them. In order to reclaim your ability to use them, you need to give that window focus again (or make it the current window). The trick is to know which window is current.

In X, the current window's title bar is highlighted. (It will therefore be distinct from the other title bars. Typically, it's a lighter and crisper color than the others.) In contrast, windows without focus have a shaded title bar. (See the following figure for an example.)

In this figure, the current window is the Xgetfile application. There are two ways you can quickly identify it as the current window:

➤ It's currently on top
➤ Its title bar is highlighted

In contrast, the Crisp text editor window has been shuffled to the back and its title bar is shaded.

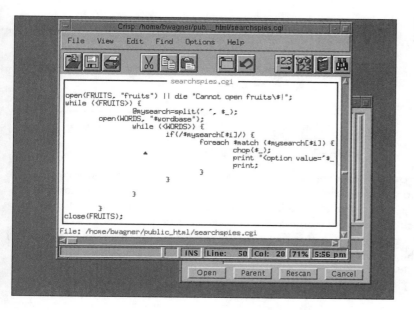

The current window title bar is highlighted. (Although difficult to see in black and white, the title bar of the window without focus is much dimmer.)

Changing the Current Window

You change the current window by bringing another window into focus. To do so, click the title bar of the window you want to bring into focus. In response, X will shuffle the other windows to the back. For example, suppose you want to bring the Crisp editor into focus. To do so, you would simply click its title bar. (The results are illustrated in the following figure.)

The Crisp editor is now the current window.

In this figure, the Xgetfile utility has been moved to the back and the Crisp editor is now the current window.

To bring any window into focus, simply click its title bar. (In some window managers, you can either single- or double-click its border).

We're Not Quite Out of Focus Yet

There are also other methods for giving a window focus. In Motif, you can place your mouse cursor over the desired window and hit Alt+F1. On Sparc systems (where you're using OpenWindows), you can place your mouse cursor over the desired window and press the Front key on your keyboard. On first examination, it might seem silly to include these extra methods. After all, if you were too lazy to click a window's title bar, you'd hardly go through the laborious process of using Function keys. However, these extra means of focusing windows have a very practical application. If your mouse fails for any reason, you can still catch a window and try to save your work by continuing with Function keys.

Special Situations: Windows and Focus

In some instances, you don't have to click the title bar of a window to bring it into focus. One such instance is where you have two windows side by side. As long as these windows don't overlap, you can make either of them current simply by moving your mouse over them.

Finally, to give a window focus, you can also click (or double-click) its borders.

Using Your Mouse to Focus

Moving your mouse over nonoverlapping windows will generally change window focus. However, in a minority of cases, this may not work. Here's why: Window manager configurations are very flexible. It's possible to set this option in the configuration files. The two common settings are click-to-focus and mouse-focus. In click-to-focus, you cannot make a window current without clicking it. In mouse-focus, merely moving your mouse into a window's work area will do the trick. Most default window manager configurations adhere to mouse-focus wherever possible. If you try this and it doesn't work, you'll have to revert to clicking for focus.

The Least You Need To Know

Windows in X can provide you with a very friendly work environment. Controlling them with your mouse and keyboard is easy once you master the simple tricks listed here:

➤ To quickly gain control of a window, click the window menu.

➤ To move a window, grab its title bar and drag it.

➤ To resize a window, grab a border and drag it.

➤ To minimize or maximize a window, click the appropriate buttons in the window's upper-right corner.

➤ To destroy a window that refuses to leave, get a process list (ps -a) and send a kill signal to that process (kill *process_number*).

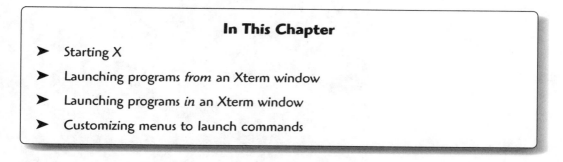

## Chapter 13

Running X and X Applications

In This Chapter

➤ Starting X

➤ Launching programs *from* an Xterm window

➤ Launching programs *in* an Xterm window

➤ Customizing menus to launch commands

X is very "plastic" in the sense that you can make it do almost anything. (In fact, X is often criticized as being a bit *too* configurable.) From this, many people draw the conclusion that not enough standardization exists in X. At first glance, that seems like a reasonable assumption.

However, in truth, X does enforce many standard rules on almost all applications. The trick is to learn how these rules work and how to use them to your advantage. That's what this chapter is all about.

Starting X

Starting X can be done in several ways. On most UNIX systems, you can start X using the `startx` command, like this:

```
startx
```

What happens after you issue this command will vary. In many cases, you'll see several messages scroll by and then suddenly, X will appear.

However, `startx` is not the only command for starting X. There are many others, including `xstart`, `X11`, and so on. At their core, these commands are really just scripts that start a program called `xinit`. Let's take a look at `xinit` now.

xinit: **The X Starter**

`xinit` is the X initializer. `xinit` starts the X server and one client on your machine. By default, `xinit` starts with the following parameters:

```
xterm  -geometry  +1+1  -n  login  -display  :0
```

This places a single Xterm window on the main desktop. (See the following figure.)

When X first starts, it generally spawns one Xterm window.

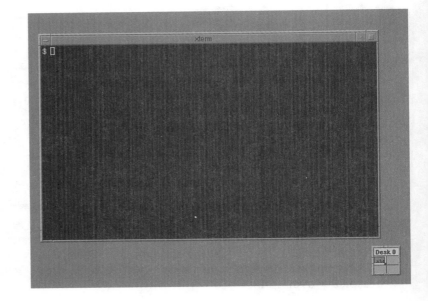

Prior to starting X, however, `xinit` looks in your home directory for a file named `.xinitrc`. This file (which is often created by your system administrator) contains additional parameters, including any programs to spawn when X starts. `.xinitrc` typically contains entries like this:

```
xsetroot  -solid  steelblue  &
oclock  -geometry  75x75-0-0  &
xterm  -geometry  +0+60  -ls  &
```

In this case, .xinitrc tells X to do several things:

➤ The first command (xsetroot) specifies the desktop's background color.

➤ The second command (oclock) starts a clock.

➤ The third command (xterm) starts an Xterm window.

This is a pretty generic .xinitrc file. You can edit it to contain your own commands.

Once you start X, you'll want to start launching programs. Let's take a look at how this is done.

Xterm: Your Window to the World

One tool that you'll use constantly is the Xterm. Xterms are shell windows or windows that offer you shell access while you're in X. Xterms also provide VT102 and Tektronix 4014 terminal emulation.

In the context of running other applications, you can use an Xterm in several ways:

➤ To monitor the output of another application

➤ To launch an application

➤ To run an application inside an Xterm

We'll cover these tasks in a moment. For now, let's discuss how to manipulate the Xterm itself.

Xterm Command-Line Options

Xterm has many, many command-line options. The more commonly used options are summarized in Table 13.1.

OpenWindows and xinit

OpenWindows, Sun's proprietary windowing system, is started with a different command: openwin, located in /usr/openwin/bin. (You should add this directory to your path). openwin is also a script that points to xinit (among other things.) To learn more about your OpenWindows system, try Sun's OpenWindows tutorial, located in /usr/openwin/demo/tutorial. To view this tutorial, change your current working directory to /usr/openwin/demo/tutorial and issue the following command:

```
start_tutorial
```

Table 13.1.   Some Xterm command-line options

Option	Purpose
-b *border-width*	Use the -b option to set the Xterm's inner border width (the space between the inside border and the text that appears in the Xterm window). The border width is assigned with a number. For example, **xterm -b 5** sets a border width of 5. (The default is 2.)
-bg *color*	-bg stands for *background*. Use the -bg option to set your Xterm's background color. For example, to create an Xterm with a white foreground and a black background, issue the following command: **xterm -fg white -bg black**.
-C	-C stands for *console*. Use the -C option when you're using your Xterm to monitor system messages. (Any Xterm created with the -C option receives console output.)
-e *program*	The -e option is probably the most important option of all. Use the -e option to execute and run an application inside an Xterm window. For example, to run pine in an Xterm window, issue the following command: **xterm -e pine**. One important note, though: This option must be the last Xterm option specified on the command line. (Any arguments or options that follow -e *program* will be interpreted as arguments to *program*, not to Xterm.)
-fb *font*	-fb stands for *font bold*. Use the -fb switch to specify which font Xterm should use when displaying bolded text. Here's an example: **xterm -fb 7x14**.
-fg *color*	-fg stands for *foreground*. Use the -fg option to set the foreground color. For example, to produce an Xterm with red text, issue the following command: **xterm -fg red**.
-font *font-name*	Use the -font option to set your Xterm's font. For example, to set a relatively large font, issue the following command: **xterm -font 7x14**. (The -font option is equivalent to the -fn option. Both specify which font is used in regular display text.)
-geometry # #	Use the -geometry option to set your Xterm's size. For example, to set a relatively small Xterm window, issue the following command: **xterm -geometry 200x200**.
-help	The -help option calls Xterm's usage summary. This is a listing of possible options and how you should use them. (When you use this command-line option, no Xterm is actually spawned.) To get Xterm help, therefore, issue the following command: **xterm -help**.

Option	Purpose
-T [*title*]	Use the -T option to set your Xterm's title. (This is the text displayed on your Xterm's top border.) For example, to assign your Xterm the title "my-Xterm," issue this command: **xterm -T my-Xterm**.
-tn	Use -tn to set your Xterm's terminal type. For example, perhaps you're not interested in the default VT102 emulation. Perhaps you want ANSI instead. If so, issue this command: **xterm -tn ANSI**.

The options described in Table 13.1 are just the beginning. Xterm has more than a dozen other options. However, it's unlikely that you'll use these anytime soon. All the aforementioned options can be used in conjunction with one another. For example, consider this command line:

```
xterm -fg white -bg black -font 7x14 -geometry 200x400 -tn vt100 -e vi
```

That's quite a command. It runs vi in an Xterm window with a white foreground, a black background, large font, a small window, and ANSI terminal emulation.

About Fonts and X

X supports many different fonts. However, in order to use those fonts, you must know their names. Typically, font specifications are expressed in name, format, and size, like this:

```
-*-helvetica-bold-r-normal-*-*-120-*-*-*-*-iso8859-1
```

Because entering this much text is too burdensome, fonts are traditionally referred to by aliases. The trick is discovering what those aliases are.

Aliases are invariably stored in a file. (For example, on Linux, the file is `/usr/X1R6/lib/X11/fonts/misc/fonts.alias`.) Table 13.2 provides a list of common fonts and their aliases.

Table 13.2. Some fonts supported by X and their aliases

Alias	Font
5x7	misc-fixed-medium-r-normal--7-70-75-75-c-50-iso8859-1
5x8	misc-fixed-medium-r-normal--8-80-75-75-c-50-iso646.1991-irv
6x10	misc-fixed-medium-r-normal--10-100-75-75-c-60-iso8859-1
6x9	misc-fixed-medium-r-normal--9-90-75-75-c-60-iso646.1991-irv
7x13	misc-fixed-medium-r-normal--13-120-75-75-c-70-iso8859-1

continues

Table 13.2. **Some fonts supported by X and their aliases**
CONTINUED

Alias	Font
7x14	misc-fixed-medium-r-normal--14-130-75-75-c-70-iso8859-1
8x13	misc-fixed-medium-r-normal--13-120-75-75-c-80-iso8859-1
8x16	sony-fixed-medium-r-normal--16-120-100-100-c-80-iso8859-1
a14	misc-fixed-medium-r-normal--14-*-*-*-*-*-iso8859-1
heb8x13	misc-fixed-medium-r-normal--13-120-75-75-c-80-iso8859-8
k14	misc-fixed-medium-r-normal--14-*-*-*-*-*-jisx0208.1983-0
kana14	misc-fixed-medium-r-normal--14-*-*-*-*-*-jisx0201.1976-0
kanji16	jis-fixed-medium-r-normal--16-*-*-*-*-*-jisx0208.1983-0
nil2	misc-nil-medium-r-normal--2-20-75-75-c-10-misc-fontspecific
olcursor	sun-open look cursor-----12-120-75-75-p-160-sunolcursor-1"
olglyph-12	sun-open look glyph-----12-120-75-75-p-113-sunolglyph-1"
olglyph-14	sun-open look glyph-----14-140-75-75-p-128-sunolglyph-1"
r14	misc-fixed-medium-r-normal--14-*-*-*-*-*-jisx0201.1976-0
r16	sony-fixed-medium-r-normal--16-*-*-*-*-*-jisx0201.1976-0
r24	sony-fixed-medium-r-normal--24-*-*-*-*-*-jisx0201.1976-0
rk14	misc-fixed-medium-r-normal--14-*-*-*-*-*-jisx0201.1976-0
rk16	sony-fixed-medium-r-normal--16-*-*-*-*-*-jisx0201.1976-0
variable	*-helvetica-bold-r-normal-*-*-120-*-*-*-*-iso8859-1

To apply an aliased font, simply add its alias to the command line. For example, to start an Xterm with 6x10 font, issue this command:

```
xterm -font 6x10
```

To append a *bold* attribute to a specific font, enter the term bold after the font's alias. For example, to get a 7x14 font in bold, issue the following command:

```
xterm -font 7x14bold
```

Because different UNIX systems store font aliases in different files, your best bet is to try finding the fonts directory, like this:

```
cd /
find . -name fonts
```

Be prepared to experiment. Most X distributions support hundreds of fonts. These can get quite specialized, as well. For example, Linux supports fonts for scientific and mathematical typesetting, astrological and astronomical symbols, Chinese characters, and even Russian characters. (These are useful if you ever visit sites in China, Russia, or Eastern Europe.)

About Colors in X

In addition to the basic colors (white, black, red, blue, and green), X supports the following colors:

AntiqueWhite	LightGoldenrod	RoyalBlue	cornsilk	pink
CadetBlue	LightPink	SeaGreen	cyan	plum
DarkGoldenrod	LightSalmon	SkyBlue	firebrick	purple
DarkOliveGreen	LightSkyBlue	SlateBlue	gold	red
DarkOrange	LightSteelBlue	SlateGray	goldenrod	salmon
DarkOrchid	LightYellow	SpringGreen	gray60	seashell
DarkSeaGreen	MediumOrchid	SteelBlue	gray70	sienna
DarkSlateGray	MediumPurple	VioletRed	gray80	snow
DeepPink	MistyRose	aquamarine	gray85	tan
DeepSkyBlue	NavajoWhite	azure	green	thistle
DodgerBlue	OliveDrab	bisque	honeydew	tomato
HotPink	OrangeRed	blue	ivory	turquoise
IndianRed	PaleGreen	brown	khaki	wheat
LavenderBlush	PaleTurquoise	burlywood	magenta	yellow
LemonChiffon	PaleVioletRed	chartreuse	maroon	
LightBlue	PeachPuff	chocolate	orange	
LightCyan	RosyBrown	coral	orchid	

Each color also has varying depth. Typically, there are four levels of depth, and you assign these by number. For example, DarkSlateGray1 is really just slightly darker than a regular gray. DarkSlateGray3, on the other hand, has an almost smoky, purplish hue to it and is quite dark.

The way these colors appear on your screen depends a lot on your color resolution and depth. If you're using the equivalent of standard VGA (8-bit) monitor, you may experience poor results. As a general rule, however, the more basic colors (or even those closely related to basic colors) show up beautifully on almost any color display.

Of course, on the other hand, you may be using a $50,000 Silicon Graphics machine, in which case, you have true 24-bit color. If so, count yourself lucky. In any event,

these colors can be used to draw any Xterm and any of its components (including its borders, title bar, text, background, foreground, bold fonts, and so forth).

About Grayscale Displays

Naturally, on grayscale displays, X cannot display colors. Therefore, "colors" appear in varying shades of gray. As a general rule, when setting colors on a grayscale display, you should stick with grays and their derivatives. If you don't, you may experience bizarre results, or X may refuse to load at all.

Running Applications Inside an Xterm Window

To run an application inside an Xterm window, open an Xterm and run the application from a prompt. In response, UNIX will run the specified application inside the Xterm. For example, to run `pico` in an Xterm, open an Xterm and issue the following command:

`pico`

`pico` will appear *inside* the Xterm window. (See the following figure.)

`pico` *running in the Xterm window.*

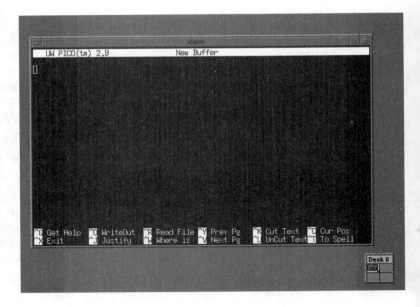

Here's an important point to note: Although Xterm windows have special capabilities (notably cut and paste), applications running inside of Xterms don't have any more functionality than they would when running from a command line. In other words, Xterms bestow no special powers on garden-variety command-line programs. For example, you cannot open `pico` in an Xterm window and place the mouse cursor anywhere in `pico` and start typing. You'll still be forced to adhere to `pico`'s mostly keyboard-based interface. (On the other hand, that doesn't prevent you from grabbing text from a `pico` window and pasting it elsewhere in X.)

About Colors, Keys, and Things

Will an application behave the same way in an Xterm as it would when executed from a command line? Maybe. Much depends on how thorough the developer was. Often, applications that have extensive color schemes from a command line appear rather bare bones when run through an Xterm.

Additionally, some command-line applications have odd key bindings (that is, the rules governing what each function key does). These key bindings might not work when funneled through an Xterm. There are several reasons for this. The most common reason is that the application's key bindings conflict with basic X key bindings. In such cases, X key bindings will naturally take precedence. If the key bindings are essential to the program's operation (and X doesn't accommodate them), it's best to run the application from the shell, not in X.

Launching Applications from an Xterm

Another way to run applications in X is to launch them from an Xterm. This is simple enough. Open an Xterm and execute the application. For example, to launch `ftptool` from an Xterm, open an Xterm and issue the `ftptool` command at the Xterm shell prompt, like this:

> **ftptool**

In response, X will launch `ftptool`. (See the following figure.)

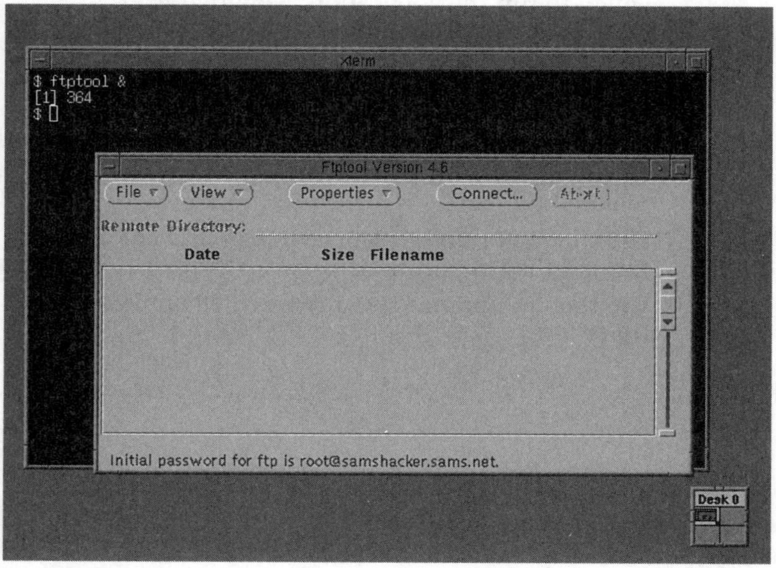

pico *running in the Xterm window.*

Most X applications support their own command-line options. These help you manipulate their behavior. In addition to these command-line options, however, there are several options that work with nearly all X applications. Let's take a brief look at those now.

Generic X Options

As mentioned earlier, most X applications behave in a similar fashion. In keeping with this, most X applications also accept basic command-line options. These options allow you to manipulate your application's look and feel. These options are briefly summarized in Table 13.3.

Table 13.3. Generic X options

Option	Purpose
-bg *color*	Use the -bg option to set the background color of the specified application. For example, to start xtetris with a gray background, issue the command **xetris -bg gray**. Use this option cautiously. For example, prior to setting the background color, make a test run of the application first. Make sure you don't set the background color to the same color as the foreground. Otherwise, you'll be unable to see the foreground at all. (For example, Xterms generally have a black foreground for text. If you set the background color to black, you'll be unable to see the text.)
-display *host display*	Use the -display option to specify the X server on which to run the application. Note that *host display* doesn't have to be the X server on your own machine. It could very well be on someone else's machine. For example, consider this command: **xtetris -display wagjag:0**. This will start an instance of xtetris (an X version of the popular game Tetris) on the first X server on wagjag, a remote host.
-fg *color*	Use the -fg option to set the foreground color of the specified application.
-fn *font-name*	Use the -fn option to set the specified application's font.

Option	Purpose
`-geometry #x#`	Use the `-geometry` option to set the initial size of the application window. This is especially useful when starting an application that was designed at much higher resolution than the current display. Such applications will appear huge, by default, often completely filling your screen and then some. The `-geometry` option is measured in standard pixel format. For example, on a PC running standard VGA, you can fill the entire screen by specifying this command: **xterm -geometry 640x480**.
`-iconic`	Use the `-iconic` option to start the application in a minimized state. (In this state, the application is reduced to an icon on the desktop.)
`-rv`	Use the `-rv` option to have the application start in reverse-video mode. For example, if an Xterm has a white background and black foreground, by default, this command will reverse that: **xterm -rv.**

About Menus and Customization

If you're brave, you can also try customizing your menus. After all, menus are nothing more than visual tools that provide a shortcut to running this or that command. (They save you the trouble of opening an Xterm and launching an application.) If you're going to run an application regularly, you may as well make it a permanent option on your menu.

Nearly all X window managers allow you to customize your menus. However, this is no task for the faint-hearted. With the exception of the Common Desktop Environment (CDE), most X window managers provide no special tools for customizing menus. Instead, you're forced to customize your menus by hand.

CDE Menu Customization

If you're using CDE, you can customize your menus using the menusetup command. This utility allows you to replace the default /dt/dtwmrc file with one of your own design. Although this doesn't make menu customization a snap, it does help considerably. If you want to try it, copy the original /dt/dtwmrc file to your home directory and study it carefully. Only after you're sure you understand how the menu structure works should you try to add menu entries. I recommend trying one menu entry at a time. In any event, the great thing about menusetup is this: If you completely bungle your customization attempt, you can use menusetup to reset the menus and recover a working system. To do so, start menusetup and choose Option 2, Revert to Default CDE Menus. Voila! Your menus will return to normal.

To customize menus, you must first find the default menu configuration file. For example, on systems using fvwm, the file is system.fvwmrc. The system.fvwmrc file defines menus in structures that are surprisingly easy to read. For example, here's an entry for a typical Utilities menu:

```
# This menu will fire up some very common utilities
Popup "Utilities"
  Title    "Utilities"
    Exec    "Netscape"      exec netscape &
    Exec    "Xterm"         exec xterm -e tcsh &
    Exec    "Big Xterm"     exec xterm -fg black -bg white -font 7x14 &
    Exec    "Top"           exec rxvt -T Top -n Top -e top &
    Exec    "Calculator"    exec xcalc &
    Exec    "Xman"          exec xman &
    Nop     ""
    Popup   "Modules"       Module-Popup
    Nop     ""
    Popup   "Exit Fvwm"     Quit-Verify
  EndPopup
```

As you can see, menu specifications start with PopUp and end with EndPopup. Everything in between describes the menu. For example, consider this entry:

```
Exec    "Big Xterm"      exec xterm -fg black -bg white -font 7x14 &
```

This places a menu item called Big Xterm on the main menu. When clicked, Big Xterm executes the following command:

xterm -fg black -bg white -font 7x14 &

To add a menu item, simply insert a new line that describes the program. For example, suppose you want to run pico in an Xterm window. You might call that menu item *PicoWindow*. To add this to the menu, simply add the following line to the Utilities menu:

```
Exec    "PicoWindow"          exec xterm -e pico &
```

Now, your new Utilities menu structure has the new PicoWindow entry. Here's what it looks like:

```
# This menu will fire up some very common utilities
Popup "Utilities"
  Title   "Utilities"
  Exec    "Netscape"      exec netscape &
  Exec    "PicoWindow"        exec xterm -e pico &
  Exec    "Xterm"         exec xterm -e tcsh &
  Exec    "Big Xterm"     exec xterm -fg black -bg white -font 7x14 &
  Exec    "Top"           exec rxvt -T Top -n Top -e top &
  Exec    "Calculator"    exec xcalc &
  Exec    "Xman"          exec xman &
  Nop     ""
  Popup   "Modules"       Module-Popup
  Nop     ""
  Popup   "Exit Fvwm"     Quit-Verify
EndPopup
```

When you restart X, the new PicoWindow menu item will be visible on the menu. Click it, and X will load an Xterm with pico running inside. This all looks pretty simple (and for the most part, it is). However, here are some rules you should follow religiously:

➤ **Make backups of original system files**—Even before you try to edit a menu configuration file, make a backup. This entails nothing more complex than copying the original file. For example, if the file is system.fvwmrc, issue this command: **cp system.fvwmrc system.fvwmrc.my-backup**. This will store the original system.fvwmrc in system.fvwmrc.my-backup. This way, if anything goes wrong, you simply copy the original back again and restart X.

Menu Don't Want to Tangle With

There are certain menus you shouldn't change. These include all menus that specify menu choices on window controls, such as Minimize, Restore, Maximize, Shuffle Up, Shuffle Down, Destroy, Delete, and Quit. Don't futz around with these, because if you do, you could potentially disable important functions. For example, imagine if you accidentally mangled the Delete or Quit function. You'd have a hard time destroying windows. Similarly, avoid the temptation to change key bindings. (Key bindings are also sometimes specified in the menu configuration file.) If you accidentally mangle the key bindings, you may lose access to important Function key operations.

➤ **Avoid creating new menus**—Until you become more familiar with menu customization, avoid trying to make new menus. Instead, add your desired programs to menus that already exist. This way, you only need to know the program's name, its command line, and what you want to call it. After you've used X a while (and customized a few menus), then you can try more fancy stuff.

➤ **Don't delete existing menu choices**—Avoid deleting existing menu choices, even if you think you'll never use them. (You may later wish you didn't delete them!) Instead of deleting existing menu choices, comment them out. This is done by placing the # symbol at the beginning of the line, like this: `#Exec      "Xman"      exec xman &`. Any line beginning with the # symbol is ignored, and for all purposes, that menu choice is disabled. If you need it later, you simply remove the # symbol at the beginning of the line. Presto! The menu choice is back.

➤ **Test your command lines first!**—Before you commit a menu addition to record, test the command line you provided to execute the application. If the command line is bad or malformed, the menu choice will not work.

Also, watch closely for wrapped lines. (Wrapped lines occur when your command is so long that your editor breaks the line somewhere before the end.) For example, suppose you added a menu choice that executes this command:

```
xterm -fg black -bg white -font 7x14 -b 5 -fb 7x14bold -geometry
➥200x400 -T MyLogFile -e pico my-log-file.txt
```

That's a gnarly command line. If you edit your menu configuration file in pico (or another editor that wraps long lines), the line will be wrapped as it is in the example. Consequently, the command will not work. There's a simple solution to this: Don't use an editor that wraps lines. If you do, then prior to saving the file, unwrap the line. (In the example, the break occurs immediately after the -geometry option.)

Finding the line break point is usually pretty easy. Most editors give you some indication that a break has occurred. For example, whenever pico wraps a line, it adds a $ symbol at the precise point where the wrap started. To remedy that line break, position your cursor after the $ symbol and hit the backspace button. This will rejoin the line and make it one, continuous run.

Also, different window managers have different configuration files. Often (in fact, most of the time), the configuration file ends in rc, as in system.fvwmrc, system.twmrc, .twmrc, and dtwmrc. However, your mileage may vary. Today, there are many new and strange window managers out there. If you can't find the configuration file, ask your system administrator or consult your manuals.

Finally, exercise caution when creating menu items that execute shell scripts. Prior to creating such a menu item, run the shell script from an Xterm window and see what happens. If you encounter unexpected results (your system halts, your display freezes, or your monitor blows up), you should probably abandon the idea of making that script a menu choice.

Changing Your Monitor Choices, Video Card, or Resolution

Stop right there. Are you considering changing your monitor, video card, or resolution specifications? Don't even think about it. At least, don't think about it unless you know absolutely everything about your monitor and video card. Here's why: X is an excellent windowing system, and it allows you every opportunity to customize your system. However, unlike Microsoft Windows, X assumes that you're an "X-pert."

Indeed, X assumes that you would never, ever set your monitor frequency to a dangerous or impossible value. Similarly, X assumes that you would never accidentally specify the wrong video card, memory allocation, or color depth. Therefore, X will attempt (to the best of its ability) to accommodate your shaky estimations about these values. If you make a mistake, this could seriously damage your monitor or video card. I'm not kidding!

Here's an example from my early experiences with X: I had an older, 15" Mag monitor that I thought was pretty cool. However, my system didn't support my video card (an ancient Trident) *or* my monitor. I thought I was slick, though, and decided to set values at the high end. (I had absolutely no idea what frequency my monitor would support, and because it was used, I had no documentation.) So, I set these cock-eyed values and started X.

The first time X almost started and then died. I heard a strange click in my machine. I figured that something went wrong but decided to try it again. The second time I

Newer Monitors Will Warn You Before They Blow Up

Many modern monitors will give you some indication that something's amiss. For example, if you set your frequency and resolution values incorrectly, X will not start and the monitor will go into a protective mode. From here, a message will flash on the screen repeatedly. Usually, it says something like this: "Out of Range!" or "Danger, Will Robinson! Danger!" (Additionally, some monitors will beep loudly if they're equipped with speakers.)

started X, I heard a terrible sound and my screen flashed several times. From that day forward, my Trident card never worked again—in any machine on any operating system. Therefore, take my advice on this. Unless you have documentation that lays out your monitor's frequency range and your video card's capabilities, leave these values alone (or call in an X super-geek). Otherwise, you may end up a very unhappy camper.

Troubleshooting Applications in X

From time to time, you may encounter problems with X applications. This following list covers some common problems and how to solve them:

➤ **Application lock**—If an application locks up (and remains unresponsive), try killing it by invoking its window menu and choosing Quit, Delete, or Destroy. If this doesn't work, open an Xterm, pull a process list (ps), and kill the process.

➤ **Color problems**—Linux and SolarisX86 users beware: Both Linux and SolarisX86 (especially older versions) support only a limited number of video adapters. If yours is not supported, you may be forced to install with only 8-bit color (or generic VGA). If so, many applications will either not load or they'll warn you that the driver cannot generate all the colors needed for the current application. In such cases, your display may look odd in some applications. (Netscape Navigator is a good example. With lower color resolutions, photographs will appear grainy or washed out.) This is not a problem with your computer; you simply have limited color capabilities. The only real cure for this is to purchase a supported video card.

➤ **Complete freeze-up**—Occasionally, X may freeze up. You'll know it, too, because none of your windows will respond to either mouse events or keyboard strokes. If you encounter this situation, hold down the Ctrl key and press the backspace key. X will immediately die, and you'll find yourself at a shell prompt. From there, you can investigate further.

➤ **Problems with clip and paste**—Sometimes (though rarely), clipping and pasting won't work from one application to another. This isn't a generalized problem, but it occurs only between applications that handle the Paste to Clipboard function differently. If you encounter this problem, open a third application and try using it as a way station. That is, clip the text from application 1 and paste it to application 2 (your way station). Once you're sure that your paste worked, copy the text from application 2 and paste it to application 3. If you're pasting just a few lines of code, this is probably too complicated. However, this is a good solution if you're pasting many dozens of pages of text.

➤ **Strange happenings**—On rare occasions, one application may cause trouble for another. For example, suppose you have two applications running simultaneously. One may enforce special rules on the mouse cursor. This may "ruin" the mouse functionality in the second application. (The mouse may become sluggish, uncontrollable, or inoperable in the second application.) The cure is to kill both applications and restart X. (This situation is more common on Linux, where many beta distributions crop up.)

The Least You Need to Know

Learning to make X behave the way you want it to is a big step toward taking control of your work environment. To do that, here's the least you need to know:

➤ X reads the .xinitrc file before loading. Any programs specified there will load when X loads.

➤ You can run applications *inside* Xterms. For example, open an Xterm and issue the **vi** command. This will run vi inside the Xterm.

➤ You can launch applications *from* Xterms. To do so, try this: Open an Xterm and in it, issue the following command: **xeyes &**. This will run xeyes on your desktop.

➤ You can customize your own menus to execute applications.

➤ Never try to change your monitor frequency or video card specification without documentation.

## Chapter 14

Cool Programs for X

In This Chapter

➤ A few good applications for X

Before writing this chapter, I carefully considered what it should contain. It was no easy decision. After all, there are hundreds of free applications for X alone (never mind all the commercial packages). What I finally settled on is a short list of useful and not-so-useful X applications that are unique and interesting. Most of them are available for nearly all UNIX flavors, and all except one are either shareware or freeware.

xv: A Graphics Tool

xv is one of the best X applications available. Written by John Bradley (formerly of Pennsylvania University), xv is a graphics viewer. It works much like Corel PhotoPaint or Adobe Photoshop and supports a wide range of image formats, including the following:

➤ BMP

➤ FITS

➤ GIF

➤ JPEG

➤ JPG

➤ PBM

➤ PCX

- ➤ PGM
- ➤ PPM
- ➤ RLE
- ➤ TIFF
- ➤ TIF
- ➤ XPM
- ➤ RGB
- ➤ Sun Rasterfile
- ➤ Targa (TGA)
- ➤ X11 bitmaps

Additionally, xv is extremely portable and has been verified to work on the following flavors:

- ➤ AIX
- ➤ Digital UNIX
- ➤ FreeBSD
- ➤ HP-UX
- ➤ Irix
- ➤ Linux
- ➤ NetBSD
- ➤ OSF/1
- ➤ Solaris
- ➤ SunOS
- ➤ Ultrix
- ➤ UNIXWare

The xv Interface

xv is well designed, compact, and exceptionally stable. When you first open xv, it displays a splash page, as shown in the following figure.

To access xv's main control panel, right-click the splash page. This will launch xv controls and you can begin working. (See the following figure.)

From xv's main control panel, you can perform many tasks, including viewing and editing graphics. xv can add many special effects to your images by applying a wide range of filters, including blur, sharpen, edge detect, emboss, and even oil painting. In addition, xv allows you to manipulate the colors, hue, and saturation of images. Finally, xv has a screen capture utility with delayed snapshots so you can even catch menus and modal dialog boxes. In all, xv is a commercial-class, industrial-strength graphics package for UNIX.

xv is available at http:// www.trilon.com/xv/.

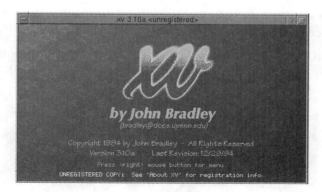

The xv opening page.

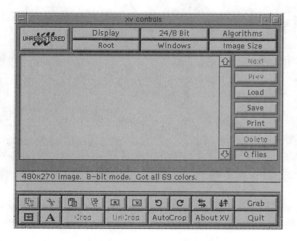

The xv main control panel.

Xgopher

Many people insist that the Gopher protocol is no longer used. Instead, they say, the WWW has obviated the need for Gopher servers. In fact, neither is true. Gophers serve primarily text-based information, but they serve it at blazing speeds. If you're doing research, you may find Gopher networks faster and more informative. There are many reasons for this, but one really stands out: Gopher servers don't carry advertisements. They primarily carry academic information.

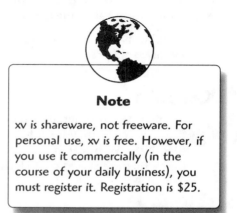

Note

xv is shareware, not freeware. For personal use, xv is free. However, if you use it commercially (in the course of your daily business), you must register it. Registration is $25.

The problem is, if UNIX systems come with a Gopher client at all, it's usually a text-based one. (Invariably, it's the tried-and-true client from the University of Minnesota.) Text-based Gopher tools are excellent for light research, but if you have more demanding needs, I recommend Xgopher.

Xgopher is to Gopher research what Netscape Navigator is to the Web. All information is conveniently displayed in windows, along with notations, bookmarks, and help. (See the following figure.)

Xgopher in action.

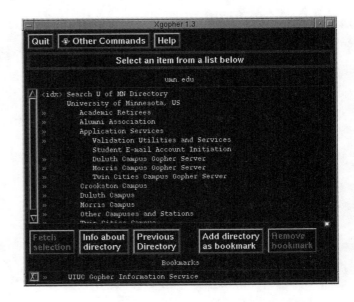

Xgopher also provides the means to configure external applications. This way, if you find a Telnet link, Xgopher will spawn an external Xterm to filter your Telnet session. In all, Xgopher is indisputably the best UNIX Gopher client available. It runs on most systems and eats a meager amount of X resources.

Xgopher is available at `http://sunsite.unc.edu/pub/X11/contrib/applications/` `xgopher.1.3.3.tar.Z`.

Xarchie

Archie is yet another antiquated protocol, and many people think that it has no practical use. Well, they need to think again. True, you can use Web search engines to find files, but a Web search accesses only a small portion of the Internet's vast resources. Many files are stored on FTP sites that are not indexed by Web spiders.

Wasn't Archie a Cartoon Character?

Archie is an archiving service. Here's how it works: FTP server administrators from all over the world report their drive contents to centralized Archie servers. You can search these servers to find files in different countries. Although Archie servers are less prevalent here in the United States, they remain a mainstay of Internet computing in many countries.

Of course, Archie wouldn't be complete unless accompanied by Veronica and Jughead. *Veronica* is the Gopher equivalent to Archie. Using Veronica, you can search Gopher server contents. Similarly, *Jughead* is a tool to search Gopher servers (although Jughead is not quite as powerful). The difference is this: Veronica is generally used to search many Gopher servers simultaneously. In contrast, Jughead is most often used to search a single Gopher server.

For example, suppose you need to find a program that was once freeware and is now commercial. Or, you need a very old version of a particular program or programming language. You could spend hours or even days trying to find it on the Web. Therefore, you should use Archie instead.

Here's one of the most valuable tips you'll ever get in a book: Whereas Americans routinely discard old programs for the latest and greatest versions, many other folks don't. Particularly in Eastern Europe and Asia, users may lack the necessary financial resources to purchase brand-spanking-new software. Therefore, they archive useful, older software on their FTP sites. If you can't find an antiquated software version on the Web, there's a four out of five chance you'll find it using Archie.

The problem with Archie servers, however, is that accessing them is a pain. The archaic method is to Telnet to archie.sura.net and conduct your query in a text-based environment. This is no longer true. Xarchie simplifies the process considerably.

Xarchie was built using the old Athena Widget set and is therefore extremely lightweight. Furthermore, its interface is simple and easy to understand. (See the following figure.)

Finding a file takes just seconds. What's more, Xarchie is loaded with dozens of Archie server addresses from all over the world. Therefore, if you can't find your file in England, try Finland, Taiwan, Korea, and so on. Eventually, you'll find the right server. All in all, Xarchie is an excellent tool. You can find Xarchie at
http://sunsite.unc.edu/pub/X11/contrib/applications/xarchie-2.0.10.tar.gz.

The Xarchie main screen.

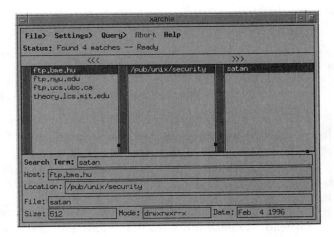

X3270

If you've ever done library or bibliographical research, you know that most university libraries and document depositories serve their catalogs via Telnet. (The actual percentage would be difficult to gauge, but it's probably on the order of 80 percent.) However, a small but significant percentage also use the old IBM TN3270.

Servers that use TN3270 cannot negotiate a typical Telnet session; therefore, you need a TN3270 client or emulator. For this, you simply must have X3270.

X3270 negotiates 3270 sessions flawlessly and even provides an auxiliary keypad function. This keypad function emulates keys found on a 3270 terminal, thus ensuring you the maximum compatibility with 3270 servers. X3270 is available at `http://www.geocities.com/SiliconValley/Peaks/7814/`.

Techno-Talk: What's a 3270?

3270 refers to a series of IBM mainframe terminals that were quite popular in the 1980s. These were used to access IBM mainframes. There were also 3270 emulators, such as the IRMAboard, that you could plug into a regular computer. These would negotiate communication between your system and the mainframe.

StarOffice

Throughout this book, you've probably been searching for some indication of a good office suite for UNIX. Something that goes beyond simple text processing or even PostScript. Something, quite frankly, like Microsoft Office. Well, such a product does exist. It's called StarOffice.

StarOffice is a mighty office suite that features word processing, spreadsheet, charting, graphing, math typesetting, image editing, and drawing packages. These packages rival Microsoft Office applications in both functionality and ease-of-use. Here's a list of the StarOffice packages:

➤ StarCalc

➤ StarChart

➤ StarDraw

➤ StarImage

➤ StarMath

➤ StarWriter

Let's take a brief look at each application and what it does.

StarCalc

StarCalc is a powerful spreadsheet tool. It's roughly equivalent to Microsoft Excel. (See the following figure.)

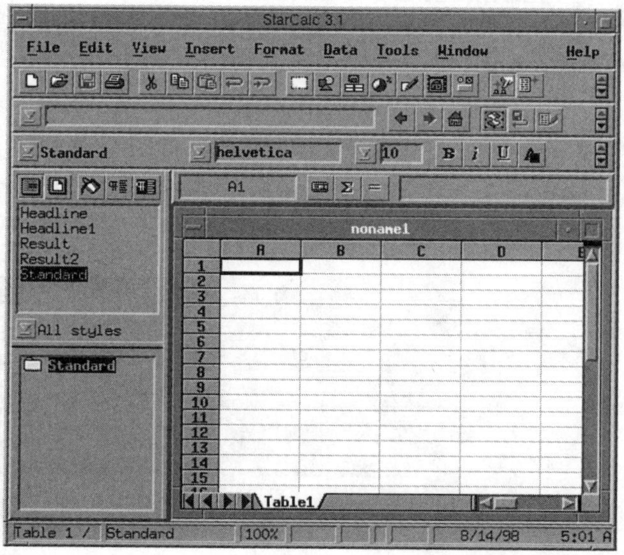

StarCalc's main screen.

StarCalc comes loaded with many preset formulas common to modern financial, scientific, and mathematical tasks. Also, like Microsoft Excel, StarCalc allows you to incisively select either portions of your worksheet or the entire table and enforce formulas on the selected block. Finally, StarCalc outputs neatly formatted reports, graphics, and charts.

StarChart

StarChart is a charting and graphing tool. It's roughly equivalent to Corel Chart. (See the following figure.)

191

StarChart's main screen.

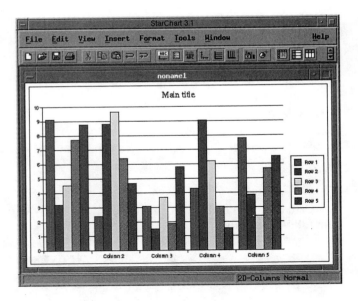

StarDraw

StarDraw is a paint tool. It's roughly equivalent to CorelDRAW. (See the following figure.)

StarDraw's main screen.

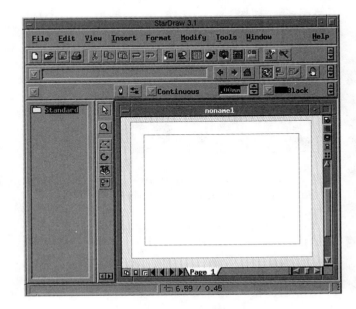

StarDraw is a vector-based drawing package, offering sharp, easy-to-manipulate images. These can be exported to a wide range of image formats. The program also creates slide shows for presentations.

StarImage

StarImage is a tool for manipulating images, especially photographs. It operates much like Corel PhotoPaint or Adobe Photoshop. (See the following figure.)

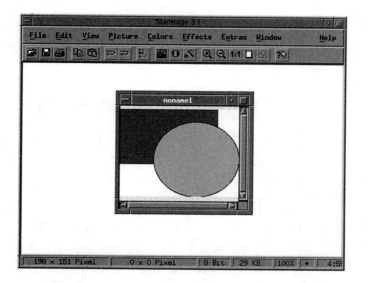

StarImage's main screen.

StarMath

StarMath is an extremely powerful tool for generating and typesetting documents that contain complex calculations. It contains special characters not found in your average word processor and is intended for high-end, scientific math development. (See the following figure.)

StarMath's main screen.

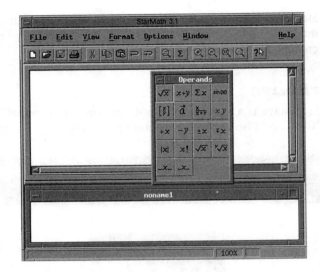

StarWriter

StarWriter is a full-featured word processor and desktop publishing tool that follows the tradition of Microsoft Word. (See the following figure.)

StarWriter's main screen.

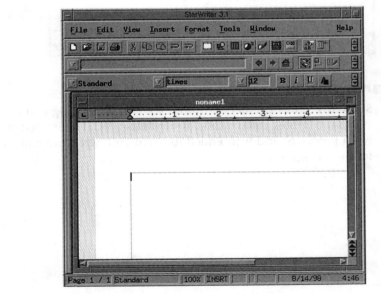

StarOffice Integration

One major feature in StarOffice is integration between applications. StarOffice applications can share data, and data elements retain their structure when clipped and pasted from one suite application to the next. (For example, images from StarDraw and spreadsheets from StarCalc can be dropped into a StarWriter document and integrated seamlessly.)

StarOffice Functionality

StarOffice relies heavily on *objectbars* (called *toolbars* in Microsoft products). These are icon bars from which you can call most functions. These functions might include inserting tables, drawing graphs, spell-checking, clipping, pasting, and so forth.

If you've ever used a Microsoft Windows or Mac OS application, you'll be right at home with StarOffice.

Bridging the UNIX/Windows Gap

One useful function in StarOffice is that you can import or export files created in many Microsoft Office applications. (For example, StarWriter will export your work to a Microsoft Word–compatible file.) This is a tremendous help in heterogeneous office network environments. Is StarOffice's export feature perfect? No, but it's pretty close. Nonetheless, I should warn you that your mileage may vary. Sometimes, bringing templates across is difficult.

Summary of StarOffice

StarOffice is a very comprehensive office suite. Interestingly enough, the product is also available for Windows, Mac OS, and OS/2. StarOffice, manufactured by Star Division, is currently in release 4.*x* and is available at `http://www.stardivision.com/`.

About X Applications in General

As I wrote at the beginning of this chapter, there are hundreds of free X applications (most are located either at `ftp://sunsite.unc.edu` or `ftp://ftp.x.org`). However, not every X developer has time to compile binaries for different platforms. Therefore, you may find that many X applications are distributed in source form only.

StarOffice and Linux

Personal versions of StarOffice (free for noncommercial use) are available with various Linux distributions. Caldera's OpenLinux product is one such distribution, available at `http://www.caldera.com`.

If you encounter a great X application that's been distributed in source form only, please refer to Chapter 10, "Working with Applications," which will give you some clue on what to do. (Typically, developers offer detailed instructions on unpacking and compiling their programs. However, on some rare occasions, you may find little accompanying documentation.)

Also, I should warn you that not all X applications distributed in source form will work on all UNIX flavors. Some are written with specialized libraries and include files that you may not have handy on your system. Whenever possible, read the README or INSTALL files prior to downloading the application. (Many software archives separate these files from the total distribution. This way, you get a chance to read them. This may save you the agony of downloading the program and later finding that it will not work on your system.)

Finally, a word of caution: Many free X applications are authored by computer science students. Some work flawlessly and others...well, others work only marginally well. Try to be forgiving whenever possible. (They've got to learn somehow.)

The Least You Need to Know

Unfortunately, it's impossible for me to list all the wonderful X applications available on the Internet. (Perhaps someone should create a book just for this purpose.) However, I can tell you that commercial vendors are porting their products to X *en masse* (for example, PhotoShop for X, CorelDraw, WordPerfect. and so on). However, before you buy a commercial package, do check the free software archives mentioned in the following list (chances are you'll find the perfect application at the best price—free):

➤ One great depository of X software is at the University of North Carolina at Chapel Hill: `ftp://sunsite.unc.edu`.

➤ Another is at the X Consortium's Home Page, located at `ftp://ftp.x.org`.

Help!

It never fails. No matter how much computing experience you have, eventually you'll find yourself staring blankly at the screen. Usually, this happens when you can't remember how to use a particular command (or when you receive a cryptic error that doesn't even remotely explain the problem). At that precise moment, you need help. That's what this chapter is all about.

Help on UNIX

By now, you've probably discovered that UNIX is a little different than almost any other operating system. UNIX programmers are often busy folks, so when UNIX reports an error, the explanation can be pretty bare. Let's try to remedy that.

Most UNIX commands have a built-in help mechanism, sometimes referred to as the *usage summary*. A typical usage summary explains what command-line flags exist and how to use them.

In a pinch, usage summaries can refresh your memory about how a particular command works. However, getting a usage summary is sometimes more complicated than you'd think.

Different programs display usage summaries under different conditions. For example, some programs will give a usage summary (or even pretty detailed help) when you issue the --help flag as an argument. For example, take a look at perl's help output:

```
$ perl --help

Usage: perl [switches] [--] [programfile] [arguments]
-0[octal]          specify record separator (\0, if no argument)
-a                 autosplit mode with -n or -p (splits $_ into @F)
-c                 check syntax only (runs BEGIN and END blocks)
-d[:debugger]      run scripts under debugger
-D[number/list]    set debugging flags (argument is a bit mask or flags)
-e 'command'       one line of script. Several -e's allowed. Omit
[programfile].
-F/pattern/        split() pattern for autosplit (-a). The //'s are
optional.
-i[extension]      edit <> files in place (make backup if extension
supplied)
-Idirectory        specify @INC/#include directory (may be used more than
once)
-l[octal]          enable line ending processing, specifies line
terminator
-[mM][-]module..   executes `use/no module...' before executing your
script.
-n                 assume 'while (<>) { ... }' loop around your script
-p                 assume loop like -n but print line also like sed
-P                 run script through C preprocessor before compilation
-s                 enable some switch parsing for switches after script
name
-S                 look for the script using PATH environment variable
-T                 turn on tainting checks
-u                 dump core after parsing script
-U                 allow unsafe operations
-v                 print version number and patchlevel of perl
-V[:variable]      print perl configuration information
-w     TURN WARNINGS ON FOR COMPILATION OF YOUR SCRIPT. Recommended.
-x[dir] strip text before #!perl line and perhaps cd to directory
```

This is probably a little more than you need, but it illustrates my point. Many times, the --help flag will call help for the specified program.

Still other programs (such as man) display a usage summary whenever you issue the command without arguments, like this:

```
$ man
usage:  man [-] [-adFlrt] [-M path] [-T macro-package ] [ -s section ]
name
```

```
man [-M path] -k keyword ...
man [-M path] -f file ...
```

This is also very helpful. Unfortunately, though, not all programs will issue a usage summary under these conditions. For example, when faced with no arguments, many programs (such as ls) will simply perform the requested operation on the current directory, like this:

```
$ ls
dick    harry   tom
```

This isn't much help. Therefore, as strange as it sounds, you can get a usage summary from such a program by purposefully issuing an erroneous command. This will force the program to exit on error and print its usage summary. For example, here's what happens when an erroneous ls command is issued:

```
$ ls -@
ls: illegal option -- @
usage: ls -1RaAdCxmnlogrtucpFbqisfL [files]
```

In this case, ls has surmised that I'm a complete idiot, so it prints a short summary of valid flags.

Therefore, to get quick help on any command, you can use any of these methods:

➤ Call the program with the --help or -h flag

➤ Issue the command without arguments

➤ Issue the command with a bad option

Hey Man! What's Happening? (The Man Page System)

Usage summaries and command-line help are great if you're just trying to remember how to use a program. However, when you need real help, it's time to turn to the man.

Manual Pages

Virtually every UNIX program ever made has manual (or *man*) pages. This is generally a text-based description of the program and its features. Man pages are broken into the following sections:

➤ Program purpose

➤ Program name

➤ Synopsis of the command

➤ Description

➤ Options and arguments

➤ Environment and operands (if any)

➤ Related files and commands

➤ Authors and credits

In most cases, a command's man page is the totality of information available about it. Let's look at how that information is retrieved and formatted.

Summoning Man Pages Using the man Command

To summon the man page for any command, issue the man command followed by the command name, like this:

```
man clear
```

UNIX will respond by loading the man page for that particular command (in this case, clear):

```
User Commands                                                    clear(1)

NAME
      clear - clear the terminal screen

SYNOPSIS
      clear

DESCRIPTION
      clear clears your screen if this is possible.  It  looks  in
      the  environment  for the terminal type and then in the ter-
      minfo database to figure out how to clear the  screen.

ATTRIBUTES
      See attributes(5) for descriptions of the  following  attri-
      butes:
| ATTRIBUTE TYPE|  ATTRIBUTE VALUE|
____|_____
____| Availability |  SUNWcsu            |
____|_____|_____|

SEE ALSO
      attributes(5)
```

On the first line of the clear man page, the following text appears:

```
User Commands                                                    clear(1)
```

That tells you that `clear` is a user command. The remaining information tells you everything you'll ever need to know about `clear` (for example, it has no options and takes no arguments).

Managing man: Isolating Specific Sections

The `man` command feeds you man pages one screen at a time. (In other words, it pauses after filling the screen. When you hit the spacebar, `man` scrolls down to the next page.) This is very useful because many commands have man pages that are ten pages long or more.

However, sometimes you don't want the entire man page. Instead, you want only valid flags and perhaps a description. To isolate only certain information, use `head` and `tail` in combination, like this:

```
man df ¦ head -20 ¦ tail
```

In 90 percent of all cases, this will isolate both the synopsis and the description. For example, here's the output of the previous command:

```
SYNOPSIS
     /usr/bin/du [ -adkr ] [ -s ¦ -o ] [ file... ]
     /usr/xpg4/bin/du [ -a ¦ -s ] [ -krx ] [ file... ]

DESCRIPTION
     The du utility writes to standard output  the  size  of  the
     file  space  allocated  to,  and  the size of the file space
     allocated to each subdirectory of, the file hierarchy rooted
     in  each of the specified files.  The size of the file space
     allocated to a file of type directory is defined as the  sum
```

Similarly, you can test whether one command appears in the text of another command's man page (this is sometimes helpful when you're studying how to perform a particular task using several commands in concert). For example, suppose you want to know which files are used in ppp sessions. To determine this, you could start by issuing the following command:

```
man ppp ¦ grep /
```

Here's the output of this search:

```
The  pseudo  device  drivers  /dev/ipd,   /dev/ipdptp,   and
     /dev/ipdcm form the IP-dialup layer.  This layer provides IP
     /dev/ipd          pseudo  device  driver   that   provides
     /dev/ipdptp       pseudo  device  driver   that   provides
     /dev/ipdcm        pseudo  device  driver   that   provides
```

From this, you know that `/dev/ipd`, `/dev/ipdptp`, and `/dev/ipdcm` are involved in the ppp process.

Finding Man Pages

Until now, I've been operating on the assumption that you know the command you want to learn more about. Maybe that's wrong. Maybe you're not looking for man pages on a particular command; instead, you want man pages on certain *types* of commands. (This is a fancy way of saying that you have only a vague idea of what you're looking for.)

If this is the case, you need to issue a more general man query (or an *apropos* query). To do this, you call man with the -k option plus a search term, like this:

man -k password

This command asks for a listing of all man pages on commands that deal with passwords. UNIX responds with this:

```
crypt (3)          - password and data encryption
passmass (1)       - change password on multiple machines
fgetpwent (3)      - get password file entry
yppasswd (1)       - NIS password update clients
getpwuid (3)       - get password file entry
conflict (8)       - search for alias/password conflicts
putpwent (3)       - write a password file entry
passwd (5)         - password file
endpwent (3)       - get password file entry
getpwnam (3)       - get password file entry
getpwent (3)       - get password file entry
yppasswdd (8)      - NIS password update server
setpwent (3)       - get password file entry
getpw (3)          - Re-construct password line entry
getpass (3)        - get a password
mkpasswd (1)       - generate new password, optionally apply it to a user
vipw (8)           - edit the password file
xlock (1x)         - Locks the local X display until a password is entered.
```

This is quite a list. Is there a way to refine this output? Yes. You can join this query with a grep command. For example, suppose you want only those entries that deal with NIS passwords. In this case, you could issue the following command:

man -k password ¦ grep NIS

This time, UNIX responds with a more relevant answer:

```
yppasswd (1)       - NIS password update clients
yppasswdd (8)      - NIS password update server
```

From here, you can check out the man pages for yppasswd and yppasswdd. Pretty cool, right? But wait, there's more. Why should you have to enter additional commands to view those man pages? Instead, why not automate the entire process? To do so, enter the following command:

```
man -k password ¦ grep NIS ¦ awk '{system ("man " $1)}'
```

That's one crazy command line! What does it do? Well, here are the steps involved:

1. man gets all man page listings on commands that deal with passwords.
2. grep discards all listings except those relevant to NIS.
3. awk grabs those names and runs man on them.

The end result is that man automatically loads man pages for both yppasswd and yppass-wdd.

Man, That's a Lot of Data!

In the example for automating man, awk causes man to execute twice (once for each match). Therefore, when you're finished reading the man page for yppasswd, man will automatically load the man page for yppasswdd. This holds true no matter how many matches you receive, so be careful when you structure your search string. If you use terms that are too general, man might load 20 man pages or more.

Finally, you can also redirect man output to a file for later viewing, like this:

```
man passwd > password_man.txt
```

However, note that man pages often contain control characters for formatting. These will show up in some editors, making the text difficult to read.

When You're Stuck in the GUI: Graphical Help Tools

Getting help from a command line is pretty easy. Because man output is plain text, you can readily manipulate it. However, what about when you're in X? Will man still work? Absolutely. man operates precisely the same in any Xterm.

However, on many systems, you can take advantage of more advanced help tools. Some are proprietary (indigenous to your particular UNIX flavor) and some are popular freeware or shareware. Let's briefly look at these.

xman

Most systems that run MIT's X Window System also have a utility called xman, a tool that allows you to view man pages in a graphical environment.

Starting xman

To start xman, open an Xterm (or other terminal window) and issue the following command:

    xman

This will load the xman control menu. (See the following figure.)

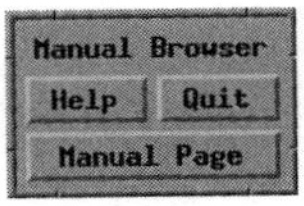

The xman control menu.

Note that your xman control menu may look slightly different than the one illustrated in the figure (for example, it may sport a different font or have thicker borders). Much depends on your version of X. However, regardless what version of X you're using, xman will behave exactly the same.

Using xman

To start using xman, choose the Manual Page button. This will load the main xman Manual Page window. (See the following figure.)

From there, choose the Sections tab on the menu bar. This will load a menu that lists various topics, such as user commands, system administration, and so on. Choose the category most likely to contain your desired command. xman will then load a window containing all commands in that category. (See the following figure.)

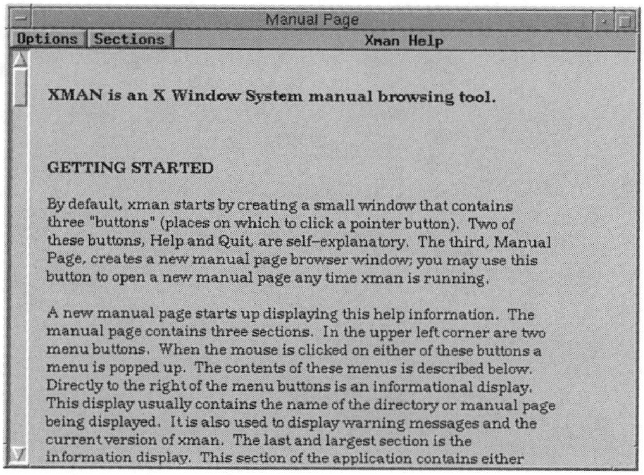

The xman viewer window.

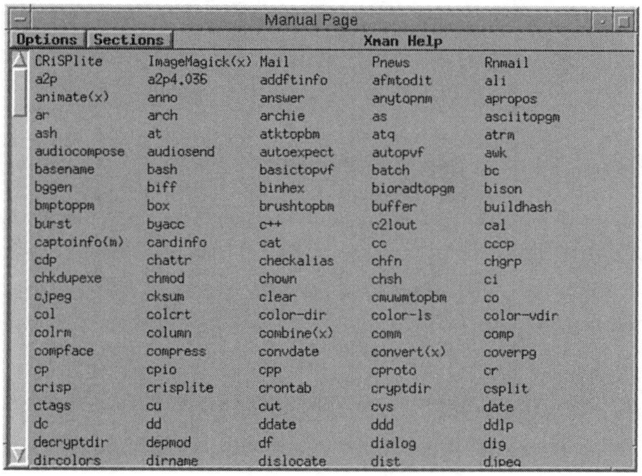

The user commands category.

Once you locate your desired command, click it once with your mouse cursor. In response, xman will load the corresponding man page. For example, if you choose ash, xman will load the ash man page. (See the following figure.)

xman is convenient because it groups similar commands together (for example, you can learn about all system administration commands by choosing the System Administration category).

The only problem with xman is this: The man pages are static. You cannot navigate these documents (except for scrolling forward and back). For this reason, many UNIX vendors have migrated their manual documentation to hypertext.

The ash *manual page.*

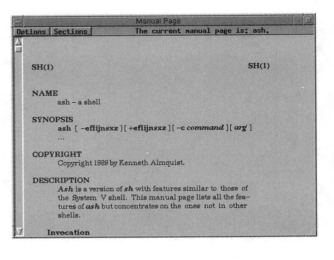

Why Is Hypertext so Hyper?

Hypertext is the text display format commonly used on Web pages. Hypertext is distinct from regular text because it's interactive. In a hypertext document, when you click or choose any highlighted word, other associated text appears. This allows for powerful cross-referencing and document navigation. Today, many UNIX help systems are based on hypertext.

The Evolution of man: TkMan

Above and beyond true hypertext help, other advances have been made to make man pages more easily accessible and user friendly. One excellent effort in this area is TkMan, a tool that allows you to access man pages through a graphical browser. (See the following figure.)

When man pages are displayed, TkMan highlights links to other commands associated with the current topic. If you click a link, TkMan displays the man page for that command. Moreover, TkMan will attempt to resolve a man page for any text you click. This opens many new possibilities.

Unfortunately, TkMan relies on the Tcl/Tk languages for its interface and functionality. These languages are also free but few shops actually install them. Nevertheless, because TkMan is platform independent, there's an excellent chance that your system will support it. Contact your system administrator and inquire about Tcl/Tk and TkMan.

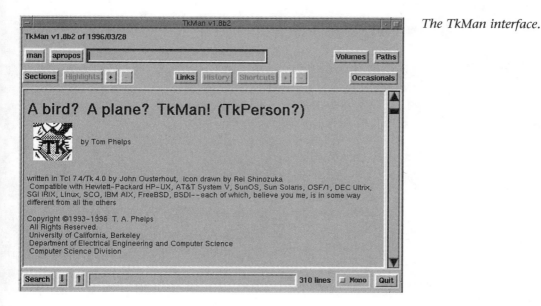

The TkMan interface.

The Least You Need to Know

There are three basic ways to obtain help:

➤ Issue a command with the -h or --help flags.

➤ Force a usage summary.

➤ Get the man page.

In addition to these avenues, your vendor may have developed well-organized and detailed help retrieval systems. Wherever possible, you should take advantage of these systems, because they are generally more comprehensive than garden-variety man pages.

Part 4

UNIX's Net Worth

Okay, so now that you know what UNIX is, where it came from, and why it's cool, you proba-bly want to take this puppy out for a drive and check the scenery. Well, it's a big world out there, but UNIX has the ponies to keep you in the fast lane.

In fact, UNIX and the Net grew up together, and in Part IV you'll learn how to take advantage of that long-term relationship. After first becoming a UNIX historian, you'll learn how to com-municate through email and chat, discover how to get the latest news, and cruise the Web with the coolest browsers. So strap yourself in and let's go!

## Chapter 16

UNIX and the Internet

In This Chapter

➤ How the Internet came about

➤ Some of UNIX's networking features

➤ Types of Internet connections

➤ Connecting to the Internet with UNIX

In Chapter 1, "I Thought UNIX Lived in Harems," I explained that the Internet's early design was based almost exclusively on UNIX. In this chapter, I want to expand on that a bit.

Out of the Ashes of a War That Never Happened

The date was October 22, 1962. After weeks of aerial surveillance, American intelligence officials had confirmed the worst: The Soviet Union was shipping missiles to Cuba. On that date, anticipating the eventuality of a Soviet first nuclear strike, President Kennedy ordered a naval blockade. Within hours, American warships surrounded Cuba.

Kennedy's aim was to place a stranglehold on Cuban ports while he delivered an ominous message to the Soviet Union: *Cease the shipment of missiles to Cuba and dismantle the Soviet-engineered missile bases there.* In those first few hours, Nikita Khrushchev, the Soviet Premier, pondered his options. In the interim, the world waited breathlessly and pondered it's own question: Would the United States and USSR engage in nuclear war?

Looking back, those events seem distant and implausible. At the time, however, American military strategists considered nuclear engagement a very real possibility. Therefore, they began generating projections of how far the destruction would reach. Not surprisingly, one chief concern was how that damage could affect the U.S. communication infrastructure.

Based on that research, the U.S. Air Force commissioned several think tanks to develop a revolutionary concept: a means of communication that could withstand and survive a nuclear war. In 1962, a fellow named Paul Baran (then with the Rand Corporation) provided an answer.

Baran took a long, hard look at the way our computer networks were designed. What he saw wasn't promising. You see, in those days, important databases were kept exclusively on mainframes.

Mainframes are designed primarily for large enterprises. Integrated into mainframe design is complex security architecture. There are many, many controls to prevent unauthorized persons from accessing sensitive, classified, secret, or top-secret data. So, from this, you'd probably draw the conclusion that mainframe-based networks were extremely secure. Unfortunately, that simply wasn't true.

Instead, the contemporary mainframe model was exceptionally vulnerable to attack. Here's why: In typical mainframe environments, all information resides on the mainframe, and dumb terminals are used to connect to this centralized database. If you knock out the mainframe, terminals cannot access that centralized data. Therefore, for all purposes, that particular network has been destroyed. (Remember that dumb terminals don't store data, they simply access it from a centralized source.)

The solution was simple enough: Instead of populating networks with dumb terminals that couldn't replicate data, why not have a network where *all* stations (whether they were mainframes, terminals, or whatever) could store and forward data?

In 1963, these ideas were presented to the Department of Defense. However, some bright folks there determined that the idea was ludicrous. (No one had ever heard of such a thing!) So, the concept was scrapped. Scrapped, that is, until 1969.

In 1969, after mulling it around for awhile, the Defense Department took a different view. Something had to be done, after all, so they went with Baran's rather offbeat idea. From there, engineers at various corporations and institutions took the idea and ran with it.

These folks started with four machines. After many months of effort, they managed quite a feat: The four machines could communicate and even replicate data redundantly. Imagine their excitement until they realized that they had overlooked one minor detail: They needed a common language by which all networked machines could communicate. They needed a set of standardized rules by which communication was conducted. In order to achieve that, they had to pick a suitable operating system.

As I explained in Chapter 1, MULTICS wasn't it. In fact, MULTICS wasn't even close to what they needed. So the search was on for something more appropriate. They found that something in UNIX.

The Ultimate Network Operating System

From that day on, UNIX's development has been almost exclusively focused on networking. Over the years, UNIX developers have found ways to network almost anything. In fact, to demonstrate just how religiously they adhered to this concept, let's take a brief detour.

In Chapter 4, "Getting In," I discuss finger, a program that snoops out data on what other users are up to and when they last logged in. Well, many years ago, someone at Carnegie Mellon University got the bright idea that a Coca-Cola dispensing machine could be wired to the Internet. (That's right. A Coca-Cola machine.) Crank up your UNIX box, connect to the Net, and issue this command:

finger coke@cs.cmu.edu

Here is what finger will return on that query:

```
[L.GP.CS.CMU.EDU]
Login: coke                          Name: Drink Coke
Directory: /usr/coke                 Shell: /usr/local/bin/tcsh
Last login Fri Jul 31 21:21 (EDT) on ttyp0 from gs77.sp.cs.cmu.e
Mail came on Mon Aug  3 04:45, last read on Mon Aug  3 04:45
Plan:
     M & M                Coke Buttons
    /—— -\          C: CCCCCCCCCCC............
    |?????|          C: CCCCCCCC....  D: CCCC........
    |?????|          C: ???????????? D: CCCCCCC.....
    |?????|          C: ???????????? D: CCCCCCCCCCCC
    |?????|                          C: C..........
    \—— -/                          S: C..........
      ¦            Key:
      ¦            0 = warm;  9 = 90% cold;  C = cold;  . = empty
      ¦            Beverages: C = Coke, D = Diet Coke, S = Sprite
      ¦            Leftmost soda/pop will be dispensed next
   —·ˆ—·           M&M status guessed.
                   Coke status guessed.
 Status last updated Mon Aug  3 06:47:31 1998
```

Take a close look at that output. Does it make any sense? Sure it does. It describes in great detail the contents of the soda-dispensing machine at Carnegie Mellon University. It shows how many soda cans are in each slot, the brand name of each, and which ones are cold.

That's just one example of many. Since 1974, UNIX has been used to internetwork almost anything you can think of.

Why Use UNIX?

Because UNIX and the Internet developed together, UNIX is an excellent platform from which to access the Net. There are several reasons for this.

First, most UNIX distributions provide both clients and servers for all the following information services:

➤ Email

➤ FTP

➤ Gopher

➤ HTTP

➤ IRC

➤ Telnet

➤ TFTP

In addition, UNIX provides the means for running programs remotely, both from command-line mode and in X. (This is something that still hasn't been perfected in the Windows/Mac OS world.)

Finally—and this is a major plus—UNIX can provide excellent Internet connectivity while still eating meager system resources (in other words, if you have an older machine, you can still enjoy fast, efficient Internet access).

Moreover, although you might not appreciate it right now, you'll eventually discover that UNIX is absolutely unmatched when it comes to automating online tasks.

Connecting to the Internet

UNIX provides several different types of Internet connectivity and several different ways to achieve it. These are the most common:

➤ **Direct connection**—This is a 24-hour-a-day connection, usually achieved through high-speed digital lines. For example, your connection may be via Ethernet through a T1 (1.5Mbps) or T3 (10Mbps to 45Mbps) digital telephone line. This is common in corporate environments. Other direct connections include ISDN, cable, fiber optics, Asynchronous Digital Subscriber Line (ASDL), and wireless. Using a direct connection means that your box has a permanent, or *static*, IP address and perhaps a hostname.

➤ **Point-to-Point connection**—This is typically a PPP connection over analog telephone lines. This is the most common connection type and is often offered by Internet Service Providers. With most PPP connections, you're assigned a temporary, or *dynamic*, IP address. This address is only yours while you're connected.

➤ **Dial-up connection**—Dial-up connections are rare nowadays. In a dial-up connection, you dial a UNIX server and connect to one of its serial ports. For all purposes, this type of connection behaves precisely like stringing a serial cable from your machine to the remote host. This is the oldest and least desirable way to hook up.

The process of configuring these connections works differently on different UNIX flavors. For this reason, it's impossible for me to provide a generic description of connecting. However, the next section provides some tips that might help.

Direct Connections

In a direct connection, you'll invariably be connected via Ethernet. Usually, this involves a cable running from your machine to a hub. The cable will have an end resembling either a television cable wire (BNC) or an oversized telephone jack (RJ45). In either case, if you have such a connection, rejoice. It's probably very fast.

In direct connections, you need to do very little (and perhaps nothing) to get up and running. In most cases, your system administrator has already assigned your workstation an IP address. The only problem you might run into is that you may need to identify your name server.

Name servers are machines that translate hostnames (`www.somewhere.net`) to IP addresses (`207.171.0.111`). If your workstation cannot reach a name server, your host lookups will fail. This is a critical problem.

To find out whether a name server has been specified, check the `/etc/resolv.conf` file, like this:

```
more /resolv.conf
```

If the `/etc/resolv.conf` file is empty or missing, contact your system administrator. He or she will fix it for you. On the other hand, if *you* are the system administrator, you can fix it yourself. To do so, edit the `/etc/resolv.conf` file and enter the name server's address.

PPP Connections

PPP connections are notoriously difficult to establish using the default tools available on most UNIX flavors. Therefore, I recommend getting ppp.

ppp

ppp greatly simplifies connecting to the Internet and currently supports the following platforms:

➤ AIX 4.*x*

➤ Digital UNIX

➤ Linux

➤ NetBSD, FreeBSD

➤ NeXTStep

➤ OSF/1

➤ Solaris 2

➤ SunOS 4.*x*

➤ Ultrix 4.*x*

ppp automates the process of logging on and reduces the time you'll spend configuring your machine. Certainly, most of the listed platforms have their own PPP services, but they're notoriously difficult to configure.

For example, getting PPP running on older Solaris boxes encompasses a document some 30 pages long. During the process of configuration, you need to alter many files that are difficult to understand. To avoid this, you should use ppp.

Getting ppp

Now I'm going to do something that authors do all the time: propose an impossible proposition. Authors routinely write about tools for connecting to the Net. The problem is, they tell you that you need to get these tools *from* the Net. That's a bit silly, isn't it? After all, if you were already connected, you wouldn't need the tools in the first place, right?

In any event, ppp is available at `ftp://cs.anu.edu.au/pub/software/ppp/`.

Setting Up ppp

Setting up ppp is very simple. In the ppp distribution, there's an executable file named pppd, which is used to automate logons. Here's a sample pppd logon script, which I call ppp-on:

```
pppd /dev/cua1 38400 connect 'chat -v "" ATDT5555555  CONNECT ""
➥"ogin:" "username" "word:" "mypassword"' modem defaultroute
```

Let's break the script down, bit by bit.

First, the script calls the program pppd and specifies the device to use for dialing:

```
pppd /dev/cua1
```

In this case, /dev/cua1 is the first modem. (The device node for your modem may differ from this. Check your system configuration to determine the correct device file.)

Next, the script specifies the modem speed and signals that this is a connection process:

```
38400 connect
```

Next, the script starts chat (in verbose mode) and handles the dial-up and logon:

```
'chat -v "" ATDT5555555  CONNECT "" "ogin:" "username" "word:"
"mypassword"'
```

Finally, the script specifies that the defaultroute should be used. (This signals the system to use whatever IP addresses are assigned at connect time.)

If this seems complicated, don't worry. To use the script, follow these simple instructions:

1. Copy the script verbatim into a plain text file named ppp-on.
2. Replace *username* with your login name.
3. Replace *mypassword* with your login password.
4. Replace *5555555* with your own dial-up number.
5. Make ppp-on executable (**chmod +x ppp-on**).
6. Run ppp-on (**ppp-on &**).

Note

In this script, "Login" and "Password" have been truncated to "ogin" and "word," because some servers issue login and password prompts with the first letter capitalized (Login, Password) and some don't (login, password).

That's it. You'll hear your modem dial out and connect. Several moments will pass and your hard disk drive will fall silent. At this point, you can check to see whether your connection is ready. Try this command:

```
ping 198.41.0.8
```

If your connection is up, you'll see a message very similar to this:

```
Reply from 198.41.0.8: bytes=32 time=238ms TTL=249
Reply from 198.41.0.8: bytes=32 time=260ms TTL=249
Reply from 198.41.0.8: bytes=32 time=243ms TTL=249
Reply from 198.41.0.8: bytes=32 time=231ms TTL=249
```

Or even this:

```
198.41.0.8 is alive.
```

Now you know your connection is alive.

Notes on Modems

Depending on your modem, you may need to provide a customized initialization string. This is a command line that only the modem understands. Table 16.1 lists the more commonly used modem codes.

Table 16.1.   Some commonly used modem commands

tip Command	Purpose
+++	Escape Code. Switch from data mode to command mode.
A	Answer Command. Answer incoming call.
A/	Repeat Last Command.
AT	Attention Code.
Bn	Bell Compatibility.
D!	Dialing Command. Hook Flash.
D,	Dialing Command. Pause.
D;	Dialing Command. Resume command mode after dialing.
D@	Dialing Command. Wait for 5 seconds quiet.
DP	Dialing Command. Pulse Dialing.
DR	Dialing Command. Reverse.
Ds	Dialing Command.
DS	Dialing Command. Dial one of the stored numbers.
DT	Dialing Command. Tone Dialing.
E	Echo Command.
E,E0	Echo Off.
E1	Echo On.
L2	Speaker Volume. Medium Volume.
L3	Speaker Volume. High Volume.
Ln	Speaker Volume.
M,M0	Speaker Off.
Z	Reset Command.

Shutting Down ppp

Shutting down pppd is a simple matter. You can basically kill the process by using the kill command. If you have Perl, here's a script that automates this process:

```
#!/usr/bin/perl

$count=0;
```

```
open(PS, "ps¦") ¦¦ die "Cannot open PS\n\$!";
while (<PS>) {
    if(/pppd/) {
    $count++;
    @my_ppp = split(' ', $_);
        system("kill $my_ppp[0]");
        print "Your PPP process [PID $my_ppp[0]] has been
terminated!\n"
        }
    }
    close(PS);
    if($count==0) {
        print "There is no PPP process running right now\n";
    }
```

This script performs a simple function: It scans the current process list for an instance of pppd. If it finds one, it kills that process and reports that the process has been terminated. If no pppd process is running, the script reports that fact to you, as well.

If you don't have Perl, you can still do this in a variety of ways. For example, using simple system commands, you can perform precisely the same task, like this:

```
ps ¦ grep pppd ¦ awk '{system ("kill
" $1)}'
```

Warning

Be sure not to kill your pppd process while data is being transferred. If you do, your files could become damaged.

pppd *Options*

pppd supports a number of options that help you control your connection. These are briefly summarized in Table 16.2.

Table 16.2. Various pppd flags and what they mean

pppd Flag	Function
crtscts	crtscts specifies that hardware flow control should be used. (*Hardware flow control* is where your hardware controls the transmission of data from your machine to the remote host. In hardware flow control, synchronization, error checking, and verification of transmissions is done at a hardware level.)
defaultroute	defaultroute specifies that the remote host should be used as a gateway. This is an easy way to avoid having to know the IP addresses of your gateway.

continues

219

Table 16.2.   Various pppd flags and what they mean
CONTINUED

pppd **Flag**	**Function**
MRU [#]	MRU stands for *maximum receive unit*. This value describes the largest byte size of received packets. (This is a way to limit the size of packets sent to you.) The minimum size you can specify is 128, but if you're using a modem, 296 is recommended. (You can go as high as 1500, but this is not recommended unless you have a high-speed connection.) To specify an MRU value, issue the MRU flag plus the value, like this: **MRU 296**.
MTU [#]	MTU stands for *maximum transmit unit*. This value describes how many bytes each packet will be when transmitted. Using a large MTU guarantees faster transfers, but it also increases the chance that errors will occur during transfer. To specify an MTU value, issue the MTU flag plus the MTU value, for example: **MTU 256**.
speed	speed is a number value. With it, you specify the top speed of the connection. For example, if you have a 33.6 modem, a good speed setting would be 38400.

Direct Dial Connections

In the unlikely event that you're ever forced to access the Net by direct dial-up, this section's for you. Almost all UNIX systems have two utilities that can help you establish a direct dial connection:

➤ cu

➤ tip

Let's briefly cover each.

Dialing Another UNIX Machine: The cu *Command*

To dial another UNIX machine directly, use cu, like this:

```
cu 18185555555
```

This will dial the system at (818) 555-5555. Pretty simple, right? Maybe and maybe not. cu has many, many options. Depending on your system configuration, you may need to use one or more of these options. The important ones are summarized in Table 16.3.

Table 16.3. A few `cu` options

cu Option	Purpose
-b [*7 or 8*]	The -b switch is for setting the bits on received data. This value is either 7 or 8. This is important. If you connect using 8 bits when the other system uses 7 bits, the text will appear in bizarre places on the screen, or perhaps not appear at all.
-c	The -c option allows you to specify a dialing device. To obtain a list of devices, check the /etc/uucp/Devices file.
-d	The -d option stands for *diagnostic*. This forces a diagnostic log of your session. (This is useful when you're trying to determine what's wrong.)
-s [*speed*]	The -s option allows you to specify a baud rate. For example, **cu -s 38400 5555555**. This tells cu to dial 555-5555 and when the connection is made, that connection will occur at 38,400bps.

In most cases, when cu finally connects, the session works much like a serial connection. Typically, you'll be faced with a login prompt. From there, you simply log in and begin working.

Still More Direct Dialing: The `tip` *Command*

Still another excellent utility for direct dial sessions is `tip`, which is a little more powerful than cu because it has some very convenient, prefabbed functions. (These are discussed later.) However, at least with regard to making the connection, `tip` works very much like cu. You can start a `tip` session by issuing the `tip` command plus either the host or the telephone number you want to dial:

```
tip some-host
```

Once the connection is made, the session will behave exactly as though you were working on a local terminal. There's virtually no difference between using `tip` and plugging a dumb terminal into the remote host. However, once you're logged in, you can do a lot with `tip`.

While connected to the remote host via `tip`, you can jump into command mode at any time by placing a tilde character (~) at the beginning of a line. Anything that follows that tilde is then interpreted as a command. Table 16.4 summarizes some legal `tip` commands that can follow a tilde.

Table 16.4.   Some `tip` commands

`tip` Command	Purpose
~!	This drops you to a shell on your own machine. (This is very useful when you need to search for a file but you don't want to cut the connection. When you exit from the shell, you're returned to your `tip` session.)
~$	This tells `tip` to send the output of local commands to the remote host for processing by the remote shell.
~. or ~+Ctrl+**D**	This tells `tip` to sever the connection.
~?	This tells `tip` to display all possible tilde-based commands currently available.
~¦	This tells `tip` to pipe the results of a remote command to a local command or process. (This is useful when you want to use a local program to examine files on a remote machine. You can print the remote files to `stdout` and pipe them to the local program.)
~<	This tells `tip` that you want to transfer a file from the remote host to your own machine. (`tip` will prompt you for a filename.)
~>	This tells `tip` that you want to transfer a file from your machine to the remote host. (`tip` will prompt you for a filename.)
~c [*directory*]	This tells `tip` to change to a particular directory—if the argument *directory* is given—or to your home directory.

Summary: Direct Dial Connections

Using a direct dial connection is probably the least desirable way to connect because you're dependent on the remote system's Internet access. Moreover, getting files to your machine is a two-part process. First, you have to download the files from the Internet to the remote machine. Then, you download them to your own box.

However, if this is the only connectivity you currently have, it helps to know how to negotiate a raw connection. If you intend to use direct dialing for any length of time, you should study the `cu` and `tip` man pages carefully. Both programs are quite versatile, and you can perform many complex tasks using them.

The Least You Need to Know

This chapter may not teach you everything you need to know about Internet connectivity, but it's a good start. However, note that many proprietary UNIX systems often have built-in Internet connectivity suites. (For example, UNIXWare now includes

MorningStar PPP, an excellent connectivity package.) Therefore, check your manuals. You may find that your UNIX has a very user-friendly method of hooking up.

Here are some key points from this chapter:

➤ UNIX is an excellent operating system for Net surfing.

➤ To simplify PPP connections, use pppd.

➤ To dial directly, use cu or tip.

## Chapter 17

Email

In This Chapter

➤ Learn about email

➤ Different email programs

On the Internet, email is the primary method of communication. It's instant (nearly), simple, and inexpensive. For example, the average letter sent airmail takes approximately eight days to get from Los Angeles, California to Sydney, Australia. In contrast, an email message can take as little as 80 seconds. Amazing.

Is email going to put the U.S. Postal Service out of business? Not likely. Email is very impersonal and lacks the warmth of a hand-written letter. However, email is an excellent medium of communication for quick notes.

In this chapter, you'll learn how to send and receive email on your UNIX system.

Return to Sender, Address Unknown: Email Addresses

Email works much like regular mail. Each message should be accompanied by at least two addresses: the sender and recipient. (The recipient, at least, is an absolute necessity.)

An email address is constructed of two values: your *username* and your machine's *hostname*. These are separated by the @ symbol, sometimes called the "at" symbol. For example, my username is bwagner and my machine's hostname is wagjag. Therefore, at least at home, my email address is this:

    bwagner@wagjag.net

This translates to "Bill Wagner at the machine wagjag." Everyone's email address will look this way, although some addresses are longer than others. I've seen some pretty radical email addresses in my time; addresses like this:

    system_administrator@mathlab.research-and-development.00022x.com

However, most folks have simple email addresses, like this:

    racerxo@pacbell.net

Whenever you send email, you must use the recipient's full email address. (There's only one exception to this: If the recipient is on the exact same machine as you, you can simply use his or her username).

Email Tools

UNIX distributions come with several programs that allow you to send and receive email. Some of these programs are rudimentary (such as mail) and some are more user friendly. Three tools are discussed in this chapter:

➤ mail

➤ elm

➤ pine

Let's take a look at these programs now.

mail

The most common UNIX program for sending email is mail, a command-line tool that makes sending email quick and painless. To send a message using mail, issue the mail command plus the recipient's address, like this:

    mail bwagner@altavista.net

In response, mail will provide a new line, and you can begin typing your message, like this:

    mail bwagner@altavista.net
    Hi, Bill. Just checking to see whether you're done with that book yet.

When you're done typing your message, enter a period (.) on an otherwise empty line, like this:

```
mail bwagner@altavista.net
Hi, Bill. Just checking to see whether you're done with that book yet.
.
```

`mail` will exit and send the message.

Reading Mail with `mail`

To read your current messages, enter the `mail` command without arguments, like this:

mail

`mail` will respond by displaying the most current message first. A typical email message will look like this:

```
From bigdave Sun Jul 26 21:21:50 1998
Date: Sun, 26 Jul 1998 21:21:49 -0700
From: bigdave
Message-Id: <199807270421.VAA06159@editors.bigdave.com>
Content-Length: 72

Hi, Bill. Just checking to see whether you're done with that book yet.
```

To view only the headers of email messages (summaries about each message), enter the following mail command:

h a

In response, `mail` will display only brief information about each message, including the sender, the message length, the date that it was sent, and so forth. Here's an example:

```
2 letters found in /var/mail/bwagner, 0 scheduled for deletion,
0 newly arrived

      2     394     dc31245     Sun Jul 26 21:22:27 1998
>     1     403     dc31245     Sun Jul 26 21:21:50 1998
```

From this list, you can pick the messages you want to read, print, or discard.

`mail` Commands

`mail` is a fairly versatile program that supports a wide range of functions and commands. Common mail commands are summarized in Table 17.1.

Table 17.1. Some `mail` commands

`mail` Command	Result
-	`mail` displays the previous message. For instance, if you're currently viewing message number 2 and you issue this command, `mail` will display message number 1.
! *command*	`mail` executes the specified command. For instance, if you're working with mail and needed to see a directory listing, you could do so by issuing the following command: **! `ls`.**
#	# represents a number. This will display a particular message number. For example, by entering the number 2, you're telling mail to display message number 2.
?	`mail` displays help on all commands.
+	`mail` displays the very next message.
a	This positions you at the first new message in your mail box.
d #	`mail` deletes the message number you specify. For example, to delete message number 2, issue the following command: **d 2.** Also, you can delete the current message (the one you are reading) by simply entering the letter **d** with no number after it.
Enter	`mail` scrolls down to the next message.
h a	`mail` displays the headers (subject lines and other data) for all current messages.
n	`mail` displays the next message. (This is the same as Enter or +.)
q	Quits mail.
r	Replies to a message.
s	Saves the current message. (The **s** command will also take a filename as an argument. For example, suppose you want to save the message in `mymail.txt` instead of the default mailbox. To do so, you would enter the following command: **s `mymail.txt`.**)
u	Use the **u** command to undelete deleted messages. (You can also specify which message to undelete. For example, to undelete message number 2, issue the command **u 2.**)

elm

elm is a text-based mail tool that's slightly more user friendly than mail. To start elm, enter the elm command without arguments, like this:

    elm

The first time you use elm, it will set up your directories and your elm mail account. (See the following figure.)

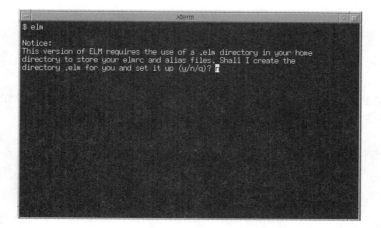

The elm mail program setup screen.

At the elm setup screen, choose Yes (enter the letter y). elm will create the necessary directories and drop you into its main program screen. (See the following figure.)

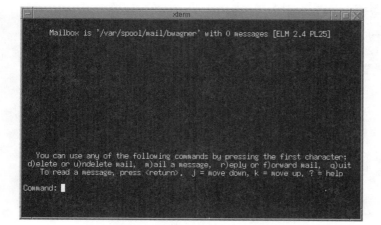

The elm mail program main screen.

Sending an Email Message with elm

To send an email message with elm, choose m from the main menu. elm will respond by asking you to identify the recipient:

```
Send the message to:
```

Here, you type in the recipient's email address. Next, elm will ask you to describe the subject:

```
Subject of message:
```

Here, type in a subject line. Finally, elm will ask if you want to send the message to additional recipients:

```
Copies to:
```

If you have no additional recipients, simply press the Enter key. At that point, elm will launch the editor.

About the elm Editor

By default, elm will use the editor your system administrator specified at installation. That editor could be ed, vi, emacs, pico, wpe, and so on. If you find that you don't like the current elm editor, you can change it. To do so, enter the command **o**. This will bring up the options menu, which looks like this:

```
                     -- ELM Options Editor --

      C)alendar file        : /home/bwagner/calendar
      D)isplay mail using   : builtin+
      E)ditor (primary)     : /usr/local/bin/lemacs
      F)older directory     : /home/bwagner/Mail
      S)orting criteria     : Reverse-Sent
      O)utbound mail saved  : =sent
      P)rint mail using     : /bin/cat %s ¦ /bin/lp
      Y)our full name       : Bill Wagner
      V)isual Editor (~v)   : /usr/local/bin/lemacs

      A)rrow cursor         : OFF
      M)enu display         : ON
      U)ser level           : Beginning User
      N)ames only           : ON


      Select letter of option line, '>' to save, or 'i' to return to index.

      Command:
```

To change the editor, choose E and specify the new program, along with its complete path.

Typing and Sending Your Message

Regardless of what editor you use with elm, the procedure for formatting and sending mail is the same. You type your message and exit the editor. At that time, elm will send the message to the recipient.

elm *Commands*

There are a handful of elm commands that you should know. These are listed in Table 17.2.

Table 17.2.   Some elm commands

elm **Command**	**Purpose**
!	Temporarily escape to the shell
/ pattern	Search for a pattern in your message headers
// pattern	Search for a pattern in your messages
?	Get help
¦	Send the current message to a system command
d	Delete a message
Enter	Display the next message
f	Forward a message
j	Go to the next message
m	Mail a message
p	Print the currently selected message or messages
r	Reply to a message
spacebar	Display the next message
u	Undelete a message
x or X	Exit

pine

mail and elm are quick and efficient tools for sending and receiving email. However, perhaps you're looking for something a bit more user friendly. If so, you should try pine.

pine is a simple mail client with a very friendly interface. To start pine, issue the pine command without arguments, like this:

```
pine
```

This will launch the `pine` interface, which is largely menu driven. (See the following figure.)

The `pine` mail program has a menu driven interface.

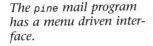

As you can see, there are a series of menu choices. The highlight bar identifies the current menu choice. (In the previous figure, the highlighted menu choice is FOLDER LIST.)

Here are the two ways to choose a menu action:

➤ Use the arrow keys to highlight the desired action

➤ Type the first letter of the desired action

Sending a Message with `pine`

To begin composing a message, use the up-arrow key to highlight COMPOSE MESSAGE (or type in the letter c) and press Enter. This will launch the COMPOSE MESSAGE interface shown in the following figure.

By default, your cursor will be positioned in the To field. There, enter the email address of your intended recipient. Next, tab down to the Subject field and enter your subject line. Finally, tab down to the main editing area and type your message.

When you're done, hit Ctrl+x. `pine` will then ask you if you really want to send the current message. Enter the letter y for Yes. That's it! Your mail is on its way.

The COMPOSE MESSAGE interface is where you write your messages.

pine *Edit Commands*

While editing your email messages in pine, you can take advantage of pine's word processor–like functions. Table 17.3 provides an explanation of pine editing commands.

Table 17.3. Some pine edit mode commands

pine Command	Result
Ctrl+c	pine cancels the current operation. (Choose this when you decide you don't really want to send mail after all.)
Ctrl+g	pine displays help on the current operation. (This is generally a summary of editing commands.)
Ctrl+j	Justifies the current text.
Ctrl+k	Cuts the current line.
Ctrl+r	Use Ctrl+r when you want to append text to the current message from a file on your disk drive. When you enter Ctrl+r, pine asks you to specify the file's path and name (for example, /home/bwagner/message.txt). pine then inserts the contents of that file into the current email message. Caution: Make sure your cursor sits clearly above or below the text you've already typed. If you don't, pine will insert the file's contents smack dab in the middle of your document. (pine inserts the text wherever your cursor is at the time.)
Ctrl+t	Initiates a spell check on the current document.
Ctrl+u	Pastes text into the current message.

continues

Table 17.3. Some pine edit mode commands CONTINUED

pine Command	Result
Ctrl+w	Ctrl+w works in pine exactly as it does in pico. Its purpose is to search for a particular string of text. When you enter Ctrl+w, pine opens a field in your status bar. In this field, type the text you want to find and press Enter. pine will find the first match. To find subsequent matches, you can hit Ctrl+w and then Enter again.
Ctrl+x	pine sends the current message. By default, pine asks for one confirmation before doing so. To affirm, type the letter y. (When you get really comfortable with pine, you'll probably master all three keystrokes as one motion: Ctrl+x+y.)

Reading Your Email with pine

To read your email with pine, start pine and choose FOLDER LIST¦INBOX. This will bring you to a screen with a list of email messages. Choose one by pressing ENTER. pine will then display the message in its entirety. (See the following figure.)

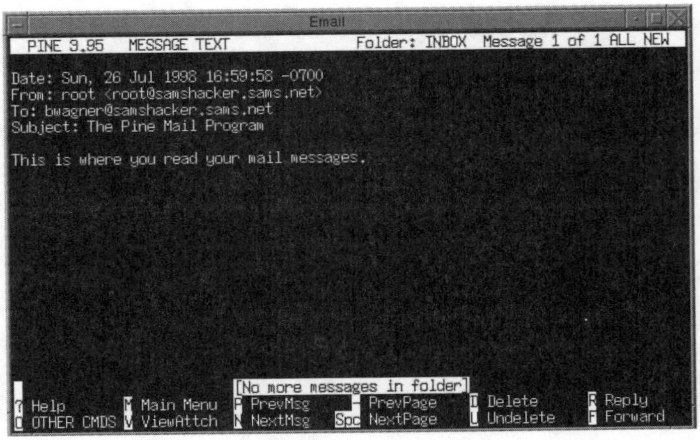

Reading email with pine.

pine Read Messages Mode

While reading your messages in pine, you have many options available to you through single-key commands. These commands are summarized in Table 17.4.

Table 17.4. Some `pine` read messages mode commands

`pine` Command	Result
?	`pine` displays help on reading and replying to messages.
d	`pine` marks the current message for deletion (deletes the message when you exit the program).
f	Is the current message just so silly that you have to send it to a third party? If so, use the f command. This stands for *forward*. When you enter the f command, pine puts you into edit mode. When you're finished appending your snide comments to the message, press Ctrl+x+y. The original message and your comments will be forwarded to the specified party.
m	`pine` leaves the current message and returns to the main menu screen.
n	`pine` displays the next message.
o+g	Use this command when you want to go back to folder view.
o+q	Use this command when you want to quit from the read messages mode.
o+s	Use this command to save the current message. (`pine` will prompt for a filename.)
o+y	Use this command when you want to print the current message.
p	`pine` displays the previous message.
-	`pine` goes to the previous page.
r	Use the r command to reply to messages. When you enter the r command, pine puts you into edit mode. There, you simply type your reply and hit Ctrl+x+y.
spacebar	`pine` displays the next page of the current message.
u	`pine` undeletes the current message.
v	`pine` shows any attachments that were appended to the email message. (Sometimes, folks send along silly things called *email attachments*. These are huge files that take years to download and usually have no practical use. The more you use email, the more of these you'll receive.)

A final note about `pine`: It also functions as a newsreader. To find out the particulars, see Chapter 19, "USENET News."

About Email in General

If you're new to email, there are a few things you should know. Unfortunately, though the majority of folks on the Internet are quite friendly, a few bad apples are out there. When you cross paths with these fellows, you're bound to encounter fakemail, spam, and even the dreaded email bomb. Let's briefly discuss these here.

The Phony Express: Fakemail and Spam

If you use the Internet for any length of time, you're bound to ride the Phony Express. That's another way of saying that you'll receive both fakemail and junk mail (and sometimes, these will be one and the same).

A recent study indicated that the average Internet user's email is comprised of almost 25 percent junk mail. (*Junk mail* usually consists of unsolicited advertisements sent to your email address. Typically, the authors of such garbage attempt to obscure their real email addresses.)

Is there any cure for junk mail and fakemail? Not really. You simply have to either ignore them or get a program that filters them out. Unfortunately, though, there aren't many commercial UNIX programs designed for this. On UNIX, mail filters are usually homegrown, meaning that UNIX users write their own.

Until you get more proficient at using UNIX, writing your own mail filtering program is clearly out of reach. Therefore, for now, just ignore your junk mail. Eventually, such mail will fade away. Lastly, whatever you do, don't reply to junk mail. (The perpetrator's email server may interpret your reply as a request for further information.)

The Dreaded Email Bomb

You can't please all of the people all of the time. During the course of using the Internet as a tool of free speech, you're bound to tick somebody off. It doesn't matter what you say, really, because there will always be someone who takes issue with your viewpoint (even if this person has absolutely no idea what you're talking about).

Sometimes, these people do more than simply berate you in public forums or over email. Instead, they take things a step further, graduating to bona fide harassment. One common harassment tool is the dreaded *email bomb*. This is where some bozo sends you the same message hundreds (or even thousands) of times.

Do email bombs actually cause any damage? No. Instead, they're a nuisance. If you should receive one, simply ignore it and delete the messages.

The Least You Need to Know

Sending and receiving messages nearly instantly to and from practically anywhere in the world is one of the great advantages of the computer age. To take advantage of the email capabilities of UNIX, here's the least you need to know:

➤ Nearly all UNIX distributions come with `mail` installed. When in doubt, use `mail`.

➤ `elm` is slightly more user friendly than `mail` but is only available in select UNIX flavors. If your system doesn't have `elm`, contact your system administrator.

➤ `pine` is the most user-friendly text-based mail client currently available. However, pine is not available on all systems.

## Chapter 18

The WWW: Browsers for UNIX

In This Chapter

➤ Various WWW browsers for UNIX

After a hard day's work with UNIX, you'll probably want to relax and have some fun. There's no better way to have fun with your system than cruising the World Wide Web.

In this chapter, you'll learn about some popular Web browsers for UNIX, as well as their advantages and disadvantages.

A Few Words about Standards

Sometimes, as progress marches on, it inadvertently complicates things so that an original idea is lost in the shuffle. This is the case with the WWW.

In 1991, a physicist named Tim Berners-Lee implemented hypertext as a medium by which users on disparate machines could view documentation. With rare exceptions, that documentation would look almost identical to Mac users, IBM users, and UNIX users. In effect, Berners-Lee's WWW served all users equally, regardless of the architecture or software used.

When the Web became more commercially viable, however, software vendors sought to extend their browsers' capabilities. To do so, they introduced special, proprietary extensions to HTML—extensions that only their browsers could understand. As a result, pages built expressly for Microsoft Internet Explorer would not work well with Netscape Navigator, and vice versa. This trend continued until the differences were so great that even basic page elements (such as buttons and list boxes) would only be visible if you used the "right" browser.

One HTML extension in particular that changed the way users see the Web is *tables*. Tables allow Webmasters to specify near-absolute positioning of elements such as text and graphics on the viewable page. In this respect, tables greatly enhanced the user's Web experience, because more beautiful and functional pages could be created. However, not all browsers support tables.

Table support (or lack of it) is probably the chief disparity among browsers. Browsers that don't support tables often display text and graphics in odd positions. Because tables are now used regularly on the Web, using a browser that's not table compliant places you at a distinct disadvantage.

To demonstrate the difference between a table-compliant and a non-table-compliant browser, I loaded both Netscape Communicator and NCSA Mosaic and then downloaded the home page of Macmillan Computer Publishing on each.

Netscape Communicator is table compliant; it interpreted the MCP home page properly. (See the following figure.)

Using Netscape Communicator to access MCP's Web site.

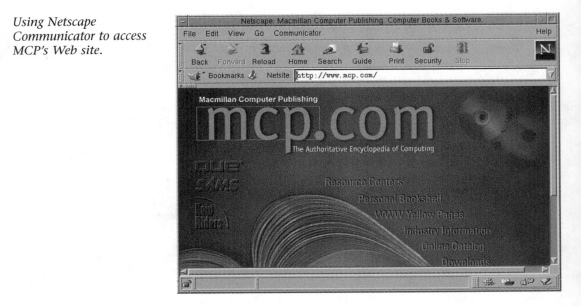

However, NCSA Mosaic, a non-table-compliant browser, was only able to load a small portion of the MCP site. (See the following figure.)

Using NCSA Mosaic to access MCP's Web site.

As you can see, Mosaic missed quite a bit. Today, the vast majority of sites implement tables in their Web pages.

Table 18.1 summarizes tables support for various UNIX browsers (as well as several other important disparities).

Table 18.1. Browser/tables compatibility

Browser	Status
Amaya	Amaya has table support, Java support, and graphics support. However, Amaya does not support JavaScript, VBScript, video, and sound.
Chimera	Chimera supports tables and graphics but does not support JavaScript, VBScript, sound, and video.
Lynx	Lynx does not support tables. Moreover, Lynx does not support JavaScript, VBScript, graphics, sound, and video.
Mosaic for X	NCSA Mosaic does not support JavaScript, VBScript, tables, sound, and video.
Navigator/Communicator	Netscape Navigator and Communicator both support JavaScript, tables, graphics, sound, and video.

The browser you use will depend on why you use the WWW. If you're in research and are seeking mostly text, it doesn't really matter which browser you use. However, if you cruise the Web for personal enjoyment and entertainment, your best choice is probably Netscape Navigator or Communicator. Both products support most of the latest technologies in Web media.

About Availability

You're probably wondering whether your system already has a Web browser installed. That's very possible. Newer UNIX distributions (particularly those released after 1997) are likely to have at least one browser included. For example, UNIXWare has Netscape Navigator, and nearly all versions of Linux have at least one browser installed (and sometimes several).

If you can't immediately determine whether your UNIX system has a Web browser, consult your system administrator.

The Browsers

The following sections cover the UNIX-based browsers you'll most likely encounter. About a dozen other Web browsers for UNIX are in various stages of development. (Even Microsoft has developed a version of Internet Explorer for UNIX. However, to date, it only supports two very specific configurations.)

NCSA Mosaic

National Center for Supercomputing Applications
University of Illinois at Urbana-Champaign
Champaign, IL 61820
http://www.ncsa.uiuc.edu/

NCSA Mosaic for X is one of the oldest WWW browsers. It was designed at the National Center for Supercomputing Applications by Marc Andreessen and Eric Bina. You might recognize Marc Andreessen's name—he founded Netscape Communications Corporation. (Andreessen's success story is now a matter of Internet folklore. When Andreessen designed Mosaic, he was making approximately $6.50 an hour. However, less than one week after he founded Netscape, he became an instant multimillionaire.)

In any event, Mosaic for X is a long-time favorite of super-geeks. Its design is extremely user friendly. In fact, it was Mosaic that opened the WWW to nontechnical users. Prior to Mosaic's 1993 release, the WWW was intimidating and difficult to use (primarily because the Net was text based). Mosaic changed all this by making navigation of the WWW a point-and-click affair.

In appearance, Mosaic for X closely resembles any Windows or Macintosh application. (See the following figure.)

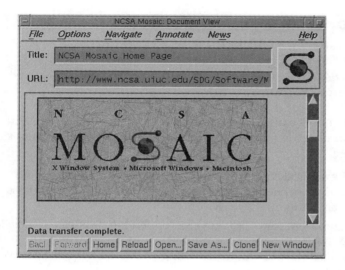

Mosaic for X.

Almost all Mosaic functions are available through drop-down menus. (A good number of functions are also available through buttons on the main screen.) Certainly, if you're doing research, Mosaic is an excellent choice. It's fast, reliable, and lightweight.

Mosaic binaries exist for the following UNIX systems:

➤ AIX

➤ Apple A/UX

➤ Bull DPX/23xx

➤ ConvexOS 11.0

➤ DESQview/X

➤ DG AVIION

➤ HP9000 (HP-UX)

➤ Linux

➤ NeXT

➤ SunOS and Solaris

➤ UNIXWare

Mosaic for X is currently in release 2.6 (although a 2.7 beta exists) and is available at
`http://www.ncsa.uiuc.edu/SDG/Software/XMosaic/`.

Pros: Mosaic is fast, free, reliable, stable, and easy to use.

Cons: Mosaic is dated and doesn't conform to many standards that have since been implemented.

Netscape Navigator and Communicator

Netscape Communications Corporation
501 E. Middlefield Road
Mountain View, CA 94043
`http://home.netscape.com`

Netscape Communicator and its earlier incarnation, Navigator, are both excellent Web browsers. In addition to being up-to-date (they support most new technologies), these browsers have several, important amenities:

➤ **Integrated email and USENET news**—Navigator and Communicator both have built-in mail and news clients, allowing you to send and receive messages without leaving the application.

➤ **Integrated document editors**—If you get a sudden creative urge to develop your own Web page, Navigator and Communicator can fix you right up. Both applications have built-in HTML editors, allowing you to build your own Web page either locally or for use on another server.

➤ **Prefabbed bookmark files**—Netscape's products come with stock bookmark files. These have endless links to cool Web sites in a dozen categories, including business, finance, entertainment, education, sports, shopping, and leisure. (Why search when Netscape's already done all the work?)

Furthermore, Netscape Communicator's interface is extremely user friendly. (See the following figure.)

Netscape Communicator for X.

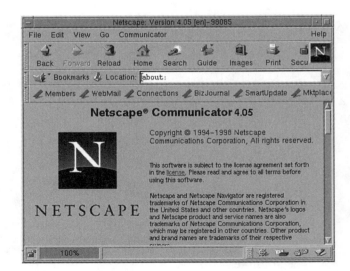

If anything, Communicator's major drawback is that it's a very large package and takes well over an hour to download over standard dial-up lines. However, Communicator's extended features more than make up for this minor shortcoming.

Netscape Navigator and Communicator are available at `http://home.netscape.com`.

Pros: Free, user friendly, comprehensive, convenient, and up-to-date.

Cons: Large in size, takes awhile to download, and eats up a lot of disk space.

Lynx

The University of Kansas
Distributed Computing Group
Lawrence, KS 66045
`http://www.ukans.edu/about_lynx/`

Lynx is a text-based browser for UNIX that also runs on the following systems:

➤ Windows 95
➤ Windows NT
➤ VMS
➤ OS/2

Now, you may wonder why anyone would develop and maintain a text-based browser. After all, with Mosaic, Netscape Navigator, and other graphical browsers available, text browsers seem pathetically obsolete. Nevertheless, there are certain instances in which text-based browsers are valuable tools.

For example, many public libraries offer Internet access but only through dumb terminals connected to a UNIX server. Effectively, then, library patrons are using UNIX shell accounts. In such an environment, a text-based browser may be the only alternative.

Also, in environments where onsite developers generate all their help documentation in plain HTML, text-based browsers can offer fast, cost-efficient access.

Using Lynx

To use Lynx, issue the `lynx` command along with a WWW destination address, like this:

```
lynx http://www.mcp.com
```

Lynx will load the requested page, and you can begin surfing. (See the following figure.)

Using Lynx to access MCP's Web site.

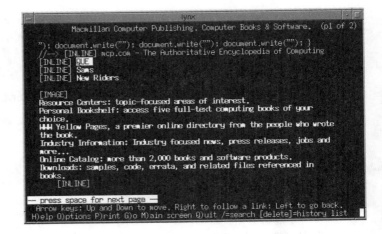

Navigation is achieved entirely through keystrokes. Table 18.2 summarizes various Lynx navigation keystrokes.

Table 18.2.   Some Lynx keystrokes

Keystroke	Purpose
!	Exit to the shell temporarily.
/	Search the current document for text strings.
?	Get help on Lynx
\	Examine the document source.
Down arrow	Move forward to the next link.
h	Get help on Lynx.
Insert	Move back two lines.
m	Go to the main menu.
p	Print the current document.
Page Down	Go to the next page.
Page Up	Go to the previous page.
Q	Emergency quit. (Use this when you have problems and absolutely need to quit without saving bookmarks or printing data.)
q	Quit lynx. (Lynx will prompt you to quit.)
Right arrow	Follow the current link.
Up arrow	Move back to the most recent link.

Generally, active links are displayed in reverse video so that they're easy to see. Although Lynx does not support tables, it does support most HTML forms.

Lynx Availability

Lynx currently runs on the following UNIX systems:

➤ AIX

➤ BSD (all flavors)

➤ Data General

➤ Digital UNIX

➤ HP-UX

➤ IRIX

➤ Linux

➤ NeXTStep

➤ Ultrix

Lynx binary releases can be obtained at
`http://www.crl.com/%7Esubir/lynx/binaries.html`.

> **Pros:** Lynx is fast, free, lightweight, and resource efficient.

> **Cons:** Lynx is entirely text based and lacks support for tables as well as many different forms of media that are now common to the Web.

Amaya

The World Wide Web Consortium
Massachusetts Institute of Technology
Laboratory for Computer Science
545 Technology Square
Cambridge, MA 02139
`http://www.w3.org/`

Amaya is the brainchild of the World Wide Web Consortium—the folks who set WWW standards. This browser has some promising features (as well as about two dozen that you'll probably never use). For example, Amaya can be used to edit complex math equations, a feature that's of interest to physicists.

Other Amaya amenities include the following:

➤ Strict adherence to WC3 standards. (And why not? After all, the WC3 wrote it.)

➤ A built-in Web page editor

➤ Support for Cascading Style Sheets

➤ Java support

Amaya's interface is also quite user friendly. (See the following figure.)

The Amaya interface.

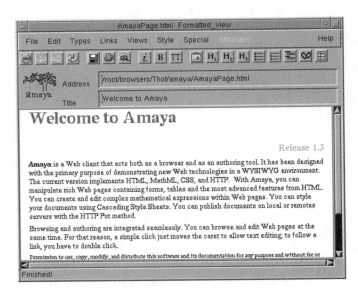

Amaya is the choice of super-geeks worldwide, primarily because it can be used in development. (The program has an extensive API.)

What the Heck Is an API?

API stands for *application program interface*. APIs specify all the allowable rules and function calls available to a programmer. Using these rules and function calls, the programmer can request an application (or operating system) to perform a particular task. In most proprietary software packages, at least some (but probably not all) of the API is published and publicly available. By making their APIs publicly available, software manufacturers allow programmers and users to access special functions that enhance the software's functionality. (These enhancements typically exceed the application's off-the-self functionality.)

Pros: Amaya supports all accepted standards, has a built-in editor, is quite user friendly.

Cons: Amaya is somewhat obscure and does not support many new media technologies.

You can obtain Amaya binaries from the WWW Consortium at `http://www.w3.org/`.

Chimera

Information Science Research Institute
University of Nevada, Las Vegas
4505 Maryland Parkway
Las Vegas, NV 89154
`http://www.isri.unlv.edu/`

Chimera is a browser for X that was built using the Athena Widget Set. What does this mean? It means that you don't need Motif to build or run it.

Chimera currently supports file retrieval for all the following protocols:

➤ HTTP (Web)

➤ FTP (File Transfer Protocol)

➤ Gopher (Gopher Protocol)

Chimera is quite small, compact, and efficient. Moreover, its interface is user friendly and fairly intuitive. (See the following figure.)

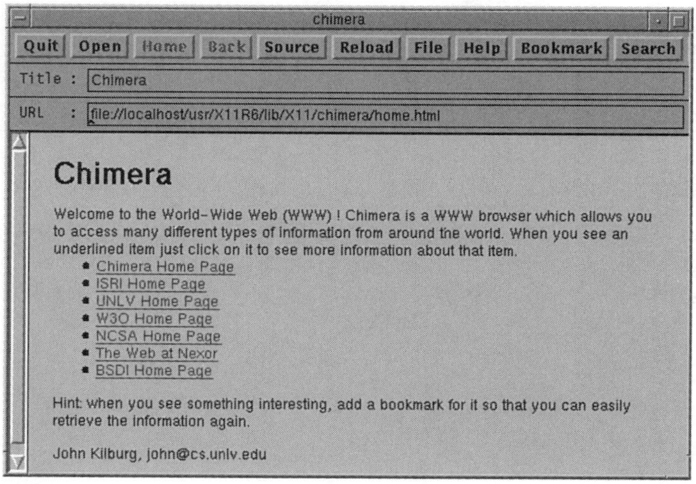

The Chimera interface.

In all, Chimera is an excellent Web browser for general use. However, it has two chief drawbacks:

➤ It comes only in source code form; therefore, you have to compile it.

➤ Chimera does not support tables.

Chimera is available at `http://www.unlv.edu/chimera/`.

The Least You Need to Know

Here's the least you need to know about UNIX Web browsers:

➤ To cruise the World Wide Web, you need a Web browser.

➤ Not all Web browsers support the latest Web technology.

➤ Your best choice is probably Netscape Communicator.

## Chapter 19

USENET News

In This Chapter

➤ What is USENET?

➤ Learning how to read USENET news

➤ A few good newsreaders

➤ Some words of caution

What Is USENET?

USENET stands for *user network*. To illustrate what USENET is and what it does, I need to reach back a few years. The story goes like this: In 1979, two universities in North Carolina tried an interesting experiment. They created a system vaguely similar to email, except that messages would be publicly available. In this respect, the system was a lot like a bulletin board. One person could post a message and many others would see it.

Eventually, additional functionality was incorporated into the system. Not only could others *see* the original post, they could also *reply* to it (and, in turn, others could reply to those replies). Thus, full-scale discussions developed. It was wonderful and all was well.

However, almost immediately after this new system was instituted, some controversy arose. You see, at the time, folks were only allowed to discuss serious and academic subjects. The gods of the USENET system frowned upon more frivolous discussions. This, of course, prompted a revolution.

To remedy this, USENET was restructured. (This period is actually known as the Great Renaming.) Forever after, USENET has been broken into groups. For example, a group named comp was created for discussion about computers. Again, everything was wonderful—computer users could have discussions, and all was well. (At least for a while.)

Eventually, however, even that wasn't enough. No sooner than the comp group was created, folks began to argue again. UNIX users didn't want to fraternize with Mac users who, in turn, hated Windows users. Therefore, the comp group was dissected into even more refined groups. If you wanted to discuss UNIX, you had to go to the group comp.UNIX.

This process of refining continued (and still continues today). In fact, once you get some experience with USENET, you won't be at all surprised to find groups with names such as this:

```
comp.UNIX.security.blue-cadillac.eye-patch.smoker.hack
```

This, of course, would be a group where UNIX security is discussed by administrators who drive blue Cadillacs, wear eye patches, and smoke three packs of cigarettes a day. (Things aren't quite that bad yet, but they're getting there.)

This refined naming scheme is called the *USENET hierarchy*. The USENET hierarchy currently houses 30,000+ groups. In these groups, folks discuss everything from gardening to ham radio. In this respect, USENET is a wonderful place to find people with interests similar to your own.

To read USENET news (the messages posted to USENET), you need a newsreader. That's what this chapter is all about: using newsreaders.

tin: **A Newsreader**

tin is a very popular text-only newsreader that's available on most UNIX systems. To start tin, enter the tin command plus the newsgroup you want to read (or at least a ballpark category, such as comp, for example):

> **tin comp**

tin will load and immediately ask you if you also want to read messages from some pretty lame groups (groups such as news.announce.newusers). Enter n (for no).

At this point, tin will retrieve all groups under the hierarchy you specified and their messages. tin will then display these groups in a scrollable list. (See the following figure.)

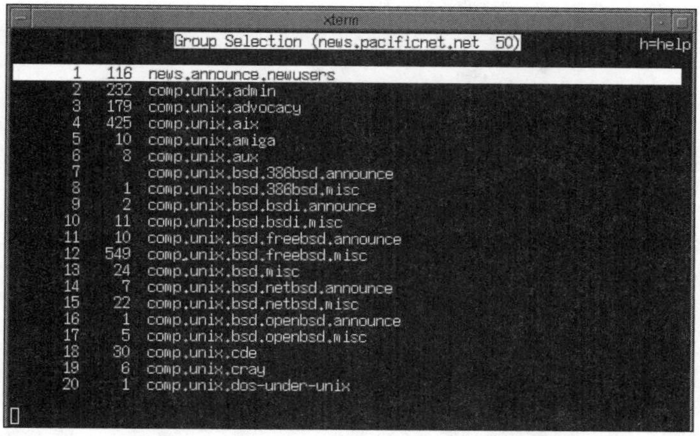

The tin *group selection screen.*

Using tin to Read Messages from a Particular Group

To read messages from any of the displayed groups, highlight one (using the arrow keys to navigate) and press Enter. In response, tin will retrieve all messages from that group and display them in a scrollable list. (See the following figure.)

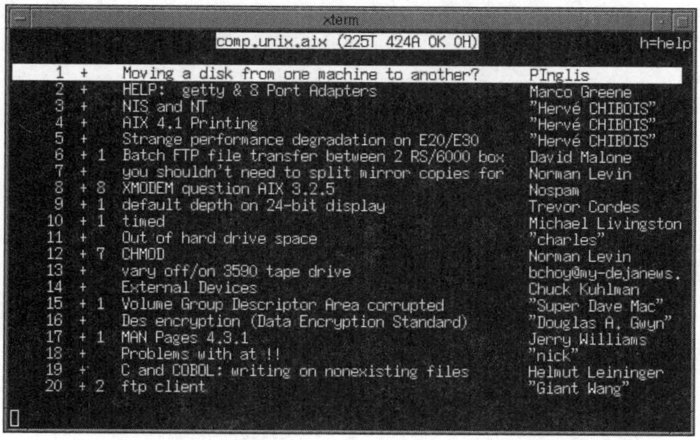

The tin *message selection screen.*

Finally, to see a particular message, highlight the subject line and press Enter. In response, tin will display the body text of the currently selected message. (See the following figure.)

Waiting for the News

Depending on your connection speed, downloading the newsgroup list can take quite some time (as little as one minute and as long as an hour). If you're using a standard PPP or dial-up account, you might want to do something else while you're waiting. (Play a game of golf, go have a beer, write your memoirs, and so on.)

The tin *message body text display screen.*

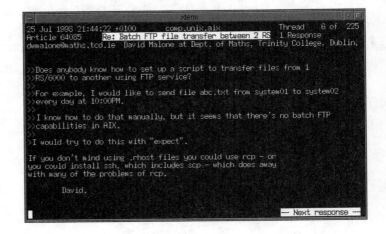

tin *Commands*

tin is almost exclusively controlled by keystroke commands. Table 19.1 describes the most critical commands and what they do.

Table 19.1.   Some important *tin* commands and what they do

tin **Command**	**Result**
#	In group mode, where # represents a number, tin goes to that particular group. For example, by entering the number 10, you're telling tin to go to group 10.
/ *pattern*	Use the / command to search forward in the current list.
? *pattern*	Use the ? command to search backward in the current list.
c	In group mode, c causes tin to display the next group.

tin **Command**	**Result**
Ctrl+**a**	In editing mode, this command positions the cursor at the beginning of the current line.
Ctrl+**b**	In editing mode, this command moves the cursor back one character.
Ctrl+**d**	In editing mode, this command deletes the currently highlighted character.
Ctrl+**e**	In editing mode, this command positions the cursor at the end of the current line.
Ctrl+**f**	In editing mode, this command moves the cursor forward one character.
Ctrl+**k**	In editing mode, this command deletes all text from the cursor to the end of the current line.
Ctrl+**k**	In group mode, this deletes the current group. Warning: Use this sparingly, because the group really gets deleted from your news configuration files. If you delete a group this way, you need to subscribe again to recover it.
Enter	In group mode, this summons messages from the currently selected group.
h	This summons the help screen.
q	This causes tin to exit. (q stands for *quit.*)
s	This subscribes you to the currently selected group.
S *pattern*	This subscribes you to any group that matches the specified *pattern*.
Tab	In group mode, this pulls up the next unread group.
u	This unsubscribes you from the current group.
U *pattern*	This unsubscribes you from any group matching the specified *pattern*.
w	This causes tin to enter edit mode. It allows you to post a message to the currently selected group.
Y	This gets any new messages that may have arrived while you were using tin.
Z	This undeletes groups you have inadvertently deleted.

tin is truly a very powerful newsreader. This table covers only a small fraction of the commands available. For more information, consult the tin man pages.

Using pine to Read News

In Chapter 17, "Email," I explain that pine can be used to read and send email. You'll be pleased to find out that you can also use pine to read USENET news. However, before you can use pine as a newsreader, you need to configure it for USENET. Let's start there.

Configuring pine *as Your Newsreader*

To configure pine as your newsreader, start it and choose Setup. (See the following figure.)

Use the arrow keys to navigate to the Setup option.

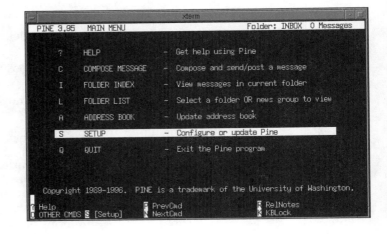

Once in setup mode, choose Config (enter the letter c on your keyboard). This will bring you to the pine Setup Configuration screen. (See the following figure.)

The pine Setup Configuration screen is where you set your options.

In your setup configuration, enter your news server's name into the nntp-server field. (See the following figure.)

Once you're sure your news server has been set, save your changes and restart pine. Congratulations! You're ready to connect to the USENET news network.

The nntp-server field

The nntp-server field is where you specify your news server.

```
xterm
  PINE 3.95   SETUP CONFIGURATION              Folder: INBOX  0 Messages

  personal-name         = Bwagner
  user-domain           = altavista.net
  smtp-server           = mail.pacificnet.net
  nntp-server           = news.pacificnet.net
  inbox-path            = <No Value Set: using "inbox">
  folder-collections    = <No Value Set: using "mail/[]">
  news-collections      = <No Value Set: using "*{news.pacificnet.net/nntp} []">
  incoming-archive-folders = <No Value Set>
  pruned-folders        = <No Value Set>
  default-fcc           = <No Value Set: using "sent-mail">
  default-saved-msg-folder = <No Value Set: using "saved-messages">
  postponed-folder      = <No Value Set: using "postponed-msgs">
  read-message-folder   = <No Value Set>
  signature-file        = <No Value Set: using ".signature">
  global-address-book   = <No Value Set>
  address-book          = <No Value Set: using ".addressbook">
  feature-list          =
              Set        Feature Name
              ---        ------------------------

  ? Help        E Exit Config  P Prev       PrevPage   A Add Value   Y prYnt
                C [Change Val] N Next    Spc NextPage   D Delete Val    WhereIs
```

Subscribing to Newsgroups

Your next step is to subscribe to some newsgroups. Before you can do this, however, you must force pine to collect all the available newsgroups. For this, restart pine and choose Select a Folder or Newsgroup to View. (See the following figure.)

What's NNTP?

NNTP is the *Network News Transfer Protocol,* the protocol by which USENET news messages are transported across the Internet. A NNTP server is any machine configured specifically to collect and distribute news. To learn more about NNTP, go to http://info.internet.isi.edu:80/in-notes/rfc/files/rfc977.txt.

This will bring you to the Folder List window. Here, under the News header, choose Select Here to See an Expanded List. (See the following figure.)

Now, you need to wait awhile. During this time, pine will collect all available newsgroups. (This will take from 2 to 30 minutes, depending on your connection speed.) Finally, pine will finish this task. When it does, you can subscribe to any newsgroup by issuing the a command plus the name of the group. Here's an example:

```
a comp.UNIX.aix
```

*Selecting the Select a
Folder of Newsgroup to
View option*

```
                                    xterm
  PINE 3.95     MAIN MENU                        Folder: INBOX   0 Messages

        ?     HELP              -  Get help using Pine

        C     COMPOSE MESSAGE   -  Compose and send/post a message

        I     FOLDER INDEX      -  View messages in current folder

        L     FOLDER LIST       -  Select a folder OR news group to view

        A     ADDRESS BOOK      -  Update address book

        S     SETUP             -  Configure or update Pine

        Q     QUIT              -  Exit the Pine program


        Copyright 1989-1996.  PINE is a trademark of the University of Washington.
  ? Help                          P PrevCmd                 R RelNotes
  O OTHER CMDS L [ListFldrs] N NextCmd                      K KBLock
```

*Opening an expanded list
of the news section.*

```
                                    xterm
  PINE 3.95     FOLDER LIST                      Folder: INBOX   0 Messages


  Folder-collection <mail/[]>  ** Default for Saves **                (Local)


                   [ Select Here to See Expanded List ]


  News-collection <News on news.pacificnet.net>                      (Remote)


                   [ Select Here to See Expanded List ]






                   [Now in collection <News on news.pacificnet.net>]
  ? Help       M Main Menu   P PrevFldr  - PrevPage     U UnSbscrbe  R Rename
  O OTHER CMDS V [Select]    N NextFldr  Spc NextPage   S Subscribe
```

In response, pine will retrieve the most recent messages from that group. During this
time, pine will notify you that it's collecting data. (See the following figure.)

*pine will collect all recent
messages in the specified
group.*

```
                                    xterm
  PINE 3.95     FOLDER LIST                      Folder: INBOX   0 Messages


  Folder-collection <mail/[]>  ** Default for Saves **                (Local)


                   [ Select Here to See Expanded List ]


  News-collection <News on news.pacificnet.net>                      (Remote)

  comp.unix.aix




                   [Now in collection <News on news.pacificnet.net>]
  ? Help       M Main Menu   P PrevFldr  - PrevPage     U UnSbscrbe  R Rename
  O OTHER CMDS V [ViewFldr]  N NextFldr  Spc NextPage   S Subscribe
```

Reading and Replying to Messages with pine

Once pine has collected recent messages in the specified group, these will be displayed in precisely the same manner that pine displays email messages. Each message's subject line will appear on the list. (See the following figure.)

```
┌─────────────────────────────xterm───────────────────────┐
│ PINE 3.95    FOLDER INDEX <News on news.pa> comp.unix.aix  Msg 1 of 419 │
│    1 Jul 26 Trevor Cordes        default depth on 24-bit display │
│    2 Jul 27 pcibrario@my-dejanews AIX filesystem and long filenames │
│    3 Jul 27 pcibrario@my-dejanews AIX filesystem and long filenames │
│    4 Jul 27 pcibrario@my-dejanews AIX filesystem and long filenames │
│    5 Jul 26 Frank da Cruz        Re: XMODEM question AIX 3.2.5 │
│    6 Jul 26 Nospam              Re: XMODEM question AIX 3.2.5 │
│    7 Jul 26 Michael Livingston  Re: timed │
│    8 Jul 26 Ross Vandegrift     Re: default depth on 24-bit display │
│    9 Jul 26 LAIX Software Consult Re: XMODEM question AIX 3.2.5 │
│   10 Jul 23 Hervé CHIBOIS       Re: AIX 4.1 Printing │
│   11 Jul 23 Hervé CHIBOIS       Re: Strange performance degradation on E20/ │
│   12 Jul 27 bchoy@my-dejanews.com Re: vary off/on 3590 tape drive │
│   13 Jul 27 bchoy@my-dejanews.com Re: Batch FTP file transfer between 2 RS/60 │
│   14 Jul 26 Chuck Kuhlman       Re: External Devices │
│   15 Jul 27 Andre Humphrey      Backup using sysback │
│   16 Jul 27 Douglas A. Gwyn     Re: Des encryption (Data Encryption Standar │
│   17 Jul 26 Super Dave Mac      Re: Volume Group Descriptor Area corrupted │
│   18 Jul 26 Jerry Williams      Re: MAN Pages 4.3.1 │
│   19 Jul 27 nick                Problems with at !! │
│          [News group "comp.unix.aix" opened with 419 messages] │
│ ? Help      M Main Menu  P PrevMsg   - PrevPage  D Delete    R Reply │
│ O OTHER CMDS V [ViewMsg] N NextMsg  Spc NextPage U Undelete  F Forward │
└──────────────────────────────────────────────────────────┘
```

The list of recent messages and their subject lines.

Once you find a subject line that interests you, highlight it and press Enter. In response, pine will retrieve the full body text of that message. (See the following figure.)

```
┌─────────────────────────────xterm───────────────────────┐
│ PINE 3.95    MESSAGE TEXT <News on news.> mp.unix.aix  Msg 19 of 419 51% │
│ Date: Mon, 27 Jul 1998 01:34:35 GMT │
│ From: bchoy@my-dejanews.com │
│ Newsgroups: comp.unix.aix │
│ Subject: Re: Batch FTP file transfer between 2 RS/6000 boxes │
│ │
│ Dear Can you not use the "cron" facilities in AIX, do  crontab -l to see what │
│ are the jobs being scheduled, simply add you job to the 'cron' table │
│ │
│ Best regards │
│ Brian │
│ │
│ In article <slrn6rjr7a.n2d.mansaxel@bartlet.df.lth.se>, │
│   mansaxel@bartlet.df.lth.se (Måns Nilsson) wrote: │
│ > In article <35B9DC4C.20CD414A@ron.com>, Tom Smith wrote: │
│ > >Does anybody know how to set up a script to transfer files from 1 │
│ > >RS/6000 to another using FTP service? │
│ > > │
│ > >For example, I would like to send file abc.txt from system01 to system02 │
│ ? Help      M Main Menu  P PrevMsg   - PrevPage  D Delete    R Reply │
│ O OTHER CMDS V ViewAttch N NextMsg  Spc NextPage U Undelete  F Forward │
└──────────────────────────────────────────────────────────┘
```

The full body text of the selected message.

At this point, you can perform several operations. These operations and the commands that perform them are summarized in Table 19.2.

Table 19.2.   Some `pine` "read messages" mode commands

`pine` Command	Result
?	`pine` displays help on reading and replying to messages.
d	`pine` marks the current message for deletion.
f	Use the f command when you want to forward the current message to a third party. When you enter the f command, `pine` puts you into edit mode. Here, you can append your commentary to the message. When you're done, press Ctrl+x+y. The original message and your comments will be forwarded to the specified party.
m	`pine` leaves the current message and returns to the main menu screen.
n	`pine` displays the next message.
o+g	Use this command when you want to go back to folder view.
o+q	Use this command when you want to quit from the read messages mode.
o+s	Use this command to save the current message. (`pine` will prompt you for a filename.)
o+y	Use this command when you want to print the current message.
p	`pine` displays the previous message.
-	`pine` goes to the previous page.
r	Use the r command to reply to messages. When you enter the r command, `pine` places you in edit mode. There, you simply type your reply and hit Ctrl+x+y.
spacebar	`pine` displays the next page of the current message.
u	`pine` undeletes the current message.
v	`pine` shows any attachments that were appended to the message.

`pine` is a very good newsreader, primarily because it presents USENET news in the same way it presents email. Therefore, if you're lucky enough to have `pine` on your system, you can use it as a total mail/news solution.

Using Netscape Communicator to Read News

If X is available on your system, you should use Netscape Communicator as a newsreader. Communicator has a built-in NNTP client with all the trimmings, and it's infinitely easier to use than `tin`, `trn`, or `pine`.

To start Communicator's newsreader, click the Message Center icon in the bottom-right corner of the screen. (See the following figure.)

The Message Center icon

The Message Center icon on Communicator's main screen.

This will open Message Center. Here, you'll see a folder named "news." (See the following figure.)

The Message Center news folder.

The News folder

If Communicator has already been configured for USENET news, you'll see another folder beneath news that bears the same name as your news server. (This name is typically the name of your provider, preceded by the word news, as in news.deltanet.com, news.pacificnet.net, news.netcom.com, and so on.) However, with all likelihood, Communicator has not yet been set up for USENET, so let's start there.

Setting Up Netscape Communicator for USENET

To set up Communicator for USENET, go to the main menu and choose File|New Discussion Server. This will bring up the New Discussion Groups Server dialog box. (See the following figure.)

Communicator's New Discussion Groups Server dialog box.

Once there, enter the name of your news server. (If you don't know your new server's name, ask your system administrator.) Once you enter your news server's name, click OK. At that point, Message Center will show the newly configured news server. (See the following figure.)

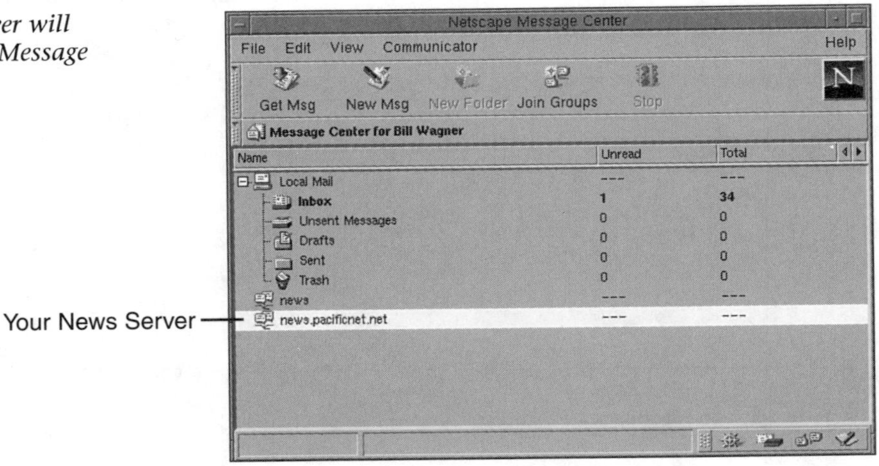

Your news server will appear on the Message Center list.

Your News Server

Next, go to the main menu and choose Subscribe. This will bring up Communicator's Subscribe to Discussion Groups window. (See the following figure.)

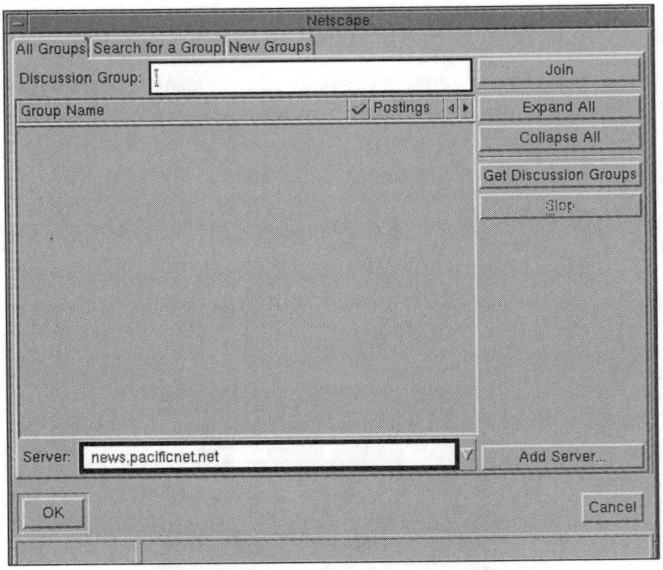

Communicator's Subscribe to Discussion Groups window.

This next step will take awhile, so you might want to catch up on your chores. Here's why: Communicator will retrieve all available USENET discussion groups. There are well over 30,000 in all, so the process can take some time. (Depending on your connection speed, this can take from 2 to 30 minutes.)

When Communicator is done gathering groups, you'll see the group list appear in the Subscribe to Discussion Groups Window. (See the following figure.)

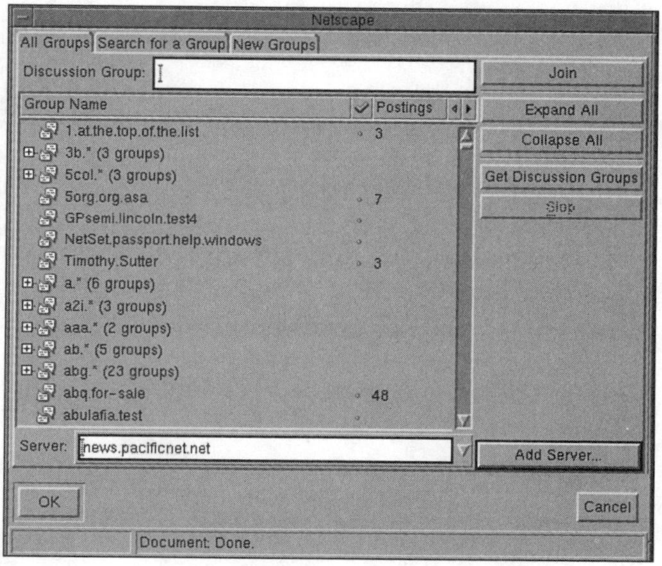

The group list appears in the Subscribe to Discussion Groups window.

Now, you can begin exploring USENET.

Subscribing to a USENET Group

Your first step is to subscribe to a group (or groups). To do so, you need to know at least part of the group's name. For example, suppose you're interested in UNIX. You could search for groups related to UNIX using Communicator's search function.

To do so, choose the Search for a Group tab on the Subscribe to Discussion Groups window. (See the following figure.)

Next, in the Search For field, enter a word or words that interest you (in this case, enter UNIX.) Communicator will search the 30,000 USENET groups for a match. The results are displayed in the bottom portion of the window. (See the following figure.)

Choosing the Search for a Group tab in the Subscribe to Discussion Groups window.

Search for a Group tab

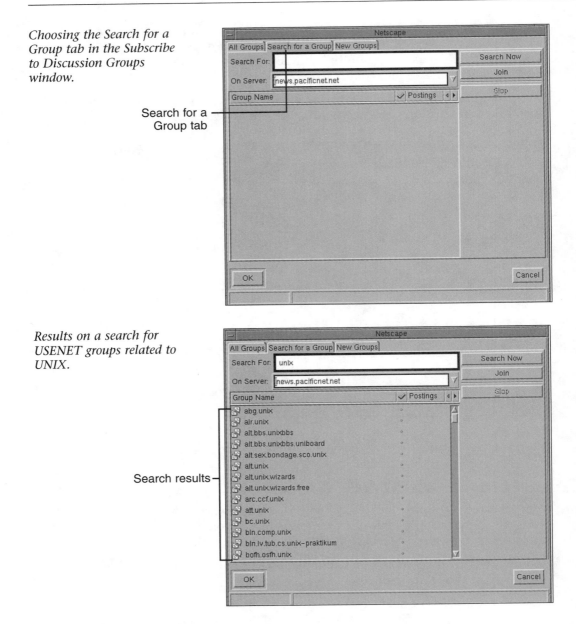

Results on a search for USENET groups related to UNIX.

Search results

To subscribe to a group, double-click it. At that point, you'll see a check mark beside the group. Now, choose OK. The Subscribe to Discussion Groups window will close. Now, if you look at your news server in the Message Center window, it has a plus sign next to it. Click the plus sign to open all newsgroups to which you're currently subscribed. In response, Communicator will retrieve the latest messages and report how many it found. (See the following figure.)

Communicator will indicate the number of new messages.

Viewing Messages from a USENET Group

To view the messages in any group, double-click the group's name in Message Center. In response, Communicator will open a new window. This window will contain all message subject headers and the body text of the first message. (See the following figure.)

The main newsreader window in Netscape Communicator.

To read the body text of any message, simply click its subject header. The body text will appear in the bottom frame of the window.

Replying to a Message

To reply to a message, choose the Reply button on the main menu bar. In response, Communicator will spawn a new Compose window. (See the following figure.)

The Compose window is for responding to a message.

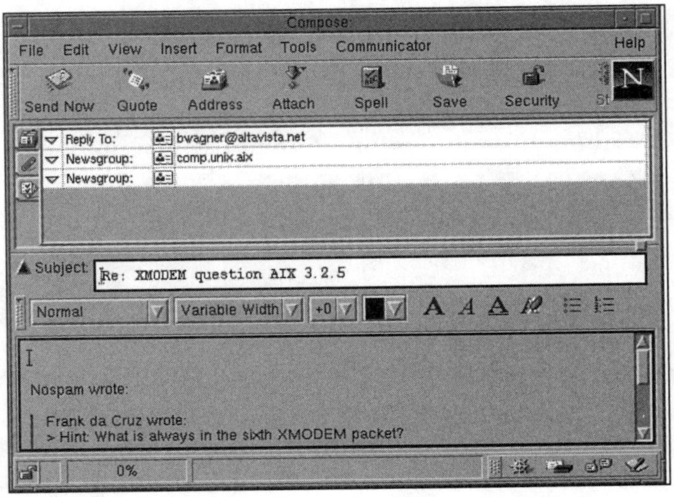

Type your response in this window. When you're done, choose Send. Voilà! Communicator will deliver your message immediately (or nearly immediately).

Get the Picture?

Netscape Communicator's newsreader makes reading and sending news as easy as reading and sending email. But that's not all. Netscape Communicator's newsreader also reads HTML and even can load images. Therefore, when folks send out fancy USENET news messages, you'll be able to see their handiwork. (Many newsreaders don't interpret HTML and cannot load graphics.)

Welcome to the Jungle: A USENET Primer

USENET, if nothing else, is uniquely American. As you'll see, it's one of the few places where folks actually speak their mind without hesitation. This has advantages and disadvantages.

Free speech is practiced in grand form on USENET. There are no police, there are no real rules, and USENET junkies take no prisoners. This means that you may often encounter people who express views radically different from your own. Moreover, they may express those views in a rather militant fashion.

These influences, however, are in the minority. Most USENET traffic is either focused (participants have serious, legitimate interests in the subject discussed) or fun (participants are just plain goofy). With all likelihood, you'll have a whale of a good time. However, here are some rules you should stick to:

➤ **Be courteous and civil**—Even if you're debating with someone, try to give them the benefit of the doubt. Also, if it's clear that you'll never agree, then agree to disagree and move on. (In other words, if your adversary's been a bone-head all his life, your posts are unlikely to change that fact.)

➤ **Stick to the group's subject**—If you're posting in a group that discusses love and romance, don't start discussions on military history. If you do, those romance lovers will probably clobber you.

➤ **Avoid advertising your business**—Unless the group invites commercial endorsements, refrain from posting promotional information about your business.

Do all USENET users follow these rules? No, not even close. However, the better half does, and that's what counts.

Also, you should carefully consider your words before you hurl them into the USENET cosmos. Remember that many thousands of people from hundreds of countries will see your post. If your words are inflammatory, you may receive hundreds of responses, and most of these will be negative.

The Least You Need to Know

USENET is a great place to get information on just about anything under the sun. To read the news, here's the least you need to know:

➤ Common UNIX newsreaders include `tin`, `trn`, and `pine`.

➤ Netscape Communicator has an excellent newsreader.

➤ USENET is a wacky place. Have fun there!

HOW WAS YOUR DAY?

## Chapter 20

Chatting

In This Chapter

➤ Types of chat systems

➤ Chatting one-on-one on your own machine or network

➤ Chatting with the world at large

➤ Some gentle words of caution

The USENET news network is great for bulletin board–type discussion, but it lacks a certain interactivity. Sometimes, you post a news message and folks don't answer it for hours or even days. Email is not much different. Therefore, when you're craving some interactive conversation, it's time to chat. That's what this chapter is all about.

What Is Chatting, Anyway?

Chatting is the process of holding a real-time conversation using your computer. Instead of actually speaking, however, you type out your sentences using the keyboard. Similarly, the person or persons you're chatting with respond by typing out their answers on their keyboard.

Chat systems differ in design. Some are truly real-time chat systems; therefore, you see the words appear as they are typed. (That is, you can see each letter appear one by one.) Other chat systems are almost in real-time, only displaying words after an entire sentence has been typed and transmitted. However, nearly all chat systems display words within seconds.

Chat System Types

Here are the three basic chat system types:

➤ **Localized chat systems**—Allow you to chat with anyone on the same network. These are typically used in corporate or academic environments.

➤ **Closed chat systems**—Allow you to chat with other authorized users. These chat systems deny access to outsiders.

➤ **Open chat systems**—Allow anyone from any host to participate.

In addition, chat systems can be either "one on one" (you can only chat with one other person) or multiphased (you can chat with dozens or even hundreds of other folks simultaneously).

Twenty-first Century Talks

Interestingly, the more antiquated chat networks and systems are now being abandoned by all but the most zealous supporters. Nowadays, it's possible to funnel chat traffic through a Web page using advanced technologies such as Java. Therefore, older chat systems will probably fade into obscurity in the next few years.

Finally, there are two classes of chat system: proprietary and nonproprietary. In *proprietary* chat systems, some special software (usually a commercial chat client or plug-in) is required. In *nonproprietary* chat systems, any garden-variety chat client will do.

In this chapter, I discuss mainly one-on-one and multiphased chats on both local and global networks.

Chatting One on One with `talk`

Not surprisingly, UNIX has a built-in one-on-one chat system. This system is called `talk`. To talk with another user on your machine, issue the `talk` command plus the desired username, like this:

```
talk bwagner
```

In response, UNIX will notify you that it's paging the user:

```
[Waiting for your party to respond]-------------------------------
```

Meanwhile, the desired user's terminal will display a message similar to this:

```
Message from Talk_Daemon@207.171.0.111 at 19:06 ...
talk: connection requested by chatme@207.171.0.111.
talk: respond with:  talk chatme@207.171.0.111
```

This message tells the user who it is who wants to talk, where this person is, and what command must be entered to initiate a chat session. In this case, based on the example, you would type the following command:

```
talk chatme@207.171.0.111
```

This connects you with chatme. At this point, your screen splits in half with a line down the middle. Words typed by you appear above the line; words typed by your chatting partner appear below it. In this split screen, words are transmitted in real-time, letter by letter.

talk is a pretty fast and efficient way to chat. On local area networks (where machines are connected via Ethernet), the lag time is so negligible that it's actually unnoticeable. This is not true over standard dial-up or PPP connections. (Of course, much depends on other traffic being sent down the wire. Given a quiet night where you and your chatting partner are the only folks using the network, talk can be pretty fast.)

Like most UNIX network utilities, talk works not just locally but over the Internet. Therefore, you can talk with users located elsewhere in the world. To do so, issue the talk command plus the full email address of the person you want to chat with, like this:

talk bwagner@pacificnet.net

On the end, the remote user responds with a talk acknowledgement and, for all purposes, the talk session works precisely as it would if he or she were on your network.

Internet Relay Chat: The Internet's Wild West

Probably the most popular chatting system of all is *Internet Relay Chat* or *IRC*. Developed in Finland in the late 1980s, IRC is the Internet's last frontier. IRC is a lawless space, where hundreds of thousands of people chat every day, unseen and unnoticed by the rest of the world.

Technically, IRC is an extension of the original talk service. However, several major differences exist, including the following:

➤ IRC allows multiple users to chat

➤ IRC allows users to chat privately if they wish

➤ IRC allows users to transfer files

➤ IRC uses a system of channels or groups

This last fact (the use of channels or groups) is what makes IRC truly unique. Here's how it works: In Chapter 19, "USENET News," I explained that newsgroups were broken down into specialized areas of interest. For example, folks who want to discuss UNIX would naturally gravitate to comp.unix.

Similarly, IRC segregates users by their interests using a system called *channels*. Each channel has a permanent name (for example, #unix) that reflects the group's topic of discussion. Such channels are like virtual rooms, separate and distinct from other channels.

Because IRC channels transmit discussions in real-time (and because those discussions are largely untraceable), IRC is often used for very curious and offbeat purposes. Typically examples include the following:

➤ Citizens of despotic states have used IRC to anonymously report news of political upheavals. (For example, reports on political instability in Russia, when a coup was apparently underway.)

➤ American military families received status reports on (and communicated with) their loved ones in Operation Desert Storm.

➤ Crackers and software pirates use IRC to traffic illegal software and discuss intrusion techniques.

➤ Political dissidents and (according to some intelligence analysts) even terrorist groups use IRC to anonymously communicate.

In all, these things sound pretty way out, but they've happened. So, what's the chance of you encountering a terrorist in IRC? Almost nil, and here's why: Folks with unlawful intent don't use standard, established chat channels. Instead, they create their own. (We'll get to that in a minute.) Therefore, their presence is hardly ever felt on IRC at large.

Instead, most folks use IRC just to shoot the breeze, and they typically do this in established chat channels. In fact, more than 30,000 IRC channels exist on a permanent basis. The greater number focus on perfectly "normal" subjects.

Equally, however, there are more challenging channels, where folks express some rather unpopular views. When you first use IRC, you may be shocked. As I indicated earlier, there are no real rules. In this respect, IRC is the ultimate free speech frontier.

Using IRC

Many different IRC clients are available for UNIX. However, the greater number are for Linux. These range from primitive (regular command-line IRC), to sophisticated (ksirc, a GUI-based client), to the eclectic (a Perl-based IRC client).

In the end, though, the most popular and generic IRC client is still ircII, a command-line IRC client that runs on almost any UNIX system. Because ircII is so widespread, I'll concentrate on it here.

To start ircII, issue the following command:

```
irc
```

Immediately, you'll know if IRC is available on your system. (Some system administrators refuse to install IRC because it poses security and administrative risks. Many would rather not have the hassle.)

If IRC is available, it will immediately attempt to connect to an IRC server. Once the connection is made, the IRC server will report some interesting statistics. (See the following figure.)

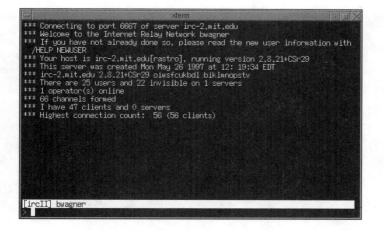

IRC clients first try to connect to well-know IRC servers.

Next, you'll want to join a channel. Do this by issuing the /join command plus the channel you want to join, like this:

    /join #unix

In response, the server will connect you to the requested channel (that is, if that channel is available). Once the server binds you to the specified channel, it will report the names of all users currently connected. (See the following figure.)

```
                              xterm
*** Connecting to port 6667 of server irc-2.mit.edu
*** Welcome to the Internet Relay Network bwagner
*** If you have not already done so, please read the new user information with
    /HELP NEWUSER
*** Your host is irc-2.mit.edu[rastro], running version 2.8.21+CSr29
*** This server was created Mon May 26 1997 at 12: 19:34 EDT
*** irc-2.mit.edu 2.8.21+CSr29 oiwsfcukbdl biklmnopstv
*** There are 25 users and 22 invisible on 1 servers
*** 1 operator(s) online
*** 66 channels formed
*** I have 47 clients and 0 servers
*** Highest connection count: 56 (56 clients)
*** bwagner (~bwagner@207.171.10.77) has joined channel #unix
*** Users on #unix: @bwagner




[ircII] @bwagner on #unix
#unix>
```

The server will log you into a channel and report who's there.

Once you're in your desired channel, you'll want to get a little help on the commands available. To do so, issue the /help command, like this:

/**help**

In response, the IRC server will forward a list of commonly used commands. (See the following figure.)

The server will display a long list of help commands.

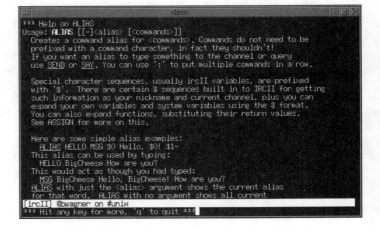

To find out what any particular command does, type the command in the status bar area. In response, the server will display the help file associated with that command. (See the following figure.)

While in an IRC channel, you can transmit a message to other channel members simply by typing a message in the status bar area and hitting Enter.

The server displays help for the specified command.

IRC Commands

IRC supports an obscene number of commands. Table 20.1 summarizes only the most important ones.

Table 20.1. Some important IRC commands

IRC Command	Purpose
/bye	Use the /bye command to exit IRC. (This is functionally equivalent to /quit.)
/clear	Use the /clear command to clear your screen. This is useful when a lot of residual text is onscreen (or when dozens of messages from different folks make it difficult to assimilate the discussion).
/help	Use the /help command to get a list of commands currently available. (This doesn't always give you the full list of IRC commands. Instead, it may often give you a context-based list, depending on what mode you're currently in.)
/ignore [user]	The /ignore command is the bozo or knucklehead option. Use this if you're being harassed by some bozo on the network. To use the /ignore command, issue the /ignore command plus the nickname of the offending party, like this: /ignore joe-stalker.
/invite [user]	Use the /invite command when you want to invite a user to engage in a private conversation. To do so, issue the /invite command plus the name of the user you want to converse with, like this: /invite bwagner.
/join [channel]	Use the /join command to join a particular chat channel. For example, to join #unix, issue the following command: /join #unix.
/list	Use the /list command to list all available chat channels. (Note that on many systems, this will only list those available locally. Only on large systems— notably university IRC servers—will this list truly all IRC channels available.) Typically, the server will list the channels, followed by their discussion topics.
/msg [user] [message]	Use the /msg command to send private messages to a particular user. (Private messages are only viewable by the specified recipient.) For example, suppose you wanted to tell user1 that user2 was a knucklehead. You would issue this command: /msg user1 User2 is a real knucklehead, don't you think?

continues

Table 20.1. Some important IRC commands Continued

IRC Command	Purpose
/nick [nickname]	Use the /nick command to set or change your nickname. (IRC allows you to use an alias or nickname. This is roughly equivalent to AOL's screen name system.) To set or change your nickname to unix-wizard, issue the following command: **/nick unix-wizard.**
/query [nickname]	Use the /query command to invite another user to engage in private conversation, like this: **/query bwagner.**
/who	Use the /who command to identify all users currently available for chat, like this: **/who.**
/whois [nickname]	Use the /whois command to ascertain the real email address and/or host origin of the specified user, like this: **/whois bwagner.**

Having a Friendly (or Even Not-So-Friendly) Chat

After using IRC awhile, you'll encounter many odd nuances and tools. For example, you'll probably learn about tools such as *scripts* and *bots*. These are automated agents that perform their specified tasks without human intervention (such as knocking everyone out of a chat channel). Although these tools seem cool, try to avoid using them. If you don't, you may find yourself banned from many chat servers. Before you do anything, check the rules of your chat server. Most strictly prohibit bots and scripts.

The Rigors of Chatting

Chatting on IRC can be great fun. However, I thought it wise to offer a few words of caution.

Like any portion of the Internet, Internet Relay Chat is practically boundless. You can chat with an unlimited number of users for an unlimited period of time. In fact, if you woke up at 2:30 a.m. and went looking for chat partners, you'd have no trouble finding one. After all, the Internet is global. You might find yourself chatting with someone in China, Russia, South Africa, or New Zealand. That's the beauty of the Net.

Unfortunately, however, that's also the danger in it. IRC can be extremely addicting. Folks have been fired from their jobs for excessive IRC use, and marriages have even been broken up by excessive IRC use. Therefore, please heed these words of caution: Chat in moderation. If you're chatting more than a couple hours a day, you probably need to slack off.

The Least You Need to Know

To chat with your co-workers, friends, and just about anyone else, here's the least you need to know:

➤ To chat one on one with someone on your own machine and network, use the `talk` command, like this: **`talk bwagner`**.

➤ To chat one on one with someone on a different network, issue the `talk` command plus the user's email address, like this: **`talk bwagner@pacificnet.net`**.

➤ To chat with the entire world (or at least those currently chatting) use IRC.

➤ Chat in moderation.

277

## Chapter 21

Other Network Services

In This Chapter

➤ Learn how to transfer files

➤ Learn about remote terminal sessions

The last few chapters focused on human communication over the Internet (including email, USENET, and so forth). These tools are great for socializing or even conducting brief business communication. However, many other UNIX services exist that can help you perform remote administration tasks and simple file transfers. That's what this chapter is all about.

Say It with Files: File Transfer Protocol

Using the File Transfer Protocol (FTP) is the chief way to move files from one host to another. (Other methods exist, but none are as fast or easy.) With FTP, three steps are involved in transferring a file:

➤ Connecting to the remote machine

➤ Logging in

➤ Transferring the file

Let's run through each step now.

Making the Connection

To begin a command-line FTP session, issue the `ftp` command plus the address of the host you're trying to reach. (See the following figure.)

Starting a command-line FTP session to sunsite.unc.edu.

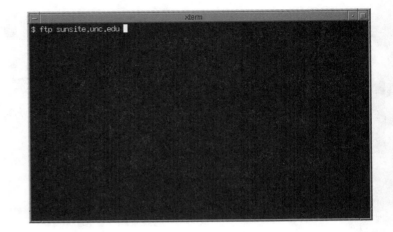

Depending on your connection speed, you may have to wait several seconds. Eventually, however, your machine will connect to the remote host. At that time, you'll receive a message similar to this one:

```
Connected to sunsite.unc.edu
```

Additionally, the remote host may send a greeting message. This message sometimes contains information on new files available for download or times when the server is scheduled for maintenance. For example, `sunsite.unc.edu` (a popular spot for down-loading UNIX freeware) uses this login message to report new directories as well as a contact email address so you can send suggestions for improving the FTP service. (See the following figure.)

The FTP greeting at sunsite.unc.edu.

```
$ ftp sunsite.unc.edu
Connected to sunsite.unc.edu.
220-                    Welcome to the SunSITE USA ftp archives!
220-
220-You can access this archive via http with the same URL.
220-
220-example:    ftp://sunsite.unc.edu/pub/Linux/ becomes
220-            http://sunsite.unc.edu/pub/Linux/
220-
220-For more information about services offered by SunSITE,
220-go to http://sunsite.unc.edu.
220-
220-WE'RE BACK TO USING WUFTPD.
220-You can still get tarred directories if you issue the following command:
220-    get dirname.tar
220-You can also get gzipped or compressed tarred directories by following
220-the .tar with .gz or .Z, respectively.
220-
220-Have any suggestions or questions? Email ftpkeeper@sunsite.unc.edu.
220-
220 helios.oit.unc.edu FTP server (Version wu-2.4.2-academ[BETA-13](6) Thu Jul 1
7 16:22:52 EDT 1997) ready.
Name (sunsite.unc.edu:root):
```

Logging In

Once connected, your next step is to log in. At that time, the remote host will request your username. (See the following figure.)

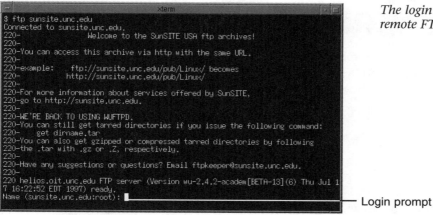

```
$ ftp sunsite.unc.edu
Connected to sunsite.unc.edu.
220-            Welcome to the SunSITE USA ftp archives!
220-
220-You can access this archive via http with the same URL.
220-
220-example:    ftp://sunsite.unc.edu/pub/Linux/ becomes
220-            http://sunsite.unc.edu/pub/Linux/
220-
220-For more information about services offered by SunSITE,
220-go to http://sunsite.unc.edu.
220-
220-WE'RE BACK TO USING WUFTPD.
220-You can still get tarred directories if you issue the following command:
220-     get dirname.tar
220-You can also get gzipped or compressed tarred directories by following
220-the .tar with .gz or .Z, respectively.
220-
220-Have any suggestions or questions? Email ftpkeeper@sunsite.unc.edu.
220-
220 helios.oit.unc.edu FTP server (Version wu-2.4.2-academ[BETA-13](6) Thu Jul 1
7 16:22:52 EDT 1997) ready.
Name (sunsite.unc.edu:root):
```

The login prompt on a remote FTP server.

— Login prompt

Depending on the type of remote server, you can log in using various methods. Here are two types of remote FTP servers:

➤ **Servers on which you have an account**—These are machines where the system administrator has assigned you an account. You, therefore, have a username, a password, and a home directory.

➤ **Servers that offer anonymous FTP access**—These are machines all over the world that allow anyone to access their software archives. These are called *anonymous FTP servers*, because they make no attempt to authenticate your identity.

Let's go through the login procedure for each.

Logging into a Server Where You Have an Account

If you have an account on the remote server, take these steps:

1. At the Name: prompt, enter your username.
2. At the Password: prompt, enter your password. (Your password will not be echoed to the screen.)

Logging into an Anonymous FTP Server

To log in to an anonymous FTP server, take these steps:

1. At the Name: prompt, type anonymous and press Enter.
2. At the Password: prompt, enter your email address. (This will not be echoed to the screen.)

281

I'm In!

The remote server will notify you when you've officially been logged in. Typically, it will display a message similar to this one:

```
230 Guest login ok, access restrictions apply.
Remote system type is UNIX.
Using binary mode to transfer files.
```

At this point, you can reassume control of the session. The ftp > prompt becomes available and you can begin navigating the FTP site.

You're Being Watched!

Just a short, cautionary note: Many FTP servers log your activity. (Some announce this when you first log in.) There are several reasons for this practice. For example, the site's system administrator may be trying to gather access statistics. More likely, however, it's a security precaution. Either way, you shouldn't feel uncomfortable about it. These days, logging is a pretty standard procedure.

To navigate a remote FTP site, you can use the same commands you use to navigate your own UNIX system. For example, when you first log in, you want to know what files and directories are available. Therefore, you begin by issuing the command ls, like this:

```
ls
```

In response, the remote server will display a directory listing. (See the following figure.)

Similarly, to change from directory to directory on a remote FTP server, use the cd command, like this:

```
cd security
```

This command changes the current directory to security. At this point, the remote FTP server will print a message indicating that the directory has been successfully changed:

```
250 CWD command successful
```

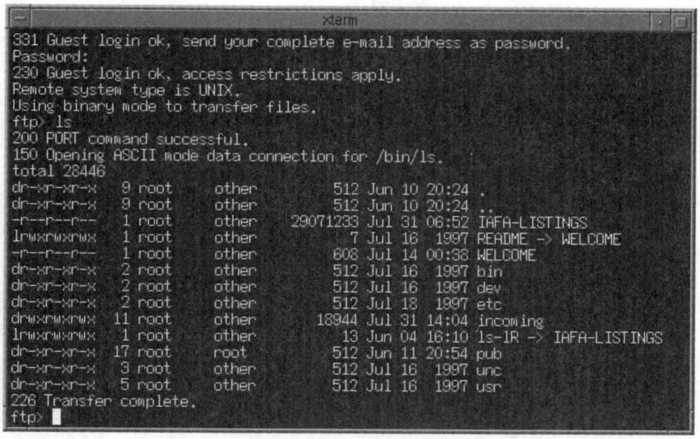

A typical directory listing on a remote FTP server.

To list the contents of the new directory, again, use ls. To view what the entire operation looks like, see the following figure.

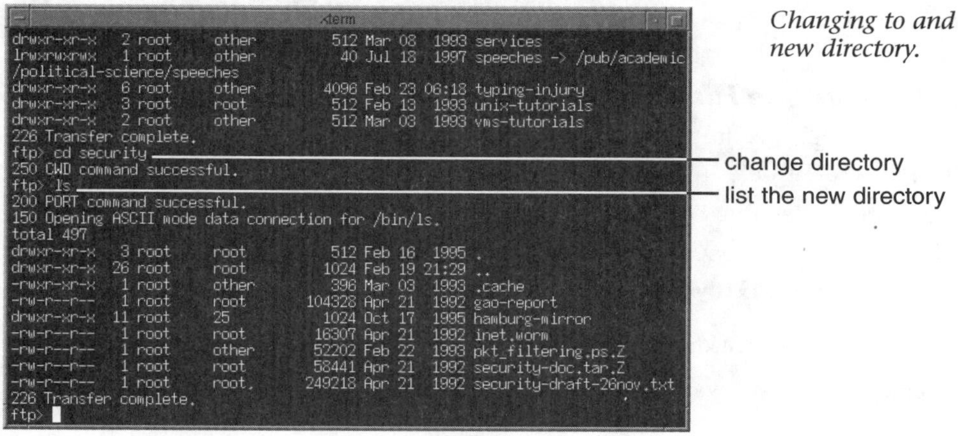

Changing to and listing a new directory.

— change directory
— list the new directory

Transferring Files

When programmers first created FTP, they wanted to make the file transfer process a simple task. Therefore, the commands to transfer files have very primitive names, such as get and put.

Let's briefly discuss those now.

Downloading Files: The get Command

To download a file, use the get command plus the name of the file you want to download, like this:

```
get inet.worm
```

This command tells `ftp` to get the file `inet.worm`. (This is a text file that describes the Internet Worm incident of November, 1988). In response, the remote server (in this case, `sunsite.unc.edu`) transfers the file. (See the following figure.)

The file is transferred to the local machine.

```
250 CWD command successful.
ftp> ls
200 PORT command successful.
150 Opening ASCII mode data connection for /bin/ls.
total 497
drwxr-xr-x   3 root     root          512 Feb 16  1995 .
drwxr-xr-x  26 root     root         1024 Feb 19 21:29 ..
-rwxr-xr-x   1 root     other         396 Mar 03  1993 .cache
-rw-r--r--   1 root     root       104328 Apr 21  1992 gao-report
drwxr-xr-x  11 root     25           1024 Oct 17  1995 hamburg-mirror
-rw-r--r--   1 root     root        16307 Apr 21  1992 inet.worm
-rw-r--r--   1 root     other       52202 Feb 22  1993 pkt_filtering.ps.Z
-rw-r--r--   1 root     root        58441 Apr 21  1992 security-doc.tar.Z
-rw-r--r--   1 root     root       249218 Apr 21  1992 security-draft-26nov.txt
226 Transfer complete.
ftp> ascii
200 Type set to A.
ftp> get inet.worm
local: inet.worm remote: inet.worm
200 PORT command successful.
150 Opening ASCII mode data connection for inet.worm (16307 bytes).
226 Transfer complete.
16629 bytes received in 6.68 secs (2.4 Kbytes/sec)
ftp> []
```

Getting Multiple Files: The `mget` Command

The `get` command is quite suitable for retrieving a single file. However, if you're downloading multiple files, you should use the `mget` command instead.

`mget` expects a filename list. (This is a space-delimited list of all files you want to download.) In this list, you can specify exact filenames, like this:

```
mget myfile.txt yourfile.txt
```

Or, you can use wildcards, like this:

```
mget *.txt
```

Uploading Files: The `put` Command

To upload a file, use the `put` command plus the name of the file you want to upload, like this:

```
put inet.worm
```

In response, `ftp` will transfer the local file to the remote server.

About Transfer Modes

Finally, prior to transferring files, you should check the transfer mode. The *transfer mode* controls the way the data is written during transfer. You'll use one of two modes when transferring files:

➤ **ASCII (American Standard Code for Information Interchange) mode**—This mode is suitable for plain-text files (including HTML files).

➤ **Binary mode**—This mode is for files that contain data (such as graphics files or compressed programs).

You need to set the proper mode prior to transfer. If you don't, you may experience unexpected results later. For example, if you transfer a shell script or Perl script in binary mode, it may not work correctly when executed. Similarly, if you transfer a program file in ASCII mode, it may later fail when executed.

Most UNIX FTP servers are set to ASCII transfer mode by default. However, to interactively set the transfer mode to ASCII, enter the following command at the `ftp` prompt:

```
ascii
```

Conversely, to set the transfer mode to binary, enter the following command at the `ftp` prompt:

```
bin
```

Spy ala Mode

You can discover your current transfer mode (and much more) by issuing the `status` command. Here's some sample `status` output (note the bolded `Mode:` section):

```
Connected to 207.171.0.111.
No proxy connection.
Mode: stream; Type: ascii; Form: non-print; Structure: file
Verbose: on; Bell: off; Prompting: on; Globbing: on
Store unique: off; Receive unique: off
Case: off; CR stripping: on
Ntrans: off
Nmap: off
Hash mark printing: off; Use of PORT cmds: on
```

FTP Interactive Commands

While using FTP, you have access to a wide range of commands. You can use these commands to manage your session, move files, create directories, and many other tasks. Table 21.1 summarizes the FTP commands you're most likely to use.

Table 21.1.   Selected FTP commands

FTP Command	Result
!	Use the ! command to temporarily return to the shell on your local machine. (You'll use this command a lot when transferring files to remote servers. For example, you may start ftp and then forget the exact name of the file you wanted to transfer. To find out, use the ! command to exit to the shell and pull a ls directory listing.)
? *command*	The remote server will display a brief help description for the command you've specified. For example, to get help on the command send, issue the command ? send.
?	The remote server will display all commands currently available to you.
close	Use the close command to end your ftp session. (This command is synonymous with the exit and bye commands. It causes your machine to disconnect from the remote server.)
delete *file*	Use the delete command to delete a remote file. (This will only work if you have the necessary privileges to do so. Only privileged users can delete files on remote servers.)
help *command*	The remote server will display a brief help description for the command you specified. (This is equivalent to the ? command.)
mkdir *directory*	Use the mkdir command to create a directory on the remote server.
rename *file*	Use the rename command to rename a file on the remote server.
status	Use the status command to view the current session's environment parameters. For example, a status report will tell you all about your current transfer mode, whether interactive prompting is on, and so forth.

FTP'ing in the Large

Command-line FTP is a quick and painless way to move files across the Internet. However, if you're moving many files located in many different directories, command-line FTP can be cumbersome. For such labor-intensive file transfers, you'll probably want an industrial-strength solution. For this, two very good graphical FTP clients for UNIX are available:

➤ Xdir

➤ Ftptool

Briefly, let's have a look at these programs.

Xdir

Xdir (more commonly known as *LLNL Xdir*) is one of the most useful tools ever created for UNIX. Written by Neale Smith at Lawrence Livermore Laboratories, Xdir can best be described as a networked file manager.

When you first start the program, Xdir illustrates the contents of your disk drive in a comfortable, intuitive interface. (See the following figure.)

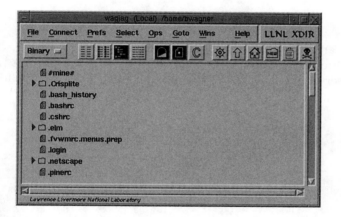

The Xdir opening screen displays your files and directories.

From the Xdir opening screen, you can view, move, delete, rename, list, and copy files. However, the program does much more than this.

To connect to a remote host, choose the Connect option on the main menu bar. This will pull down a connection menu. (See the following figure.)

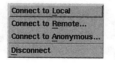

The menu for connecting.

Let's stick with the example of connecting to an anonymous FTP server (in this case, sunsite.unc.edu). To do so, choose the Connect to Anonymous option. In response, Xdir will display a screen where you can enter the targeted host, your username, and your password. (See the following figure.)

The Connect to
Anonymous screen.

Here, you enter the necessary values. What happens next is very cool. Once Xdir connects and gathers initial directory information, it displays a new window. In this window, files on the remote server are displayed as though they were local. (See the following figure.)

The remote server's files
are displayed in a sepa-
rate window.

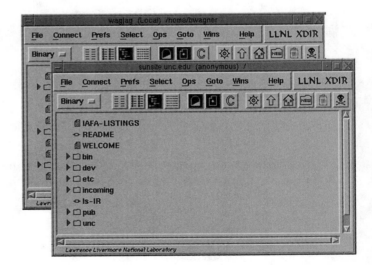

To move a file from the remote host to your own, simply highlight it with your mouse and drag it to your local window. (To move multiple files, select the desired files first and then drag the entire block over.)

Xdir runs on a wide range of UNIX systems, including the following:

- ➤ AIX 3.2.5 and 4.1.2
- ➤ Convex OS 10.1
- ➤ Digital UNIX V4.0
- ➤ DomainOS 10.4
- ➤ FreeBSD
- ➤ HP-UX A.09.01 and 10.10
- ➤ IRIX 5.3 and 6.2
- ➤ Linux
- ➤ MachTen
- ➤ MkLinux
- ➤ Solaris 2.3 (Sun and Meiko)
- ➤ Sun OS 4.1.3
- ➤ Sunsoft Interactive UNIX 4.0
- ➤ ULTRIX V4.3
- ➤ UNICOS 7.0.6.2 and 9.0.2.4
- ➤ UNIXWare

Additionally, even though Xdir's interface was based on Motif, many binaries are available that do not require Motif; therefore, almost anyone can use Xdir.

Xdir is an essential tool if you're doing many file transfers. To obtain Xdir, go to the Xdir home page on the WWW, located at `http://www.llnl.gov/ia/xdir.html`.

Ftptool

Still another excellent graphical tool for FTP transfers is Ftptool. Although Ftptool does not offer the file management capabilities of Xdir, its fast, efficient, and extremely easy to use.

To start the program, issue the `ftptool` command from a shell prompt. This will load Ftptool's main screen. (See the following figure.)

To connect to a remote server, choose the Connect option on the menu bar. In response, Ftptool will display the Host Information window. (See the following figure.)

In this window, enter the target host, your username, and your password. Finally, when you're sure all this information is correct, choose Connect. After several seconds, Ftptool will display the opening directory of the remote host. (See the following figure.)

The Ftptool main screen.

The Ftptool Host Information window.

The remote server's opening directory.

Here, you must take two steps to transfer a file:

➤ Highlight the file

➤ Choose the Copy to Local option

Highlighting files is easy; simply click your mouse once over the filename. Ftptool will highlight the file with a shaded bar. (See the following figure.)

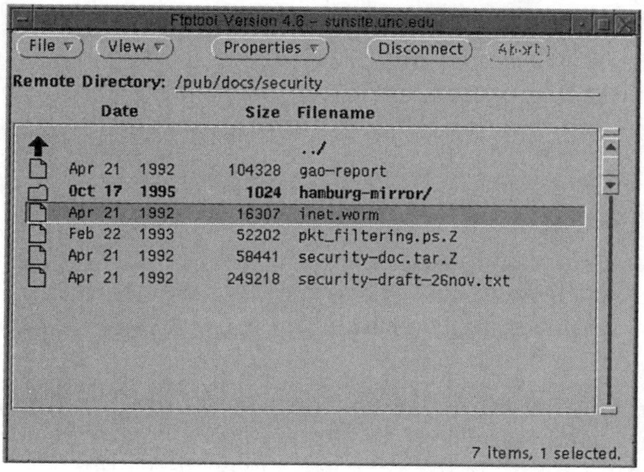

Ftptool highlights selected files with a shaded bar.

Finally, to transfer the file, right-click it. In response, Ftptool will display the Remote File List menu. (See the following figure.)

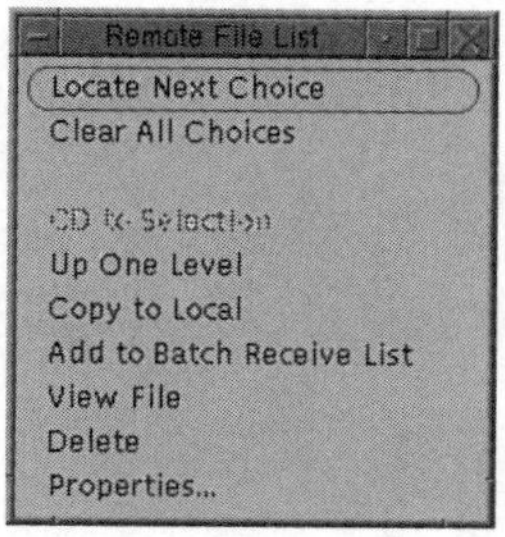

Ftptool's Remote File List menu.

To move the file, choose the Copy to Local option. That's it! Ftptool will transfer the specified file.

Ftptool is available for several UNIX flavors, including the following:

➤ For SunOS and Solaris, you can get Ftptool at
http://sunsite.unc.edu/pub/solaris/freeware/ftptool-4.6.gz.

➤ For Linux, you can get Ftptool at
ftp://ftp.x.org/contrib/utilities/Ftptool4.6.tar.gz.

➤ For FreeBSD and BSD variants, you can get Ftptool at `ftp://unix.hensa.ac.uk/mirrors/FreeBSD/packages-current/net/ftptool-4.6.tgz`.

Conclusion on File Transfer

The File Transfer Protocol can be used in several ways. Certainly, if you're transferring just one file, it's silly to load X. Therefore, for quick, simple transfers, command-line FTP is fine. On the other hand, if you need to transfer many files, you should probably use a graphical FTP tool.

However, what if you don't need to transfer files? Instead, suppose you want to execute some commands on a remote host. For this, you need `telnet`, `rlogin`, or `rsh`.

`telnet`: A Remote Login Program

If you do Web design, system administration, or networking with UNIX, sooner or later you'll end up using `telnet`, a remote networking tool. Through `telnet`, you can work on a machine in Tokyo as though that machine was located in your home or office.

`telnet` is used not only to provide remote access to shell accounts but also to provide interactive gateways to online databases. Electronic library catalogs provide a good example. Using `telnet`, you can search library catalogs all over the world.

To start a `telnet` session, issue the `telnet` command plus the address of the desired remote host. (See the following figure.)

Initiating a `telnet` session.

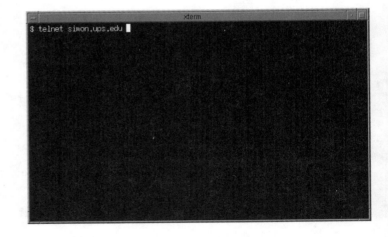

`telnet` will notify you when the connection has been made. At that time, the remote server will ask you to log in. (See the following figure.)

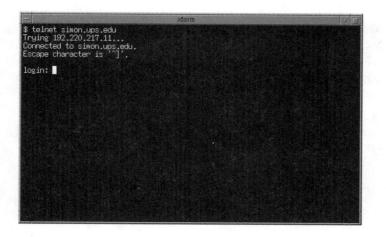

The remote host login screen.

After you enter your login name and password, you'll be dropped into a UNIX shell. From then on, you can operate the remote system as though it were local.

Terminal Ills

If you use `telnet` to access a remote server and find that your screen displays text in odd positions, the problem could be the terminal emulation. What's terminal emulation? Well, over the years, terminal manufacturers have created a wide range of terminals for accessing mainframes and UNIX systems. Unfortunately, manufacturers often develop their own specifications for how text is displayed. Therefore, some terminals display more columns and rows than others do.

Occasionally, you'll encounter remote systems that use a different terminal emulation than your own. Whenever you encounter this problem, a cure-all solution can be used: Set the terminal emulation to VT100. In sh-like shells, this can be done with the following command: **TERM=vt100**. In csh-like shells, issue this command: **set TERM=vt100**. Then, clear the screen and wait. Within seconds, the text should be readable again. To find out all the terminal types supported by the remote host, look at `/etc/termcap` on that machine.

Automating Remote Logins: The rlogin Command

rlogin is very much like telnet. In fact, once you log in using rlogin, things will work exactly as if you were using telnet. The difference is that rlogin is designed to automate logins between machines that trust one another. For example, suppose your network had three machines:

```
apples.mycompany.com
oranges.company.com
pineapples.mycompany.com
```

Furthermore, suppose you have an account under the username farmer on all three machines. If you use telnet to log in to apples, oranges, and pineapples, you have to enter a username and password every time. To avoid this, use rlogin instead, like this:

rlogin apples

Because apples already knows you, it logs you in immediately without bothering to ask for a username or password. (rlogin only works this way if your username is known. If it isn't, rlogin will still ask for a username and password.)

Executing Remote Commands: The rsh Command

rsh (which stands for *remote shell*) is a tool that allows you to execute commands on remote UNIX servers. For example, suppose you want to list the directory contents of / on the machine "bowser." You would issue the following command:

rsh bowser "ls -l /"

rsh is generally available only in private networks, and here's why: rsh can be a security hazard (for example, outsiders could potentially execute commands on your server). If you're unsure whether rsh is available on your network, consult your system administrator.

Copying Files Remotely: The rcp Command

To copy a file from a remote machine, use the rcp command (which stands for *remote copy*).

At a minimum, rcp takes two arguments: the targeted host and the file you want to copy. For example, to copy the file /etc/termcap from the host apples.mycompany.com, you would issue the following command:

rcp apples.mycompany.com:/etc/termcap

About Privileges

Even if rsh is available, you may have to execute it as another user. For example, suppose your username on the local machine is tom. Perhaps the user ID tom does not have the necessary privileges to execute the specified command on the remote machine. (For example, suppose tom wants to examine a file created on host dick by user harry. Because harry's files can only be viewed by harry, tom must use rsh as harry). To execute a command as another user while using rsh, use the -1 option (as in **rsh -1 harry**). When you use this option, rsh prompts you for a password.

The Least You Need to Know

Here's the least you need to know about remote services:

➤ To transfer files from one host to another, use the ftp command.

➤ To conduct an interactive terminal session across a network, use telnet or rlogin.

➤ To execute a command on a remote UNIX host, use the rsh command.

Part 5
System Administration

You're well on your way to becoming a UNIX guru, and it may be that you're thinking, as much of a kick as UNIX is, it might not be a bad thing to get paid to play with it all day. Well, obviously you're not alone, and in this part of the book, you'll learn the basics of UNIX system administration.

How does a UNIX system administrator wile away the day? What powers does the administrator hold over unsuspecting users, and even entire groups of users? How can system security be maintained in a world rife with hackers and crackers itching to invade? For the answers to these and other questions, enter your password . . . or turn the page.

## Chapter 22

So You Want to Run a UNIX Server

In This Chapter

➤ Learning about permissions

➤ Learning about assigning permissions

➤ Adding and removing users

It's unlikely that you'll be managing a UNIX server anytime soon. However, here at Que, we like to be thorough. Therefore, this chapter briefly touches on system administration.

A system administrator (that's you) is responsible for adding and removing users, maintaining system security, and, basically, running the entire show. A lot of responsibility is attached to this post. In fact, if you run a UNIX system, you'll spend your days answering silly questions posed by other users. (I hope you can answer some of those questions using this book.)

A system administrator must know—at a minimum—how to manage system permissions and add and remove users. This chapter, therefore, focuses on these tasks.

Getting to the Root of the Problem

Your first step to successful system administration is understanding how UNIX privileges are assigned. We'll start there.

UNIX is a multiuser system, meaning that many folks can use the same machine simultaneously. To keep track of multiple users, UNIX employs a very structured approach.

Each user has an account, which consists of a username, a password, and a home directory (for example, /home/bwagner). When users first log in, they're positioned in their home directories. On a typical UNIX box in a corporate environment, there can be as many as 200 accounts and, hence, about 200 home directories.

To manage these accounts, UNIX makes use of a special or *privileged* account. This account is called *root* (and is often referred to as the *super-user*, because you can access it remotely by logging in under the user ID "su"). Let's discuss that account now.

It's a Bird, It's a Plane, It's Super-User!

What makes root such a super user? Here it is in a nutshell: Whereas regular users can generally only make changes to their own files, root can make changes to any file. At least, in the most basic sense, this is the concept of root. In the larger picture, however, root is much, much more. To understand root and the power it wields, you need a crash course in computer security.

In shared, networked environments such as UNIX, users can run around the system, checking out files, directories, and other resources at will. To prevent that, UNIX employs a technique called *Discretionary Access Control* (or *DAC*).

DAC is present in any system that allows a centralized, human authority to permit or deny users access (and to do so incisively, based on file, directory, or machine).

At root, you enforce these rules through something called *permissions*. Here are the different types of permissions:

➤ **Execute**—Allows users to execute the specified file.
➤ **Read**—Allows users to read the specified file.
➤ **Write**—Allows users to alter the specified file.

These permissions are attached to files, directories, and devices. Each permission is represented by a token. Here are the permission tokens:

➤ r (read access)
➤ w (write access)
➤ x (execute access)

To ascertain the permissions on a file or directory, list it in long format, like this:

```
ls -l
```

Here's some sample output:

```
drwxrwxrwx   2 bwagner   other      512 Jun 25 22:35 Consent
drwxrwxrwx   2 bwagner   other      512 Jun 25 22:35 Instructions
drwx------   2 bwagner   other      512 Aug  8 18:41 mail
-rw-rw-rw-   1 bwagner   other      324 Aug 11 16:34 ppp-off
-rw-rw-rw-   1 bwagner   other      121 Aug 11 16:34 ppp-on
-rw-rw-rw-   1 bwagner   other    46188 Aug 11 16:33 pppd-man.txt
-rw-rw-rw-   1 bwagner   other       58 Aug 11 20:43 pppkill
drwxrwxrwx   8 bwagner   other      512 Aug  1 01:32 public_html
```

For purposes of clarity, let's extract the fourth line:

```
-rw-rw-rw-   1 bwagner   other      324 Aug 11 16:34 ppp-off
```

Notice that the line is broken into fields. Here, you're concerned only with the first field:

```
-rw-rw-rw-   1 bwagner   other      324 Aug 11 16:34 ppp-off
```

The first field consists of ten characters: -rw-rw-rw-. Let's break down what those ten characters mean.

The first character tells you the type of file you're dealing with. There are two tokens or this:

➤ - (represents a file)

➤ d (represents a directory)

In the example, the first character is -. Therefore, you know that you're dealing with a file:

```
[-]rw-rw-rw-
```

The remaining nine characters are actually three sets of three. Let's break them down, three at a time. The first set (reading from left to right) represents the permissions of the current user:

```
-[rw-]rw-rw-
```

In this case, the current user (that's me) has read and write but not execute permissions. In contrast, the second set (again, reading from left to right) represents the permissions of the current group:

```
-rw-[rw-]rw-
```

Again, group users have read and write access. Finally, the last set represents what permissions the rest of the world has:

-rw-rw-**[rw-]**

As you can see, the rest of the world also has read and write access. That's easy enough, because everybody has the same permissions on this file. Suppose, however, that the permission table looked like this:

drwxr-xr-x   2 root   sys   512 May 21   1997 cron

This is a different situation altogether. First, you know that this resource is a directory, because the first character is a d:

drwxr-xr-x   2 root   sys   512 May 21   1997 cron

Also, you can see that root (the owner) has read, write, and execute privileges:

d**rwx**r-xr-x   2 root   sys   512 May 21   1997 cron

However, both the current group (sys) and world can only read and execute—they cannot write:

drwx**r-x**x**r-x**   2 root   sys   512 May 21   1997 cron

To reiterate, here are the key points:

➤ The first character tells you the type of file you're dealing with (typically, a regular file or directory).

➤ The next three characters tell you the owner's privileges.

➤ The second set of three tells you the group's privileges.

➤ The last set of three tells you the world's privileges.

Now, let's briefly cover how you establish these permissions.

Setting Permissions: The chmod *Command*

To set permissions on an individual file or directory, use the chmod command. chmod accepts three operators: -, +, and =. Each performs a different function:

➤ The - symbol *removes* permissions.

➤ The + symbol *adds* permissions.

➤ The = symbol *assigns* permissions.

Table 22.1 summarizes what permissions these operators can remove, add, or assign.

Table 22.1. The chmod permissions

chmod Permission	Explanation
r	The r character adds or subtracts read permissions. For example, **chmod +r *filename*** adds the read permission to *filename*.
w	The w character adds or subtracts write permissions. For example, **chmod -w *filename*** takes away write permission from *filename*.
x	The x character adds or subtracts execute permission. For example, **chmod +x *filename*** adds the execute permission to *filename*.

Using letters (r, w, x) to assign permissions on individual files and directories is fine. However, sometimes, you'll want to set permissions for everyone at the same time. For example, you may want to set permissions for the file's owner, the owner's group, and, finally, the rest of the world. For this, it's easier to use the octal system. Let's discuss how that works.

chmod *and the Octal System*

In the octal system, permissions are represented by number. Table 22.2 summarizes the octal number scheme and what each number represents.

Table 22.2. The chmod octal permissions

chmod Octal Permission	Explanation
0	The octal value 0 is equivalent to - - - (or no permissions at all).
1	The octal value 1 is equivalent to - -x, (or only execute permissions).
2	The octal value 2 is equivalent to -w-, (or only write permissions).
3	The octal value 3 is equivalent to r- -, (or only read permissions).
4	The octal value 4 is equivalent to -wx, (or only write and execute permissions).
5	The octal value 5 is equivalent to r-x, (or only read and execute permissions).
6	The octal value 6 is equivalent to rw-, (or only read and write permissions).
7	The octal value 7 is the whole shebang: it's equivalent to rwx (or read, write, and execute permissions).

You can use the octal scheme to perform widespread permission changes. For example, consider this command:

```
chmod 751 filename
```

In this case, *filename* has the following permissions:

➤ The owner can read, write, and execute it.

➤ The group can read and execute it.

➤ The world (outsiders) can only execute it.

You should be careful when applying permissions. You can accidentally place permissions that are to restrictive and then no one will be able to access anything. Conversely, if your permissions are too liberal, folks can overwrite and access files that they shouldn't.

Adding and Removing Users

Part of your job as system administrator is to add and remove users. For a first-time system administrator, these can be hazardous undertakings, but they needn't be. You have several ways available to you to accomplish these tasks, depending on your configuration:

➤ **Using proprietary, graphical tools**—Many modern UNIX systems (including Solaris, AIX, HP-UX, and UNIXWare) have graphical tools for adding and removing users.

➤ **Using command-line tools or scripts**—Some systems (such as Linux) have automated scripts or command-line programs to add and remove users.

➤ **Editing the passwd file manually**—On many older systems, you have to edit the passwd file manually and create the /home directory for each user.

Consult your system manuals to determine which option is available to you. Because I cannot guess your specific configuration, I'll simply offer an explanation of generic procedures.

/etc/passwd: *The Password File*

User login and password information is stored in a central database called passwd, which is located in the directory /etc. On older systems, the /etc/passwd file looks something like this:

```
root:uXonr7RoTwQWs8:0:0:root:/root:/bin/bash
bin:*:1:1:bin:/bin:
daemon:*:2:2:daemon:/sbin:
```

```
adm:*:3:4:adm:/var/adm:
lp:*:4:7:lp:/var/spool/lpd:
sync:*:5:0:sync:/sbin:/bin/sync
shutdown:*:6:0:shutdown:/sbin:/sbin/shutdown
halt:*:7:0:halt:/sbin:/sbin/halt
bwagner:yPf3M5qMgglUc:101:10:Bill Wagner:/home/bwagner:/bin/bash
```

All this probably looks very confusing. In reality, however, the file's structure is quite simple. Each line consists of seven fields, separated by colons:

➤ The user's login ID

➤ The user's password (in encrypted form)

➤ The user's user ID (or *UID*), a numeric value to identify the user

➤ The user's group ID (or *GID*), a numeric value to identify the group the user belongs to

➤ The user's real name

➤ The user's home directory

➤ The user's shell

Consider my entry:

```
bwagner:yPf3M5qMgglUc:101:10:Bill Wagner:/home/bwagner:/bin/bash
```

From this, you can ascertain the following:

➤ My username is bwagner

➤ My password, in encrypted form, is yPf3M5qMgglUc

➤ My user ID is 101

➤ My group ID is 10

➤ My real name is Bill Wagner

➤ My home directory is /home/bwagner

➤ My preferred shell is bash.

To remove a user, you need only remove his or her entry from the passwd file and delete his or her home directory. However, adding a user is a bit more complicated. Let's discuss that now.

Adding a User

The only data in /etc/passwd that can't be entered manually is the password itself. Therefore, to add a new user, edit the passwd file and add the other six values by hand. For this, you can use any editor; however, on BSD-based systems, the preferred editor is vipw.

Warning

vipw behaves just like vi. If you don't know how to use vi, do not use vipw to edit the passwd file. There's a strong chance that if you have no experience with vi, you could potentially bungle the pass-wd entries. Also, because vipw only checks for root entry integrity, you might accidentally lock out other users.

vipw: *An Editor for* passwd

vipw is a simple tool for editing the passwd file. Its advantage is this: vipw will not save a passwd file that has a corrupted root entry. Because of this, vipw guards against root passwd lockouts. This is very important. (This can prevent you from doing something really silly, like accidentally bungling the root passwd entry.)

Whichever editor you ultimately use, the procedure goes like this: Jump to the end of the passwd file to add a new line. That new line will be constructed as follows:

```
username:blank-password:userid:groupid:real-
name:home-directory:shell
```

During this process, you have to carefully choose both the user ID (UID) and group ID (GID). Let's briefly discuss those now.

The User ID: UID

The UID can be any number between 0 and 32767. However, in general, you should make the UID greater than 100 but less than 19000. As long as the number is unique, however, it will suffice.

The Group ID: GID

Likewise, the GID can be any number between 0 and 32767. However, you should check /etc/group or /etc/groups to see which groups already exist. It's best to add new users to a group that already exists. This way, when you make global changes to that group, the changes affect all users in the group. (This makes your life much easier.) Here are the contents of a typical /etc/group file:

```
root::0:root
other::1:
bin::2:root,bin,daemon
sys::3:root,bin,sys,adm
adm::4:root,adm,daemon
uucp::5:root,uucp
mail::6:root
tty::7:root,tty,adm
lp::8:root,lp,adm
nuucp::9:root,nuucp
staff::10:
daemon::12:root,daemon
```

```
sysadmin::14:
nobody::60001:
noaccess::60002:
nogroup::65534:
```

After You Edit the Password File: Creating Home Directories

Once you add the user to the passwd file, the next step is to create his or her home directory. This is typically a subdirectory of /home. For example, for user bwagner, the home directory is /home/bwagner. (You can make any directory home, but making it /home/*username* is a good idea. This way, when you need to automate a system administration task, you can do so wholesale to all users in the /home directory hierarchy.)

Finishing Up

Finally, once you've added the user to /etc/passwd and created his or her home directory, you should set his or her initial login password. This is done with the pass-wd command, like this:

```
passwd bwagner [some-password]
```

passwd will prompt you for verification and then commit the new password to the passwd database. That's it! You just created a new user.

Token Passwords

Newer UNIX distributions usually have special tools for adding new users. Therefore, in all likelihood, you'll never have to follow the previous procedure. If you do, though, here's a tip: Many UNIX systems do not store the encrypted password in /etc/passwd. Instead, this password is replaced by a token. For instance, examine this sample passwd file:

```
root:x:0:1:Super-User:/:/sbin/sh
daemon:x:1:1::/:
bin:x:2:2::/usr/bin:
sys:x:3:3::/:
adm:x:4:4:Admin:/var/adm:
lp:x:71:8:Line Printer Admin:/usr/spool/lp:
smtp:x:0:0:Mail Daemon User:/:
uucp:x:5:5:uucp Admin:/usr/lib/uucp:
nuucp:x:9:9:uucp Admin:/var/spool/uucppublic:/usr/lib/uucp/uucico
listen:x:37:4:Network Admin:/usr/net/nls:
nobody:x:60001:60001:Nobody:/:
```

```
noaccess:x:60002:60002:No Access User:/:
nobody4:x:65534:65534:SunOS 4.x Nobody:/:
bwagner:x:101:10:Bill Wagner:/home/bwagner:/bin/bash
```

Notice that the character x occupies the password field. This is a placeholder for the real, encrypted password that resides elsewhere on the disk drive. When you edit the passwd file on such systems, instead of a blank password field, add the token.

A Few Words about Security

This book is really too short to give you a decent primer on security. However, here are some basic rules to live by:

➤ **Don't log in as root unless you have to**—While logged in as root, you can make changes to any file. This is a dangerous situation, because in many cases, your mistakes will be permanent. Therefore, use the root account sparingly.

➤ **Never give anyone the root password**—The root password gives you access to everything. If someone gets your root password, he or she can seize control of your machine. Protect that password with your life. Don't write it down, and make sure that it isn't easy to guess. (For example, don't make the root password your birthday, your social security number, or even any word found in the average dictionary.)

➤ **Backup the entire system on a regular basis**—Backups often comprise the only evidence you'll ever have that a security breach has occurred. If you have more than a few users, you should backup weekly (at a minimum).

➤ **Buy a good book on security**—UNIX security is a very complex field that's evolved over some 25 years. If you really intend to secure your server, you need expert advice. For this, I recommend the following book:

Garfinkel, Simson and Gene Spafford. *Practical UNIX and Internet Security*. O'Reilly & Associates, 1996. ISBN 1565921488.

This will take you step by step through the paces of UNIX security.

The Least You Need to Know

As a UNIX server administrator, you have enormous power to affect the system for good and for ill. To be effective, here's the least you need to know:

➤ Manipulate user permissions using chmod.

➤ To add users, add their entries to the passwd file.

➤ Never give anyone your root password.

Part 6
Troubleshooting

Now that you've learned how to make UNIX do your bidding, it's time for the final lesson. Yes, you, even you, the UNIX sage, might make a mistake. Hard as it may be to believe right now, it'll probably happen. But you're in good company; no matter the level of experience or expertise, at one time or another we've all screwed up and had to scramble to recover our data and dignity. The good news is that we who have gone before took notes, and in Part VI you'll reap the benefits.

In the following chapters you'll discover what the most common mistakes are and how to avoid them. From creating backups to guarding against corrupted password files to controlling a wild X session, the advice you need is here. You'll also find the meaning of life . . . or at least how to live in the land of the cryptic UNIX error message. Twenty of the most common are deciphered here for you. So, brave pilgrim, you may continue on your journey with confidence.

## Chapter 23

Common Mistakes

In This Chapter

➤ Some common mistakes that UNIX newcomers make

➤ Backups

➤ Corrupted password files

➤ Terminal problems

➤ Problems in X and how to avoid them

Your first few weeks with UNIX will be frustrating. During that time, you'll make many mistakes and encounter many problems. This short chapter addresses some of these problems and how to avoid them.

Backups

The most devastating mistake of all is having no backups. In computing, there's one immutable rule: Eventually, your data *will* get corrupted. There's no sense in denying it, and it makes no difference how much experience you have. Eventually, something terrible will happen.

Often, these disasters can have serious consequences. For example, imagine creating an entire intranet site consisting of hundreds of Web pages. Suddenly, your disk drive dies. If you don't have backups, forget it. You must redo every shred of work that took you months to accomplish. Don't let this happen to you. Back up often.

About Backups and UNIX

UNIX has two main backup tools:

➤ cpio

➤ tar

These are available on every UNIX system and are not third-party tools. Third-party solutions exist, but they cost extra.

Because I cover tar in Chapter 10, "Working With Applications," I'll concentrate on cpio here.

A Backup Tool: The cpio Command

cpio is an archiving tool. It creates archives of your files and directories for storage or transport. (cpio actually stands for *copy in, copy out*.)

To use cpio for basic backups, issue this command:

```
ls / | cpio -o > [device]
```

Here's what this command does:

➤ It gets a directory listing.

➤ The listing is piped to cpio.

➤ cpio copies the information to standard output.

➤ Standard output is redirected to [*device*].

Which device you actually send the data to depends on your hardware and the size of the device media. For example, for simple backups, you could send data to a floppy disk. (Devices are discussed in the following section.)

cpio Command-Line Switches

cpio accepts several command line switches that control the data flow and how that data is written. These switches are summarized in Table 23.1.

Table 23.1. Selected cpio command-line switches

cpio Switch	Purpose
-d	This option instructs cpio to create directories within the archive (or in extracting an archive) as needed.
-E [*source-file*]	This option instructs cpio to get filenames (for inclusion in the archive) from a source file. That source file should contain one filename per line.

cpio Switch	Purpose
-f [*pattern*]	This option notifies cpio that you'll supply a pattern and that any files matching that pattern should *not* be copied.
-i	This option instructs cpio to copy files from standard input. This is used when extracting files from a cpio archive.
-L	This option instructs cpio to follow symbolic links to get the files associated with those links. (This option must be set at backup time. Otherwise, by default, cpio will not follow symbolic links.)
-o	This option instructs cpio to copy files from standard output. (Files are also copied *to* standard output.)
-r	This switch instructs cpio to interactively query whether you want to change filenames. (In other words, whether you want to rename the files being copied.) This is useful when you're unpacking an archive that might conceivably have filenames that already exist locally.

Regardless of how you decide to perform your backup, you'll need to specify a backup device. This is a hardware device that has media to record your backup (for example, a tape or floppy drive). Table 23.2 lists a few common device types and their filenames.

Table 23.2. Some typical backup target devices

Name	Device
/dev/cdrom	CD-ROM drive (possibly a write-once or WORM)
/dev/fd0	Floppy disk drive
/dev/mnt0	BPI tape drive (9-track)
/dev/rfd0	Floppy disk drive
/dev/rst0	SCSI tape drive
/dev/rxt0	Exabyte 8mm tape (NeXT)
/dev/sd2x	Optical disk drive (or other SCSI drive)
/dev/sr0	CD-ROM (NeXT)
/dev/st0	SCSI tape drive
/dev/tape	SCSI tape drive

Check to see which devices actually exist on your system. (You may want to consult with your system administrator if you're unfamiliar with backup hardware.) For example, to back up a file list to tape using tar, you could issue this command:

```
tar -cf /dev/rst0 filelist
```

313

Here's how to use `cpio` to back up an archive to a floptical drive:

```
find . -print ¦ cpio -o > /dev/sd20
```

When Is a Good Time to Back Up?

You're probably wondering how often you should perform a backup. That depends. If you're using UNIX for business purposes, you should back up every day, archiving at least these resources:

➤ User directories and files

➤ Any changes to your business documents and databases

➤ All your logs

I recommend having several copies: for example, one for the office, one for the safe, and one for safekeeping elsewhere. (Fire safes are not secure. In a fire, your backup tapes will melt, even when deposited in a fire safe.)

In addition, these days, better solutions than backup tapes or backup floppies exist. Instead, you should consider write-once media such as CD-ROMs or floptical drives. Not only are these more durable and more reliable (tapes can break or get stretched out), but write-once media guarantees against tampering. If you have any security concerns, this is a must.

If, on the other hand, you're not using UNIX for business purposes, you should still back up weekly.

Corrupting the `passwd` File

The next most critical mistake you can make is to corrupt the `/etc/passwd` file. Here's why: Anytime a login takes place, UNIX checks the `passwd` file to verify the user's identity. If that file is corrupted, UNIX will refuse to log that user in. (Even booting into single user mode may not work.)

Most often, corruption takes place when you edit the `passwd` file and accidentally make a typographical error. (Other possibilities include deleting the file, replacing it, or inadvertently damaging it.)

To hedge against this, you should be extra careful when editing the `passwd` file. Moreover, you should always retain at least one backup copy. (Store this backup copy on a floppy disk in a safe place.)

If you have no backup of your `passwd` file, don't panic. You can still restore a basic `passwd` file using your installation media. (All installation packages contain a very sparse `passwd` file.) The problem is that you have to find the `passwd` file.

To do so, take the installation CD-ROM and put it in another machine. Now you can search for the passwd file, which is usually compressed. To do this on a UNIX machine, use the find command:

```
find . -name *passwd*
```

If the nearest machine is running Microsoft Windows, choose Start|Find|Files or Folders and enter passwd*.* as a search string.

Once you know the location of the passwd file, reboot with the installation media, mount the desired disk, and copy the passwd file from the installation media to the hard disk. (This works because the root account has no password on installation media. The root password isn't set until after the installation is complete.)

On the other hand, your password shadow file can sometimes get corrupted. If this happens (and your passwd file is still intact) you may be able to recover the shadow file using the pwconv command. pwconv will rebuilt the shadow file. (pwconv is available on many UNIX flavors, including HP-UX, Solaris, and Linux.)

The Shadow Knows

On newer UNIX systems, encrypted passwords are never stored in /etc/passwd; instead, they're stored in a shadow file. UNIX uses this file to authenticate passwords. On rare occasions, your shadow file can become corrupted. When this happens, even legitimate logins will fail. The cure is to boot with installation media and run pwconv to recover your shadow password file.

Cruising As Root

Whether on your own machine or someone else's, if you have root access, you need to be extra careful. Sure, it's easy to fall into a pattern of behavior where you log in as root and stay that way. However, you must resist that temptation, because if you don't, you'll eventually meet with disaster. There are several reasons for this.

First, while you're root, you're essentially a god on that particular machine. This is not a good thing. Humans are curious creatures and not well suited to "god" status. You may go tooling around from directory to directory, tinkering with binaries that you know nothing about. That's where the trouble begins.

The human spirit is such that when faced with a mysterious object, we have a tendency to poke and prod it until something interesting happens. This curiosity has resulted in everything from the discovery of fire to the development of the atomic bomb.

In UNIX, certain commands available to root are irrevocable or can cause irrevocable results. Moreover, root can create or destroy almost any file. Therefore, by cruising around as root, you're taking the following risks:

➤ You might accidentally delete important system files.

➤ You might accidentally overwrite important files.

➤ You might inadvertently change something that you don't have enough experience to restore to its original state.

Additionally, surfing the Net as root poses a special risk. Many Web sites employ executable content through applets. *Applets* are small programs that can be executed in a Web browser. Most applets are written in a powerful networking language from Sun Microsystems called Java.

Although Sun has done much to improve Java security, Java still poses a security risk. The degree of that risk depends on how far Java can reach into your system. Typically, malicious Java code can only do as much damage as your user ID's privileges allow.

When you cruise as root, you have privileges to do anything, to any file. Therefore, when malicious Java code compromises your security while you're root, it gains root access to resources that are generally not available to "regular" users. For this reason, you should not surf the Net as root.

Dangerous Commands

UNIX has many dangerous commands that can potentially damage or destroy valuable data. Here are few:

➤ **cp (the copy command)**—This command doesn't warn before overwriting files. If you're unsure whether you're about to overwrite a file, give the copy a unique name.

➤ **fdisk (a disk formatting utility)**—fdisk can format disk drives. If you make a mistake using fdisk, you may inadvertently destroy a system partition. If so, your system will be destroyed, and you'll have to reinstall. Be extremely careful when using fdisk.

➤ **format (a disk formatting utility)**—format formats disk drives and, in this respect, format is just as dangerous as fdisk. Be extremely careful when using format to format disk drives.

➤ **rm (the remove command)**—rm removes files. Until you become more capable with UNIX, always use the -i switch. This will force rm to prompt you before removing each file. For each time rm prompts you this way, think carefully before choosing Yes.

➤ **rmdir (the remove directory command)**—rmdir removes directories. Although rmdir will not automatically remove a directory that has files, know this: Some directories are essential, even if they're currently empty. (A good example is /tmp. Many programs use /tmp, and the code to access /tmp is hard-coded into these applications. As an interesting experiment, remove /tmp for a day; you'll soon discover which programs can live without it and which can't.)

However, this list is by no means inclusive. There are many, many UNIX commands that, when used improperly or rashly, can render a system either temporarily or permanently inoperable. To avoid complete disaster, here's a good rule: For the first six months of your UNIX experience, use asterisks as seldom as possible (if at all). Coupling asterisks with destructive commands can cause widespread damage. Only when you're absolutely certain that your asterisks are placed safely should you use them.

For instance, never use asterisks in UNIX as you would in DOS. Here's an example:

```
rm *.
```

Remember that the . symbol can represent any character. The above command could potentially destroy many, many files.

Additionally, "power" switches are available that can override certain behaviors of programs. For example, consider this command:

```
rm -r [something]
```

The -r switch instructs rm to operate recursively. In other words, if [something] is a directory, that directory, all its subdirectories, and all its files will be removed. This command could be devastating. Therefore, try to avoid using power switches until you have more experience.

Terminal Problems

One of the most common problems you'll encounter involves terminal types and terminal emulation. The problem, in a nutshell, is this: When you connect to a remote machine, chances are, you may not know its make and manufacturer. In many cases, you don't need to know this information; however, occasionally, knowing makes a world of difference.

You see, not all computers display data in precisely the same manner. For example, some terminals display data in vertical columns, like this:

Product	Item No.	Description	Price
CDROM	1233	CDROM Disk Drive	$100.00
Floppy	1234	Floppy diskette drive	$30.00

317

Other terminals display only a certain number of lines across and down. Lastly, some terminals display data inside of special windows, with special characters forming each window's frame. Here's a good example:

```
aaaaaaaaaaaaaaaaaaaaaaaaa
a                        a
a    The data gets       a
a    displayed here      a
a                        a
aaaaaaaaaaaaaaaaaaaaaaaaa
```

At or before connection time, you're supposed to set your terminal emulation correctly. (*Terminal emulation* refers to your local terminal's ability to mimic the behavior of foreign terminal types.) If you don't set your terminal emulation correctly, things can get funky. For example, instead of this:

```
aaaaaaaaaaaaaaaaaaaaaaaaa
a                        a
a    The data gets       a
a    displayed here      a
a                        a
aaaaaaaaaaaaaaaaaaaaaaaaa
```

You'll see this:

```
a
a a     a
aaaaaaaaaaaaaaaaaaaaa
a
a
a
The
data
gets
a
displayed
here
a
a
aaaaaaaaaaaaaaaaaaaaa
```

In anything but the simplest operation, this can completely undermine your session. (If you can't read the data properly, you may as well not read it at all.)

To remedy this, most UNIX machines support a wide range of terminals. However, not every UNIX system will automatically detect remote terminal types. Therefore, you need to set those types manually. To do so, you can query the remote server by reading its $TERM variable, which specifies the current terminal type. To do so, enter the following command:

echo $TERM

The remote machine, in turn, will respond with its current terminal type:

ansi

Once you know this value, you can disconnect and reset your own terminal. In bash, you set your terminal like this:

TERM=ansi

In csh, you set your terminal like this:

setenv TERM=ansi

Once you set your terminal, you can reconnect. You'll find that things look much neater now.

There are literally hundreds of terminal types. However, in the course of daily business, you'll probably encounter only a handful. These terminal types and their identifiers are summarized in Table 23.3.

Table 23.3. Some common terminal types

Terminal Identifier	Terminal Type or Specification
2621	HP 2621
2640b	HP 264*
4107	Tektronix 4107 graphics terminal
4112	Tektronix 4110 series
4115	Tektronix 4115
5520	NEC 5520
ansi	ANSI terminal
arpanet	ARPANet
dumb	Unknown
hp	Hewlett-Packard
hp2648	HP 2648 graphics terminal
ibm	IBM 3101-10
ibmpc	IBM PC/IX
pty	Pseudo teletype
rxvt	Terminal emulator common to Linux
sun	Sun Microsystems workstation console

continues

Table 23.3. Some common terminal types CONTINUED

Terminal Identifier	Terminal Type or Specification
sun1	Old Sun
sun-cmd	Sun Microsystems console
terminet1200	GE terminet 1200
ti745	TI silent 745
ti800	TI omni 800
trs100	Radio Shack model 100
trs2	Radio Shack model II (CP/M)
trs80	Radio Shack trs-80
vc303	Volker-Craig 303
vc404	Volker-Craig 404
vt100	DEC vt100
vt100-nav	DEC vt100 132 cols
vt100-s	vt100 with status line (top)
vt100-s-bot	vt100 with status line (bottom)
vt102	DEC vt102
vt200	DEC vt200
vt50	DEC vt50
wy85	Wyse-85
wyse50	Wyse 50
wyse75	Wyse 75 terminal
x1720	XEROX 1720
xterm	Xterm terminal emulator (X)

To set your terminal emulation for one of these terminals, use the terminal identifier. For example, to set it for Xterm, issue the following command:

```
TERM=xterm
```

If you don't know which terminals your machine supports, you can quickly find out. A comprehensive list of supported terminals (and their capabilities) can be found in the file /etc/termcap. To find out if a particular terminal is supported, use grep to search /etc/termcap, like this:

```
grep "¦vt100" /etc/termcap ¦ awk -F"¦" '{print $2}'
```

Here's some sample output from my Sparc:

```
vt100-np
vt100
```

```
vt100-nam
vt100-s
vt100-s-bot
vt100-nav
vt100-w
vt100-w-nam
```

Entries in /etc/termcap describe the capabilities of each terminal in excruciating detail. Check the man page on termcap for more information.

Xcruciating Peccadilloes

Chances are, you'll take a few weeks to get acclimated to X. Not only does X have a different look, it has a different feel. Above and beyond that, though, there are some common pitfalls to watch for when using X. This next section discusses those pitfalls.

Windows from Hell

One of the first things you'll notice is that not all X windows are uniformly sized. In fact, many X applications open in odd positions on the screen. Some even fill the entire screen. For example, a graphics demo called xgc spans several screens when it first opens. (See the following figure.)

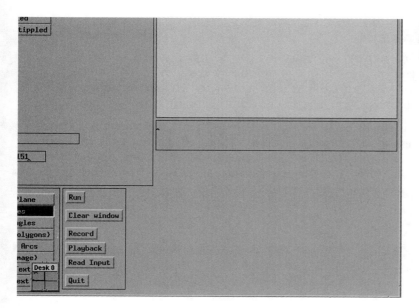

xgc fills several screens, making it impossible to see your desktop!

A lot of X applications behave this way. So, what's the deal? Are X developers deliberately trying to irritate you? No, not quite. Instead, the truth is more banal: Many X applications are designed on systems with huge monitors. Because these monitors have resolutions that far exceed the norm (the norm being 640×480), applications designed on them appear huge when displayed at normal resolutions.

Often, huge X applications can interfere with your work, making it impossible for you to reach other windows. The cure is to grab the offending application by its edges and resize it. (Usually, you need to resize it just a little; enough to grab it again and find the maximize button. Usually, clicking the maximize button will force the offending application to fill only the viewable screen. From that point on, you can safely and efficiently manipulate the application.)

On the other hand, in rare instances, the application may not respond. (The edges may be beyond your reach or the graphics libraries used do not provide for resizing from the corners or sides.) If so, there's only one solution: Hit Ctrl+backspace to kill X and restart. Once you're back in X, open an Xterm and restart the application. This time, however, try using the geometry command-line option, like this:

```
program-name -geometry 200x200
```

If the developer adhered to standard programming rules, the application should open at 200×200 resolution. If it doesn't, there's a problem, and you should send the developer an angry email. (Just kidding.)

The Killing Fields

Another problem is data entry field behavior. For example, certain fields will not accept data unless your mouse cursor is positioned over the field. This is common with applications designed using the Athena Widget Toolkit. No cure exists for this. If you encounter this problem, you *have* to position the mouse cursor over the field.

Likewise, some development packages produce fields that fail to recognize a destructive backspace. (A *destructive backspace* is where you use the backspace key to destroy all characters to the cursor's left.) There may be a cure for this. Some applications (Crisp is one) allow you to swap the backspace and Delete keys. However, if the developer made no such provision, you're out of luck. In this case, you'll probably have to use the Delete key.

The Least You Need to Know

UNIX is a very powerful and complex operating system. In order to avoid as much frustration as possible when you're learning it, here's the least you need to know:

➤ Perform backups regularly to avoid data loss.

➤ Always preserve a copy of your passwd file.

➤ Be extremely careful when using destructive commands.

➤ Use asterisks or other wildcards sparingly and carefully.

➤ Always try to ascertain foreign terminal types.

➤ X can be funky, so be prepared for strange behavior.

➤ Don't panic!

## Chapter 24

The 20 Most Common Error Messages and Their Causes

In This Chapter

➤ Common error messages and how to recover from them

UNIX error messages are in a class by themselves. They're probably the most cryptic error messages you'll ever encounter. In this chapter, the most common error messages are unraveled for your viewing pleasure.

Command Not Found

Command not found is probably the most common UNIX error message. What does it mean? You invoked a command but UNIX can't find it. Here are some possible reasons why:

➤ You misspelled the command name.

➤ The program is in a different directory (one not in the path). To learn how to set your path, refer to Chapter 5, "Surviving Shell Shock."

➤ The program you want is missing.

You can find the problem through the process of elimination. First, check your spelling. Better than half of all errors are caused by typos. If that doesn't work, try issuing the command with the full absolute path. For example, instead of using this:

pico filename

Try using this instead:

```
/usr/local/bin/pico filename
```

If you don't know the full path, try finding it. If the file is a system binary, for example, you can probably find it quickly using the following command:

```
whereis command
```

If the whereis database hasn't been built (or if whereis cannot find the file), try searching the entire disk:

```
cd /
find . -name "command"
```

If you search the entire disk and still can't find the command, it probably doesn't exist or has been deleted.

Relax and Take a Break

If you use the find command as described, you should pull up a chair and relax. On many systems, a full find search can take up to three minutes. In fact, if you try this over a modem connection to your Internet Service Provider, you could be waiting five minutes or more. Many ISPs have hard disk drives that are dozens of gigabytes in size. find can take quite a while to traverse all those directories. Additionally, conducting find queries over a network can take forever, depending on the target host's system load.

No Such File or Directory

If you receive the No such file or directory error, you requested statistics on a file that UNIX can't find. Here are a few possible reasons why:

➤ You misspelled the filename.

➤ The file is located in a different directory.

➤ The file doesn't exist.

➤ UNIX doesn't like you. (Just kidding.)

First, try retyping your command, being careful to spell the filename correctly (be sure to check for case, as well). If that doesn't work, try locating the file and using the absolute path when calling it.

Argument List Too Long

Almost every UNIX command will take multiple command-line arguments. For example, `cat` will display a list of files if you issue the following command:

```
cat file1 file2 file3
```

However, some UNIX commands limit the number of arguments you can use. If you receive the `Argument list too long` error, you exceeded the maximum allowable number of arguments. For this, a simple solution exists: Use fewer arguments.

Cannot Access (Cannot Open, No Such File or Directory)

If you receive the `Cannot access` error (or any variation of it), UNIX cannot find the specified file. Here are some possible reasons why:

➤ You misspelled the file's name.

➤ The file exists, but it's in another directory.

➤ The specified file doesn't exist.

First, check your spelling and case; then try again. If that doesn't work, try using the file's absolute path. If this also fails, the file may be missing, or you might not have the necessary permissions to view the file.

Cross-device Link (Different File System)

If you receive the `Cross-device link` error, `ln` cannot link the specified directory.

You receive the `Cross-device link` error when you try to create a link but UNIX can't find the source directory. Here are a few possible reasons why:

➤ You misspelled the source or destination directory name.

➤ The specified a file system doesn't exist.

➤ The source directory doesn't exist

➤ Your system doesn't support linking

As always, you should check your spelling and try again. If that doesn't work, make sure the source directory exists and that your system supports linking. First, though, you should make sure you have adequate permissions to create the link.

Login Incorrect

You receive the `Login incorrect` error when UNIX cannot verify your identity. Here are some possible reasons why:

➤ You misspelled your username or password.

➤ Your account has been terminated.

➤ The /etc/passwd file is corrupted.

➤ You're a hacker trying to break in.

About Linking Across Machines

It's also possible (but less likely) that you tried to link across hosts and the network connection is down. Before you give up, you might want to check this, as well.

In all cases but the last, try logging in again, making sure this time you type your username and password correctly. (You'll encounter this error often if your username or password is difficult to type. For example, if your password has both uppercase and lowercase characters in it, you can easily mistype it.) If you retype your username and password correctly and still get this error, contact your system administrator. Your account may have been terminated. (On the other hand, if you're a hacker trying to break in, you're going about it the wrong way. Each time you provide a bad username/password pair, this is logged. Find another technique of getting in or give up hacking.) Finally, if none of the above suggestions work, check that you're connecting to the right host.

No Manual Entry (No Manual Entry for Command)

You receive the No manual entry error when you request a manual page but UNIX can't find it.

Possible reasons include the following:

➤ You misspelled the command name.

➤ The man page exists but was never installed.

➤ No man page exists for the specified command.

First, check your spelling. If you've spelled the command name correctly and still receive a No manual entry error, it's possible that the man page was never properly installed. This sometimes happens when the command is a third-party program.

For example, this can happen when you download software from the Net. Many freeware and shareware packages (especially for Linux) are "bare bones." When you unpack these distributions, the documentation is often in plain text, or the man page is not formatted. You can check by examining the directory to which the package extracted. Often, the man page is in a file with a .1 extension. For example, the filename might be man.1 or command.1. If you find such a file, you can quickly view the man page by issuing the following command:

```
nroff -man command.1
```

Also, some software developers (although admittedly few) dispense with the man system altogether. Instead, they provide their documentation in PostScript, HTML, or PDF formats. If you can't find a man page file, try looking for documentation in these other formats.

Finally, if these approaches fail, the man page might have never been installed. In this case, contact your system administrator.

Host Name Lookup Failure

You received the Host name lookup failure error because you told UNIX to contact an Internet host but that host was unreachable. Possible reasons include these:

➤ You forgot to provide a name server address.

➤ Your machine is not connected to the Internet.

First, check that you've specified at last one name server in the /etc/resolv.conf file. (Without a name server, your system will be unable to resolve hosts). If your name server configuration is in order, check to see whether your Internet connection is hot. It's possible that your modem got dropped or that a hub on your LAN is down.

No Route to Host

You generally receive the No route to host error because you told UNIX to contact an Internet host but that host was unreachable. A possible reason is that your machine is not connected to the Internet.

Check to see whether you're connected to the Internet. For example, try pinging a known host, like this:

```
ping internic.net
```

Device or Resource Busy

You generally receive the Device or resource busy error message because you tried to access a device or swap partition that's already being used.

If you tried to access a swap partition and received this error, don't sweat it. The swap is already active. (For example, in Linux, swaps are typically activated at boot time.)

If you tried to access a device (such as a modem), a stale process may have it locked up or the device may simply be in use. Check the process list (using ps) to see what's going on.

Is a Directory

You receive the Is a directory error when you try to delete a directory using rm but UNIX cannot complete the task. (rm is designed for deleting files.)

This problem is easily solved: Use rmdir instead.

Nothing Appropriate

You receive the Nothing appropriate error when you issue an apropos or man -k command looking for relevant manual pages, but UNIX cannot find any that apply.

Try shortening your search string or reforming your query. For example, if you're searching for man entries related to printing, try several combinations, such as these:

➤ man -k printing

➤ man -k printers

➤ man -k printer

➤ man -k print

Additionally, sometimes you can find what you're looking for by examining man pages of similar commands. Every man page ends with a list of commands that are related to the current command. For example, the lp man page also refers to many other man pages, including the following:

➤ postprint

➤ pr

➤ lpadmin

➤ lpfilter

➤ lpforms

➤ lpsched

It's also possible that no documentation exists for the command you want.

Kernel Panic (Unable to Mount Root File System)

You generally receive the Kernel panic error when you try to boot to a partition that doesn't house the root file system. This error is common on Linux systems using LILO (particularly from a floppy disk). You may have specified the wrong partition or your boot disk may be corrupted. Double-check your partition information and try again. For example, suppose the system had three partitions:

➤ /dev/hda1 (Linux swap)

➤ /dev/hda2 (Linux swap)

➤ /dev/hda3 (Linux native)

If you tried to boot to /dev/hda1 or /dev/hda2, you'd get a Kernel panic error. Similarly, if you used a boot floppy from a different Linux system (one that had root on a different partition), you would also receive this error. For example, you used a Linux boot disk that specified a SCSI root partition target when your machine only has IDE.

Try changing your root target partition. On most Linux systems, you can specify this target from a command line. As an example, you could type this at the boot prompt:

root=/dev/hdx#

Here, x is the drive letter and # is the partition number. For example, if the root file system is located on /dev/hda3, your command would look like this:

root=/dev/hda3

Permission Denied

You receive the Permission denied error when you try to access a file, directory, or other resource that you don't own.

No easy solution exists for this problem. UNIX has a built-in security system that prevents you from accessing files owned by other users. In particular, you'll be unable to access any resource owned by root. To determine the file's owner, issue the following command:

ls -l filename

The results will reveal who owns the file. For example, to check the owner of /etc/passwd, you would issue this command:

ls -l /etc/passwd

Here's the output:

```
-rw-r--r--   1 root     other     467435 Jun 26 13:39 /etc/passwd
```

You can tell from this that /etc/passwd is owned by root. Therefore, you will not be able to alter this file.

If you're the system administrator, log in as "root" and alter the file. However, if you're not the system administrator, you should exercise caution. This is especially the case when you're trying to access files owned by root. The system administrator will discover your activity and interpret it as an attempt to breach system security.

Terminal Type Unknown

You receive the Terminal type unknown error when a remote UNIX system doesn't recognize your current terminal emulation. A possible reason is that you connected to another UNIX system and forgot to set your terminal type.

Most UNIX systems recognize a wide range of terminals. However, terminal support can occasionally vary. In any event, terminal emulation is very important when you're connected via telnet.

Your best bet is to disconnect and reset your terminal type to VT100, which is recognized by most UNIX systems.

To set you terminal to VT100 in bash (or sh), issue the following command:

```
TERM=vt100
```

In csh, issue this command:

```
set TERM vt100
```

Once you set your terminal to VT100, you can reconnect.

Not a Directory

You receive the Not a directory error when you try to access a file or directory but UNIX can't do it.

The most probable cause is that your target is not a directory. For example, if you try to delete a file using rmdir (or try to change the directory to a file using cd), you'll receive this error. Try using a command that works on files instead.

Insufficient Arguments

UNIX couldn't complete the command because you failed to provide all the necessary information. Most UNIX commands will accept multiple command-line arguments and nearly all UNIX programs accept at least one.

The solution to this problem is very simple: Try your command again, but this time provide at least one command-line argument.

Not Enough Space

You receive the Not enough space error when your system is busy. This error usually arises when processes have eaten up all available memory. This can sometimes occur when you share your machine with others. (For example, perhaps your box serves as a shell access box for everyone in the office.)

Solutions vary. One simple solution (although not very palatable) is to simply wait awhile. This will allow time for some of those processes to die out. However, if don't have the time to wait, you might want to search out and kill any processes that you think are stale. (Provided, of course, you can get the system to respond.)

Illegal Option

You receive the Illegal option error when you try to use an unsupported command-line switch. If you know which switch is bad, you can reissue your command with the corrected option. On the other hand, if you're completely mystified as to why the command failed, check the man page.

Valid command-line switches are always identified at the beginning of every man page. For example, the ls man page opens with a list of available command-line switches:

```
/usr/bin/ls [ -aAbcCdfFgilLmnopqrRstux1 ] [ file... ]
```

Is that an incredible list of switches, or what? You can use this to refresh your memory. To display this information quickly, you should issue the command man command ¦ head -15. This will fill half the screen with the switches but still leave you ample room to retype your command.

If you need further information, read the entire man page.

Read-only File System

You receive the Read-only file system error when you try to access a read-only file system. There's no real solution to this. Try contacting your system administrator.

The Least You Need to Know

This chapter quickly covered common UNIX errors. However, there are hundreds more. Whenever you're faced with an error message not covered in this chapter, remember these two rules:

➤ When in doubt, first check your spelling and case. These are the most common causes of errors.

➤ Always check whether the command you want is in the path. If it's not, put it there.

If you always observe these two rules, you'll often be able to avoid problems with UNIX.

Part 7
Reference

Well, you made it. UNIX, formerly that subject of awe, trepidation, and mystery, is now old hat. You can legitimately append the coveted "U.L." to your name: UNIXUM Literatum. And like any good scholar, what you need now are reference materials, the stripped-down diamond core of knowledge and a road-map of resource. Boy, are you in luck! That's just what Part VII is all about.

In the three appendixes that follow, you'll find a command reference detailing 96 of the most useful UNIX commands, enough to keep you up and running for as long as you like. There's also a compilation of on-line resources where you can find free software, UNIX documentation, and places to locate other UNIXphiles. Finally, even with all your new knowledge, you'll probably want to peruse the glossary so you can really impress friend and foe alike!

Command Reference

This command reference contains quick summaries on 94 of the most commonly used UNIX commands.

apropos

Purpose: apropos searches for manual page names.

Example: `apropos print` (the same as `man -k print`).

arch

Purpose: arch gets the machine architecture description.

Example: `arch`. Here's a sample arch report:

    sun4

Compare this command with `uname`, which is discussed in this command reference as well as in Chapter 4, "Getting In."

ash

Purpose: is the ash shell, only available on some flavors.

Example: `ash`. This starts in instance of the ash shell. (To learn more about shell, refer to Chapter 5, "Surviving Shell Shock.")

at

Purpose: at is used to time the execution of commands.

Example: `at 9:00am December 31`

awk

Purpose: awk is a pattern scanning and processing language.

Example: `awk '{print $1}' file.txt`. This prints the first field of `file.txt`. (To learn more about awk, refer to Chapter 7, "Regular and Not-So-Regular Expressions.")

bash

Purpose: bash is the GNU Bourne-Again shell.

Example: `bash [options]`. This starts the bash shell, which is an enhanced, sh-compatible shell. The prompt for bash is $. (To learn more about bash—and shells in general—refer to Chapter 5.)

biff

Purpose: biff notifies you if you've received mail.

Example: `biff y`. This tells biff to notify you when new mail arrives. (Note that for biff to work, you must also be running sendmail.)

cancel

Purpose: cancel cancels pending print jobs.

Example: `cancel 23`. This cancels print job number 23. (To learn more about cancel—and print jobs in general—see Chapter 9, "Printing.")

cal

Purpose: cal displays a plain-text calendar.

Example: `cal`. Here's some sample cal output:

```
August 1998
 S  M Tu  W Th  F  S
                   1
 2  3  4  5  6  7  8
 9 10 11 12 13 14 15
16 17 18 19 20 21 22
23 24 25 26 27 28 29
30 31
```

cat

Purpose: cat concatenates files and displays their contents.

Example: cat myfile.txt. This displays the contents of myfile.txt. (To learn more about cat, see Chapter 7.)

cc

Purpose: cc is the C compiler on many systems.

Example: cc myfile.c -o myfile. This compiles the source of myfile.c and outputs an executable file named myfile.

cd

Purpose: cd changes the current directory.

Example: cd /usr/bin. This changes your current directory to /usr/bin. (To learn more about cd, refer to Chapter 6, "Manipulating Files and Directories.")

chfn

Purpose: chfn changes your finger information.

Example: chfn (you will be prompted for changes).

chgrp

Purpose: chgrp changes the group ownership of files.

Example: chgrp users /home/bwagner/*. This gives everyone in the group "users" access to my files.

chmod

Purpose: chmod changes permissions on the specified files.

Example: `chmod =r myfile.txt`. This changes the permissions on `myfile.txt` to read-only.

chown

Purpose: chown changes the ownership of files.

Example: `chown bwagner myfile.txt`. This transfers the ownership of `myfile.txt` to me.

clear

Purpose: clear clears your screen.

Example: `clear`.

comm

Purpose: comm compares two files by line.

Example: `comm myfile.txt yourfile.txt`. This compares `myfile.txt` and `your-file.txt`.

compress

Purpose: compress compresses files and gives them a .z extension. Compare this with gzip.

Example: `compress myfile.txt`. This compresses `mylfile.txt` and gives it a .z file-name extension. The resulting file is `myfile.txt.Z`. (To learn more about compress—and compression tools in general—see Chapter 10, "Working with Applications.")

cp

Purpose: cp copies files.

Example: `cp myfile.txt yourfile.txt`. This copies `myfile.txt` to a file named `yourfile.txt`.

csh

Purpose: csh is the C shell.

Example: csh. This starts the C shell. When you start csh, you'll know it because your prompt will change from $ to %. (To learn more about csh—and shells in general—refer to Chapter 5.)

cu

Purpose: cu calls up another system using standard dial-out lines.

Example: cu 5555555. This calls up a system with the telephone number 555-5555.

cut

Purpose: cut removes columns or lines from files.

Example: cut -c2 myfile.txt. This cuts the second column from the file myfile.txt. (The reverse of cut is paste. See paste for more information.)

date

Purpose: date gets the date and time.

Example: date. Here's a sample of date's output:

```
Wed Aug  5 19:10:42 PDT 1998
```

df

Purpose: df reports free disk space available.

Example: df. Here's some sample df output:

```
/          (/dev/dsk/c0t1d0s0 ): 7471596 blocks    508254 files
/proc      (/proc            ):       0 blocks       905 files
/dev/fd    (fd               ):       0 blocks         0 files
/tmp       (swap             ):  258544 blocks      9551 files
```

diff

Purpose: diff compares two files and reports the differences between them.

Example: diff myfile.txt yourfile.txt. This compares myfile.txt and yourfile.txt. diff will display all lines that differ between the two files. Compare this with the comm and uniq commands.

dir

Purpose: dir lists directory contents on some platforms.

Example: dir. (dir performs precisely the same function as ls, but with less options. dir isn't available on all UNIX systems.)

du

Purpose: du reports on disk usage.

Example: du. Here's some sample du output:

```
66      ./public_html/assets/images
16      ./public_html/assets/auto_generated_images
6       ./public_html/assets/duplicate1
96      ./public_html/assets
38      ./public_html/html
146     ./public_html
64      ./mail
4       ./News
30      ./cig
58      ./.tin/.index
124     ./.tin
2       ./.elm
18      ./Mail
512     .
```

echo

Purpose: echo displays the specified text.

Example: echo "This is my workstation.". This will print the following message:

```
This is my workstation.
```

ed

Purpose: ed is a simple, no-frills text editor.

Example: ed. (For more information on ed, see Chapter 7.)

egrep

Purpose: egrep searches for patterns in files. When it finds the specified pattern, it prints the lines that match.

Example: egrep "I am bored" myfile.txt. This will search the file myfile.txt for the string I am bored. (For more information about egrep and other text scanning utilities, see Chapter 7.)

elm

Purpose: elm is a popular UNIX mail client.

Example: elm. This launches the elm mail reader. (To learn more about elm, see Chapter 17, "Email.")

file

Purpose: file reports the data type of specified files.

Example: file *. Here's a sample file report:

```
Mail:          directory
News:          directory
b:             commands text
cig:           directory
dead.letter:   ascii text
mail:          directory
mytester:      ascii text
public_html:   directory
```

find

Purpose: find will find files in a directory hierarchy.

Example: find . -name *gif. This will find all files in or beneath my home directory with a .gif extension. Here's a sample find report:

```
./public_html/assets/images/dot_clear.gif
./public_html/assets/images/link3a.gif
./public_html/assets/images/link2a.gif
./public_html/assets/images/link1a.gif
./public_html/assets/images/link5a.gif
./public_html/assets/images/link6a.gif
./public_html/assets/images/link4a.gif
./public_html/assets/images/now30_button.gif
./public_html/assets/images/Sun.gif
./public_html/assets/images/javalogo52x88.gif
```

finger

Purpose: `finger` will report user information.

Example: `finger bwagner`. This will pull all the information currently available on me. Here's the output:

```
Login name: bwagner              In real life: Bill Wagner
Directory: /home/bwagner         Shell: /sbin/sh
On since Aug  5 19:38:44 on pts/7 from traderights.pacificnet.net
Mail last read Wed Aug  5 19:39:09 1998
No plan.
```

(To learn more about `finger`, refer to Chapter 4.)

fsck

Purpose: `fsck` checks and repairs file systems.

Example: `fsck /dev/dsk/c0t1d0s0`. `fsck` is a potentially dangerous command. Read `fsck`'s man page before using this command.

ftp

Purpose: `ftp` is for transferring files between hosts.

Example: `ftp traderights.pacificnet.net`. This connects to traderights.pacific-net.net. `ftp` has many, many options and flags. Check its man page for further information. (`ftp` is discussed in Chapter 21, "Other Network Services.")

g++

Purpose: `g++` is the GNU project C++ compiler.

Example: `g++ myfile.c -o myfile`. This compiles a program written in C++ and outputs it to an executable file named `myfile`.

gawk

Purpose: `gawk` is the GNU free version of `awk`.

Example: `awk '{print $1}' file.txt`. This prints the first field of `file.txt`.

gcc

Purpose: `gcc` is the GNU project C and C++ compiler.

Example: `gcc myfile.c -o myfile`. This compiles the source code of `myfile.c` and outputs an executable file named `myfile`.

grep

Purpose: `grep` searches lines for a pattern and prints all lines that match.

Example: `grep ecoli hamburger.txt`. This finds the word `ecoli` in the file `hamburger.txt`. (To learn more about `grep`, see Chapter 7.)

gunzip

Purpose: `gunzip` compresses or expands files (usually those with a `.gz` extension).

Example: `gunzip myfile.txt.gz`. This unzips or extracts `myfile.txt`.

gzip

Purpose: `gzip` compresses or expands files.

Example: `gzip myfile.txt`. This zips up `myfile.txt`, resulting in an archive file named `myfile.txt.gz`. This can be unzipped with either `gzip` or `gunzip`. (Compare with `gunzip`. Both `gzip` and `gunzip` are discussed further in Chapter 10.)

halt

Purpose: `halt` halts the system.

Example: `halt`.

head

Purpose: head will output the first ten lines of any file by default.

Example: `head myfile.txt`. This will display the first lines of `myfile.txt`. To learn more about head, see Chapter 7.

hostname

Purpose: hostname will print out your machine's hostname.

Example: `hostname`.

ispell

Purpose: ispell is an interactive spell-checking program available on Linux.

Example: `ispell myfile.txt`. This will start the ispell environment and check the file `myfile.txt` for spelling errors.

kill

Purpose: kill will terminate a process.

Example: `kill 529`. This will kill process number 529.

ksh

Purpose: ksh is the Korn shell.

Example: **ksh**. This will start the Korn shell. (The Korn shell is discussed in Chapter 5.)

last

Purpose: last reports the dates and time when a user has logged in.

Example: `last bwagner ¦ head -3`. This will get the last three times I logged in. Here's the output:

```
bwagner pts/0 ppp-208-19-49-21 Wed Aug 5 19:28 - 19:29 (00:00)
bwagner pts/0 ppp-208-19-49-21 Wed Aug 5 19:10 - 19:28 (00:17)
bwagner pts/1 ppp-208-19-49-22 Wed Aug 5 17:11 - 17:11 (00:00)
```

ln

Purpose: ln makes links between files.

Example: ln myfile.txt another-file.txt. This creates a link from myfile.txt to another-file.txt. Once this link exists, any changes made to one will also be committed to the other.

lp

Purpose: lp sends files to the printer.

Example: lp myfile.txt. This sends myfile.txt to the printer. (To learn more about lp, see Chapter 9.)

lpr

Purpose: lpr sends jobs to the printer. (lpr is the Berkeley equivalent of lp.)

Example: lpr myfile.txt. This sends myfile.txt to the printer. (To learn more about lpr, see Chapter 9.)

lprm

Purpose: lprm removes jobs from the printer queue.

Example: lprm 23. This remove job 23 from the printer job list. (To learn more about lprm, see Chapter 9.)

lpstat

Purpose: lpstat reports on the status of pending print jobs.

Example: lpstat. (To learn more about lpstat, see Chapter 9.)

ls

Purpose: ls lists directory contents.

Example: ls /home/bwagner. This will list the contents of the directory /home/bwagner. (ls is discussed more thoroughly in Chapter 6.) Typical command-line switches for ls include -a (list all files, including hidden ones) and -1 (list directory contents in long format).

mail

Purpose: mail allows you to send and receive email.

Example: `cat myfile.txt ¦ mail bwagner`. This will mail me the contents of myfile.txt. (mail can also be used interactively, simply by issuing the command `mail`. To learn more about mail, see Chapter 18.)

man

Purpose: man is an interface to UNIX reference manuals. These are typically called *man pages*.

Example: `man mail`. This will summon the mail man page. (To learn more about man, see Chapter 15, "Help!")

mkdir

Purpose: mkdir creates the specified directory.

Example: `mkdir bozo-mail`. This will create a directory called bozo-mail. (To learn more about mkdir, see Chapter 6.)

more

Purpose: more displays file contents one screen at a time.

Example: `more myfile.txt`. This will display the contents of myfile.txt, one screen at a time. This allows for easy viewing of files that are longer than 40 lines.

mount

Purpose: mount mounts and unmounts file systems.

Example: `mount /dev/fd0 /mnt/floppy`. This mounts the first floppy drive in the directory /mnt/floppy.

mv

Purpose: rename renames files.

Example: `rename myfile.txt yourfile.txt`. This renames myfile.txt to yourfile.txt. (To learn more about mv, see Chapter 6.)

nroff

Purpose: `nroff` formats text files for line printers or the terminal screen.

Example: `nroff myfile.txt`. This results in a clean, nicely formatted output.

passwd

Purpose: `passwd` can be used to change your password.

Example: `passwd` (you will be prompted for changes).

paste

Purpose: `paste` merges lines of files or output.

Example: `who ¦ awk '{print $1}' ¦ paste - -`. This grabs the current user IDs and prints them in column format. The two - symbols specify the column layout.

perl

Purpose: `perl` (Practical Extraction and Report Language) is a powerful text-scanning language.

Example: `perl -e 'print "Hello World\n";'`. This will display the following message:

```
Hello World
```

`perl` can be used to make complex programs. However, these generally aren't entered at the command line. Instead, they are stored in `perl` script files (text files that contain many `perl` commands).

pico

Purpose: `pico` is a free text editor available on some versions of UNIX (especially Linux.)

Example: `pico myfile.txt`. This launches `pico` to edit `myfile.txt`. (To learn more about `pico`, see Chapter 8, "Opening, Editing, and Saving Files.")

pine

Purpose: pine is a freely available email and USENET package. (Many UNIX systems may have it, although pine is most often seen on Linux.)

Example: pine. This starts the pine mail reader. (To learn more about pine, see Chapter 17.)

ping

Purpose: ping checks to see whether other hosts are alive and well.

Example: ping 207.171.0.111. Here's a sample ping report from a Sparc:

```
207.171.0.111 is alive
```

On still other systems, ping reports may look different. Here's an example:

```
Reply from 207.171.0.111: bytes=32 time=176ms TTL=247
Reply from 207.171.0.111: bytes=32 time=157ms TTL=247
Reply from 207.171.0.111: bytes=32 time=156ms TTL=247
Reply from 207.171.0.111: bytes=32 time=150ms TTL=247
```

printenv

Purpose: printenv will print all the current environment variables.

Example: printenv. Here's some sample printenv output:

```
HOME=/home/bwagner
HZ=100
LOGNAME=bwagner
MAIL=/var/mail/bwagner
PATH=/usr/bin::/usr/local/bin
SHELL=/sbin/sh
TERM=ansi
TZ=US/Pacific
```

(To learn more about printenv, see Chapter 5.)

ps

Purpose: ps reports the status of current processes.

Example: ps -a. This prints all current processes. Here's some sample ps output:

```
PID TTY      TIME CMD
9757 pts/12  0:00 telnet
3159 pts/23  0:02 pine
9694 pts/9   0:00 sh
8463 pts/7   0:00 sh
2503 pts/4   0:00 tcsh
8102 pts/2   0:00 csh
9741 pts/0   0:01 telnet
9753 pts/12  0:00 csh
9161 pts/1   0:00 sh
```

pwd

Purpose: pwd displays the current directory name.

Example: pwd. This prints the name of the current directory.

rcp

Purpose: rcp copies files from remote hosts.

Example: rcp tigger:/home/poo/files.txt files.poo.txt. This copies the file files.txt from host "tigger" and gives that file a local name of files.poo.txt.

rlogin

Purpose: rlogin stands for *remote login*. rlogin automates logins on networks where user ID information is consistent across hosts.

Example: rlogin tigger. This starts a remote session between your machine and the host "tigger."

rm

Purpose: rm removes the specified file.

Example: rm myfile.txt. This removes myfile.txt. (To learn more about rm, see Chapter 6.)

rmdir

Purpose: rmdir removes empty directories.

Example: rmdir /mydirectory. This removes /mydirectory. (To learn more about rmdir, see Chapter 6.)

sh

Purpose: sh is the UNIX shell.

Example: sh. This starts the UNIX shell. (To learn more about shells, see Chapter 5.)

sort

Purpose: sort will sort text files by line.

Example: sort myfile.txt. This will sort the contents of myfile.txt.

stty

Purpose: stty displays or changes your terminal settings.

Example: stty *[options]*. There are a million stty options. (Refer to the stty man page for more information.)

tail

Purpose: tail displays the last ten lines of the specified file by default.

Example: tail myfile.txt. This will display the last ten lines of myfile.txt. You can also specify how many lines to display, as in tail -50 myfile.txt, which would print the last 50 lines of text.

talk

Purpose: talk allows you to chat with another user.

Example: chat bwagner. This will page me for a chat.

telnet

Purpose: telnet allows you conduct remote sessions with other hosts.

Example: telnet 207.171.0.11. This initiates a connection to 207.171.0.111. (To learn more about telnet, see Chapter 21.)

traceroute

Purpose: traceroute traces the route that packets must take from point A (your machine) to point B (some remote host). This is typically used to determine whether there's trouble on the network.

Example: `traceroute mcp.com`. Here's some sample `traceroute` output:

```
traceroute to mcp.com (204.95.236.226), 30 hops max, 40 byte
packets
 1  cisco-t3.pacificnet.net (207.171.0.1)  3 ms  3 ms  2 ms
 2  206.171.134.33 (206.171.134.33)  9 ms  4 ms  4 ms
 3  edge1-fe8-0-0.lsan03.pbi.net (206.13.29.130) 5 ms 4 ms 4 ms
 4  165.87.157.86 (165.87.157.86)  6 ms  5 ms  5 ms
 5  165.87.32.109 (165.87.32.109)  16 ms  68 ms  11 ms
 6  165.87.230.202 (165.87.230.202)  19 ms  16 ms  17 ms
 7  165.87.33.131 (165.87.33.131)  18 ms  18 ms  18 ms
 8  mae-west.nap.net (198.32.136.13)  18 ms  18 ms  21 ms
 9  207.112.247.157 (207.112.247.157)  94 ms  91 ms  94 ms
10  207.112.247.153 (207.112.247.153)  97 ms  108 ms  112 ms
11  * chi-f0.iquest.net (206.54.225.250)  96 ms  96 ms
12  204.180.50.9 (204.180.50.9)  104 ms  98 ms  101 ms
13  iq-ss6.iquest.net (206.246.140.166)  97 ms *  102 ms
```

tty

Purpose: tty displays the name of the current terminal.

Example: `tty`.

uname

Purpose: uname will get system information, including architecture, operating system, and processor type.

Example: `uname -a`. Here's some sample `uname` output:

```
SunOS wagjag 5.6 Generic sun4u sparc SUNW,Ultra-1
```

uniq

Purpose: uniq will find and remove duplicate lines from the specified file.

Example: `uniq myfile.txt`.

uptime

Purpose: uptime reports how long the system has been running.

Example: uptime. Here's some sample uptime output:

```
9:31pm up 4 day(s), 20:36, 14 users, load average: 0.00, 0.01,
0.02
```

vi

Purpose: vi is a text editor.

Example: vi myfile.txt. This starts vi to edit myfile.txt. (To learn more about vi, see Chapter 8.)

wall

Purpose: wall sends the specified message to all terminals.

Example: wall work sucks!! This will print the following message to all terminals:

```
work sucks!!
```

wc

Purpose: wc will count and display the number of bytes, words, and lines in the specified file.

Example: wc myfile.txt. This will display statistics on myfile.txt.

whatis

Purpose: whatis displays a brief description about the specified command.

Example: whatis whatis. This will display the man page description for whatis. Here's the output:

```
whatis (1)              - display manual page descriptions
```

whereis

Purpose: whereis locates files.

Example: whereis traceroute. This launches a search for the file traceroute.

who

Purpose: who displays statistics on users currently logged on.

Example: who. Here is some sample who output:

```
ldaly    pts/0    Aug  5 20:54    (usr2-3.pacificnet.net)
gabgar   pts/1    Aug  5 20:12    (pm3b-45.pacificnet.net)
uno      pts/2    Aug  5 19:17    (pm3j-27.pacificnet.net)
alijah   pts/3    Aug  5 21:08    (pm31-25.pacificnet.net)
bwagner  pts/7    Aug  5 19:38    (207.171.0.10)
```

whoami

Purpose: whoami displays your current user ID.

Example: whoami.

Online Resources

For the price, this book isn't bad. However, there will come a time (probably fairly soon) when you'll need more information about UNIX. When that time comes, you should turn to the Internet. The Net houses the world's largest collection of UNIX information, and much of that information is free.

This appendix is all about getting supplemental information.

Documentation on Various UNIX Distributions

You can never have enough sources about your operating system. This next section provides links to a wide variety of sources, including the following:

➤ Technical support centers

➤ Software archives

➤ Searchable knowledge bases and document archives

A/UX

A/UX sources are becoming more and more difficult to find. A/UX has really faded from the scene. These days, Mac/UNIX users favor Machten, instead. However, here's a list of several good A/UX links:

➤ **A/UX Glossary of Terms**—This document was reportedly generated by the Support Information Services at Apple. It defines terms that you'll encounter while installing and using A/UX.

   http://www.geo.tu-freiberg.de/docs/apple/aux/aux_glossary.html

➤ **The A/UX Software Archive**—This site houses software and technical documentation for A/UX. It's one of the few A/UX archives still around.

`ftp://mirror.apple.com/mirrors/jagubox.gsfc.nasa.gov/pub/aux/`

➤ **The AUX FAQ**—This document answers frequently asked questions about A/UX.

`http://jagubox.gsfc.nasa.gov/aux/FAQ.aux.`

AIX

➤ **AIX Public Domain Software Library**—Need a free or shareware tool for your AIX system? This site has it all.

`http://aixpdslib.seas.ucla.edu/aixpdslib.html`

➤ **IBM Redbooks**—The Redbooks collection has many useful tips and tutorials on system administration and maintenance (one sample title is "Safe Surfing: How to Build a Secure WWW").

`http://www.rs6000.ibm.com/resource/aix_resource/Pubs/`
`redbooks/redbooks.html`

➤ **IBM Technical Support for AIX**—This site houses recent (and past) technical support documents for AIX and the RS/6000 product family.

`http://service.software.ibm.com/`

➤ **The IBM FTP Server**—This site houses experimental and research software that IBM has made publicly available. Many good tools are available here.

`ftp://software.watson.ibm.com/pub/`

Digital UNIX

➤ **Digital UNIX Freeware Index at Cornell University**—This site houses links to many freeware packages for Digital UNIX.

`http://www.lns.cornell.edu/public/COMP/TEI/tei-osf-free-tblpkg.htm`

➤ **DIGITAL UNIX Online Books**—This page houses useful Digital UNIX documentation on everything from installation to system administration. (Most of the available documents are very comprehensive.)

`http://www.unix.digital.com/faqs/publications/pub_page/`
`doc_list.html`

➤ **Frequently Asked Questions for Digital UNIX**—This document answers frequently asked questions about Digital UNIX.

`http://www.eecis.udel.edu/~carver/digital_unix_faq.html`

➤ **The Digital UNIX Reference Page Directory**—This page is a searchable gateway to Digital UNIX man pages (as well as related documentation).

`http://www.unix.digital.com/bin/webman40d`

HP-UX (Hewlett-Packard)

➤ **The Advanced Light Source HP-UX Tutorial at the Lawrence Berkeley National Laboratory**—This site houses a no-nonsense tutorial to getting started with HP-UX.

    http://www-als.lbl.gov/als/als_ee/training/hp-ux/contents.html

➤ **The HP Manual Page Searchable Index at the University of Illinois**—This site provides a search engine for HP-UX manual pages. (All pages are also cross-referenced and hyperlinked.)

    http://forrest.cso.uiuc.edu/cgi-bin/rman.cgi

➤ **The HP-UX FAQ**—This list contains frequently asked questions about HP-UX. It also includes many useful tips and tricks on running your system.

    http://www.faqs.org/faqs/hp/hpux-faq/preamble.html

➤ **The HP-UX Software & Porting Archive**—This site houses hundreds of free programs that have been ported to HP-UX (everything from games to neural network tools).

    ftp://hpux.csc.liv.ac.uk/hpux/

➤ **The Interworks USENET Archive**—This site houses postings to the USENET group comp.sys.hp.hpux. (This collection dates back to 1990.) If you have an obscure question about HP-UX, you'll undoubtedly find an answer here.

    ftp://interworks.org/pub/comp.hp/

IRIX

➤ **IRIX Hints, How-To's, and Patches at Canada's Institute For Biodiagnostics**—This site houses technical documents, patches, fixes, and general advice on running IRIX.

    http://zeno.ibd.nrc.ca:80/~sgi/patches/index.html

➤ **Public Domain IRIX Software**—Links to sites containing freeware for IRIX (with programs ranging from system utilities to animation software).

    http://reality.sgi.com/employees/billh_hampton/anonftp/

➤ **SGI Freeware Index**—This site houses many useful freeware packages for IRIX.

    http://freeware.sgi.com/index-by-alpha.html

➤ **The IRIX Freeware Archive at Madness.net**—This site houses arguably the largest collection of IRIX freeware.

    http://www.madness.net/software/

➤ **The Uman IRIX Man Page Browser**—This site houses a searchable archive of IRIX manual pages.

    http://reality.sgi.com/cgi-bin/uman

Linux

➤ **The Sunsite Archive at the University of North Carolina at Chapel Hill**—This site is the largest collection of free Linux software in the world. If you can't find it here, it doesn't exist.

`http://sunsite.unc.edu/pub/`

➤ **The RedHat Documentation Archive**—This site houses everything from installation guides to system administration primers. Although the site was intended for RedHat users, most of the information applies to any Linux distribution.

`http://www.redhat.com/support/docs/rhl/`

➤ **The Searchable Linux Software Map at Colorado State University**—This site makes finding Linux software very easy. Search results are verbose, giving detailed descriptions of each software package. Here's a sample listing:

```
Title:  xv
Version:  3.10
Entered-date:  22DEC94
Keywords:  gif jpeg pbm rasterfile bmp pm iris photo retouch
Description:  graphics viewer and manipulator for X11
Author:  bradley@cis.upenn.edu (John Bradley)
Maintained-by:  jem@sunsite.unc.edu (Jonathan Magid)
Primary-site:  sunsite.unc.edu /pub/Linux/X11/graphics
Alternate-site:  tsx-11.mit.edu pub/linux/packages/X11/banjo-
incoming xswarm.tar.Z
Original-site:  ftp.cis.upenn.edu /pub/xv
Platforms:  X11 2.x with shared libjpeg and libtiff
Copying policy:  Shareware
```

In most cases, the original site will be up-to-date. However, if it isn't, you can still obtain the software. Here's how: Use the Linux Software Map to locate the filename and go to `sunsite.unc.edu` to retrieve it. Except in extremely rare cases, Sunsite will have the file.

`http://www.vis.colostate.edu/cgi-bin/lsmb/`

➤ **Linux How-To's**—This site houses all Linux How-To documents. How-To documents are usually detailed explanations on how to configure your Linux system. Typical examples include how to set up Ethernet or how to write CD-ROMs.

`http://www.linux-howto.com/`

➤ **The Linux Applications and Utilities Page**—This site also simplifies finding Linux software because the author has broken down Linux applications down into categories.

`http://www.xnet.com/~blatura/linapps.shtml`

Solaris

➤ **The Solaris Man Page Gateway at Australian National University—**
This site provides a searchable interface to Solaris man pages. (All pages are cross-referenced and hyperlinked.)

`http://cres20.anu.edu.au/cgi-bin/man`

➤ **The Sun Archive at Sunsite (University of North Carolina, Chapel Hill)**—Sunsite is the mother of all FTP sites. This site holds copious documentation on Solaris, including journals, patches, fixes, tutorials, whitepapers, and other documents likely to contain good, quick answers to almost any Solaris question.

`ftp://sunsite.unc.edu/pub/sun-info/`

General Links

➤ **UNIX Installation Tutorial from the UNIX Workstation Support Group (UWSG) at Indiana University**. This is an excellent introduction to UNIX system installation and management.

`http://www.uwsg.indiana.edu/usail/index/`
`➥install.html`

➤ **The UNIX Reference Desk at Geek-Girl**—Jennifer Myers (a.k.a. Geek Girl) maintains this site. It boasts many good links to UNIX software and documentation.

`http://www.geek-girl.com/unix.html`

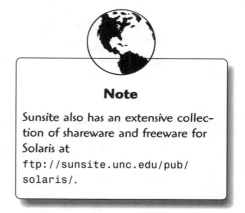

Note

Sunsite also has an extensive collection of shareware and freeware for Solaris at
`ftp://sunsite.unc.edu/pub/`
`solaris/`.

➤ **Bugtraq Archives**—This is a searchable index of UNIX security issues archived from the bugtraq mailing list. If you're going into system administration, visiting BUGTRAQ is a must.

`http://geek-girl.com/bugtraq/`

➤ **Shareware.com**—Looking for interesting or unusual UNIX software? Shareware.com archives thousands of shareware products for UNIX (and other operating systems). The Shareware.com site is particularly useful because it offers a search engine.

`http://www.shareware.com`

➤ **The Freebird Project**—This site is the ultimate archive of UNIXWare freeware. (The Freebird Project also offers a search interface to SCO's technical support library.) This is probably the most comprehensive UNIXWare site on the Internet.

`http://www.freebird.org/`

➤ **UNIX Resources Directory at the University of Texas at Austin**—This is a resource site that provides links to important UNIX information including documentation, vendors, software, and standards.

➤ **The UNIX Guru Universe**—This is an excellent place to start if you're interested in system administration. (The site authors have also designed a very nice beginner's page with many fine tutorials.)

`http://www.ugu.com/`

➤ **UNIXhelp for Users**—A simple, straightforward guide to the most commonly used UNIX commands. This is a must-see for any UNIX beginner.

`http://unixhelp.ed.ac.uk/`

➤ **The Free Software Foundation and GNU Project**—Here, you'll find dozens of free UNIX applications, including the GNU C and C++ compilers.

`http://www.fsf.org`

➤ **The UNIX Glossary at Engineering Computing**—This glossary is pretty comprehensive, and many entries are cross-referenced.

`http://www-ec.njit.edu/ec_info/home/help/Unix/glossary/`
`unixIndex/glossary_e.html`

Patch Sources for Selected UNIX Flavors

To keep your system relatively healthy and free of risk, you should keep up with patches. The wisest way to do this is to retrieve your patches over the Internet. The Table B.1 provides URLs for selected patch distribution sites.

Table B.1.   Patch distribution points

Flavor	Distribution Point
AIX (IBM)	`http://www.ers.ibm.com/tech-info/index.html`
FreeBSD/OpenBSD	`ftp://ftp.openbsd.org/pub/OpenBSD/patches/`
HP-UX	`http://us-support.external.hp.com/`
IRIX	`http://www.sgi.com/Support/security/patches.html`
NeXT	`ftp://ftp.next.com/pub/NeXTanswers/Files/Patches/`
SCO	`ftp://ftp.sco.com/SLS/`
SunOS/Solaris	`http://sunsolve.sun.com/sunsolve/pubpatches/`

USENET Newsgroups

The following USENET newsgroups center on UNIX discussion (see Table B.2). You'll find that visiting them periodically is very worthwhile. Often, you can quickly find answers to your questions even without posting a message.

Table B.2.   UNIX-oriented USENET newsgroups

Newsgroup	Discussion
comp.unix	General discussion about UNIX
comp.unix.admin	UNIX system administration
comp.unix.aix	Using IBM's AIX
comp.unix.amiga	UNIX on the Amiga platform
comp.unix.aux	Apple's version of UNIX
comp.unix.bsd	Using BSD
comp.unix.bsd.386bsd	Using 386BSD
comp.unix.bsd.bsdi	Using BSDI/OS
comp.unix.bsd.freebsd	Using FreeBSD
comp.unix.bsd.netbsd	Using NetBSD
comp.unix.bsd.openbsd	Using OpenBSD
comp.unix.cde	Using the Common Desktop Environment
comp.unix.machten	Using Machten on the Macintosh
comp.unix.osf	The Open Software Foundation's UNIX
comp.unix.shell	Using the UNIX shell
comp.unix.solaris	Using Solaris
comp.unix.unixware	Using UNIXWare
comp.os.linux	Using Linux

Online Periodicals

The following periodicals will help you keep up-to-date on the very latest developments in the UNIX community:

> ➤ **Linux Journal**—*Linux Journal* is a full-featured, monthly periodical that covers the latest Linux developments. The content is generally technical. However, articles are often written to a wide audience, including newcomers. The journal is solution oriented, with contributing authors often focusing on ways to solve common, everyday problems.
>
> http://www.linuxjournal.com/

➤ **The Linux Gazette**—I'm not sure how or why the editors chose this name, but the publication is very good. Beginner and intermediate users often write articles, explaining their trials, tribulations, and, finally, triumphs in solving various problems. If you're new to Linux, this is an excellent place to start.

http://www.ssc.com/lg/

➤ **SunWorld**—*SunWorld* is an Internet magazine that focuses on Sun Microsystems hardware and software issues. *SunWorld* is a great source of information on the latest developments in Solaris and Java.

http://www.sunworld.com/

➤ **UNIX Review**—*UNIX Review* is a print and Web publication that focuses on UNIX performance and enterprise computing. The magazine has a search engine so you can quickly scan archived issues for articles of interest.

http://www.performancecomputing.com/unixreview/

➤ **UNIXWorld Online**—*UNIXWorld Online* is an excellent source for reviews and editorials on up-and-coming strategies and products.

http://www.unixworld.com/

➤ **The HP Chronicle**—*The HP Chronicle* is a monthly tabloid that focuses on HP-UX systems. Content typically consists of upcoming product reviews and comparisons, system administration, and general interest.

http://www.pcinews.com/business/pci//hp/

Security Literature

The following documents will help you bolster the security of your UNIX system:

➤ **Securing Internet Information Servers**—This document will take you step-by-step through securing anonymous FTP, Gopher, and WWW services on your UNIX system.

http://ciac.llnl.gov/ciac/documents/CIAC-
2308_Securing_Internet_Information_Servers.pdf

➤ **Securing X Windows**—Lawrence Livermore National Laboratory Computer Incident Advisory Capability. This document will help you understand the basic weaknesses in X and how to shore up X security on your server.

http://ciac.llnl.gov/ciac/documents/CIAC-2316_Securing_X_Windows.pdf

➤ **Electronic Resources for Security Related Information**—This document will provide you with a comprehensive list of UNIX-related resources for security.

http://ciac.llnl.gov/ciac/documents/CIAC-
2307_Electronic_Resources_for_Security_Related_Information.pdf

➤ **The AUSCERT (Australian CERT) UNIX Security Checklist**—This document is a comprehensive collection of UNIX security information.

```
ftp://caliban.physics.utoronto.ca/pub/
unix_security_checklist_1.1
```

➤ **Computer Security Policy: Setting the Stage for Success**—National Institute of Standards and Technology, CSL Bulletin. This document will assist you in setting security policies in your network.

```
http://www.raptor.com/lib/csl94-01.txt
```

Speak Like a Geek: The UNIX Bible

;   A shell metacharacter used to separate commands that will be executed sequentially.

!   The bang symbol. Used in the C shell (csh) to recall used commands by their history number. (See *history*.)

$ In the C shell, this symbol is used for variable substitution. A variable assigned via the set statement (for example, set name) can be later recalled using the $ symbol ($name).

*   Used to match any character in pattern matching.

?   Used to match any character in filename searches.

@   In PERL, this symbol is used for array substitution—for example, @friends=('tom', 'dick', 'harry'). Otherwise, the @ symbol is used in email addresses (bwagner@altavista.net).

<   Used to redirect input to the specified file or process.

>   Used to redirect output to the specified file or process.

>>   Used to redirect (and append) data to a file. (This differs from the > symbol. The >> symbol appends information to a file, adding text to the end without overwriting it.)

A/UX   A version of UNIX that runs on Apple computers.

absolute path   The specified file's full path, beginning at the root. For example, the full path of csh is actually /bin/csh. (Absolute paths are also sometimes used in specifying URLs. For example, to the outside world, your WWW page could be located at `http://www.myprovider.com/~my-user-name/`, but you can also access that directory internally at `/export/home/my-user-name/public_html`.

access control   Any system that controls user access to files, directories, or system resources. (For example, you can specify that users can only access your machine at certain hours.) There are two types of access control: *discretionary* (DAC) and *mandatory* (MAC). In DAC, humans set the access controls. In MAC, access controls are written into the operating system (in other words, the machine sets the controls).

AIX   A flavor of UNIX created by International Business Machines (IBM). AIX runs on RISC workstations and the PowerPC.

alias   Short nicknames for commands. You use these to save time or to customize your system. For example, suppose you use Xdir and you prefer your windows with a gray background and black text. Every time you start Xdir, you would have to issue the following command: `/usr/X11/bin/xdir -fg white -bg black`. You can avoid this by setting an alias for the command: `alias xdir="/usr/X11/bin/xdir -fg white -bg black"`. From then on, you could just type `xdir`.

Alpha   A proprietary architecture, workstation, and processor developed by Digital Equipment Corporation. Alphas are extremely fast and capable of 64-bit processing.

anonymous FTP   An FTP service available to the public that allows anonymous logins. Any user can access anonymous FTP with the username "anonymous" and his or her email address as a password.

ANSI   The American National Standards Institute. ANSI develops data processing standards. Visit ANSI at `http://www.ansi.org`.

argument   A command-line value you pass to a program. Arguments always appear after the specified command. For example, suppose you want to delete three files in your home directory: `hickory`, `dickory`, and `dock`. To delete them, you would issue the command `rm hickory dickory dock`. These filenames are arguments for `rm`. (An argument can also be what UNIX and Windows users do when faced with one another.)

APRANet   Advanced Research Projects Agency Network. This was the original Internet.

array   A list used to store values that have similar characteristics. For example, you could create an array called `@fruits`. Inside of `@fruits`, you could store `apples`, `oranges`, `pears`, and so on.

ASCII   American Standard Code for Information Interchange. ASCII is a common standard by which all operating systems treat simple text.

awk   A pattern-scanning language that's named after its inventors: Alfred Aho, Peter Weinberger, and Brian Kernighan. `awk` is fast, lightweight, and powerful. It allows you to scan and manipulate text, as well as conditionally execute commands depending on what text appears in a file.

background   A space where programs run but hide their output until they're finished. Sometimes, if you expect a process to take a long time to complete, you'll run it in the background. This prevents the process from printing status reports to your screen until the job is done. You send a command into the background by appending the ampersand symbol to the end of your command line, like this: `grep http dtabase.txt &`. (Compare with *foreground*.)

bash   The Bourne-again shell, a `sh`-compatible command interpreter for UNIX. `bash` was created by Steven Bourne. (Compare with *csh*, *ksh*, and *tcsh*.)

bin   A directory where executable files are kept.

Bourne-again shell   (See *bash*.)

BSD   Berkeley Software Distribution. A UNIX flavor originating at the University of California at Berkeley.

buffer   An area of memory that stores temporary values.

C   The C programming language. C is often used to build operating systems. (UNIX was written in C and so was Microsoft Windows.)

C shell   A command interpreter for UNIX with syntax that resembles the C programming language.

C++   A powerful, object-oriented programming language (created by Bjarne Stroustrup) and a close cousin to C.

case sensitivity   A condition where the system differentiates between uppercase and lowercase letters.

cat   A UNIX command designed to concatenate files. You use the `cat` command to display a file's contents. For example, to view the file `letter.txt`, you issue the command `cat letter.txt`. UNIX responds by displaying the contents of `letter.txt`.

cc   The UNIX C compiler, `cc` is used to generate executable applications from raw source code.

cd   The `cd` command is used to travel from directory to directory. For example, to change your working directory to `/usr/X11`, you would issue the command `cd /usr/X11`.

CGI   Common Gateway Interface. CGI is a programming standard that allows Web clients (WWW browsers) to send and receive data.

chfn   You use `chfn` to change your `finger` information. (This is the information that appears when someone fingers you.)

chmod   A UNIX program used to change the permissions on a file.

client   Software designed to interact with a specific server application. For example, WWW browsers such as Netscape Communicator and Internet Explorer are WWW clients. They are specifically designed to interact with Web or HTTP servers.

client/server model   A programming model in which a single server can distribute data to many clients. (For example, the relationship between a Web server and Web clients or browsers.) Most network applications and protocols are based on the client/server model.

Common Desktop Environment (CDE)   A windowed desktop environment often included in modern UNIX distributions. CDE was designed to standardize desktop environments on diverse UNIX flavors. (Up until recently, there was a lack of standardization in this area. Therefore, the X Window System desktop looked and worked differently on AIX than it did on Solaris. CDE was a collaborative effort among various UNIX vendors to cure this problem.)

compress   A UNIX utility that compresses files.

core dump   This is a file left behind by a program that failed. Core dumps are used to debug the problem.

cp   A UNIX command used to copy files. You can use cp to copy files to the working directory (**cp myfile myfile.backup**) or to another directory (**cp myfile /home/bwagner/backup/myfile.backup**).

cracker   Someone who, with ill-intent, unlawfully breaches system security (or someone who writes programs that circumvent copyright restrictions on commercial software).

date   A UNIX program that prints the current date and time. (date has many command-line options to manipulate date output. Check the date man page for details.)

df   A UNIX program that reports the number of free blocks on the specified file system.

diff   A UNIX program that compares two text files and reports the differences between them.

directory   An area on your hard disk drive where files are stored.

dot files   Files that have a period as the first letter of their name. These usually hold configuration or preferences information. (Also see *hidden files*.)

du   A UNIX program that reports disk usage by directory.

dumb terminal   Usually a text-mode terminal used to connect to UNIX servers or mainframes. Dumb terminals have no disk drives or mice—they consist only of a terminal and a keyboard.

echo   A UNIX program that prints specified text to the terminal screen. For example, to have UNIX display the text "The program is finished," you can use echo, like this: echo "The program is finished".

emacs   An extremely powerful and versatile text editor for UNIX. Linux systems generally come with emacs preinstalled.

Encapsulated Postscript   A file format used to import and export PostScript language files. (PostScript is a language used to construct documents. The documents are "described" in terms of curves and lines. These values can be interpreted by a PostScript interpreter, which, in turn, will reconstruct these values into humanly readable documents.)

executable file   A program or application. When you issue an executable filename at a command prompt, the program associated with that name runs.

file   A UNIX program that identifies the specified file's data type. For example, if you want to find out what type of data is stored in /etc/passwd, you could issue the following command: **file /etc/passwd**. file responds by reporting this: /etc/passwd: ascii text.

find   A UNIX program that searches for the specified file. Use find to find files on your system. For example, to find all files with a .txt extension, issue the following command: **find . -name "txt"**.

finger   A UNIX program that gathers personal information on the specified user, including his or her username, real name, shell, directory, and office telephone number (if available). You can use finger locally (**finger username**) or across the Internet using the specified user's email address (**finger username@acme.net**).

foreground   A space in which programs run where you can see their output in real-time. For example, when you use grep to search a large database file for a particular string, you see grep's output as it occurs. Each time grep finds a match, it prints this output to the screen. (Compare with *background*.)

fork   A program flow event that occurs when UNIX creates a new (or child) process. During this event, UNIX makes a copy of the original (or parent) process. The child then continues to work independently of the parent.

Free Software Foundation   The Free Software Foundation (FSF) promotes the development and use of free software. (Free in this context refers to copyright and distribution restrictions.) Check FSF out at its WWW site (http://www.fsf.org).

FTP   File Transfer Protocol. FTP is the most commonly used means of transferring files from one Internet host to another.

g++   The Free Software Foundation's version of C++. g++ is actually an extended functionality of gcc, the FSF's C compiler.

gateway   A point on a network where two (or more) network protocols are translated into other protocols. Typical examples of such translation include TCP/IP to basic Ethernet or even proprietary protocols.

gcc   The Free Software Foundation's C compiler. (See *C*, *C++*, and *g++*.)

GNU   GNU stands for *GNU's Not UNIX*. This refers to a series of free UNIX programs written by the Free Software Foundation. These programs are free for distribution and use and are compatible with most UNIX distributions.

371

grep   A UNIX program that searches files for regular expressions or text strings. For example, to search /etc/passwd for everyone who uses csh or tcsh, issue the following command: **grep csh /etc/passwd.**

group   A value denoting a collection of users. This value is used in UNIX file permissions. All users belonging to this or that group share similar access privileges.

gzip   A compression utility. Files compressed with gzip generally have a .gz name extension (for example: mytext.txt.gz).

hack   As a verb, hack means "to write program code or to use all your knowledge and skill to solve a problem in an interesting way." As a noun, hack refers to any act that solves a problem in an interesting way.

head   A UNIX program that prints the first few lines of the specified file. You can customize head output by specifying how many lines to print. For example, to print the first 20 lines of /etc/passwd, issue the following command: **head -20 /etc/passwd.** (If you fail to specify line numbers, head will print the first ten lines of the specified file.)

hidden file   A file that doesn't normally appear in the directory list. (For example, when you issue the ls -l command, hidden files will not appear.) Hidden filenames start with a period, and such files typically contain setup or environment information. To view the hidden files in your directory, issue the following command: **ls -al.**

history   Your command history. If you use csh, you can review your command history by issuing the following command: **history.** csh will print all commands you've recently used. A number will precede these. By issuing a bang symbol (!) followed by the command history number, you can force UNIX to execute the command again. For example, if command number 33 was **ls -l ¦ grep a.out**, you can issue that command again using the following abbreviated command: **!33.**

home   Your home directory. This is the directory you end up in when you first log on. Typically, it will be named something like /home/bwagner. The home directory is allocated specifically for you.

HP-UX   A flavor of UNIX created by Hewlett-Packard.

HTTP   Hypertext Transfer Protocol. The protocol used to transport hypertext over the World Wide Web. (See *hypertext*.)

hypertext   A text display format commonly used on Web pages. Hypertext is distinct from regular text because it's interactive. In a hypertext document, when you click or choose any highlighted word, other associated text appears. This allows powerful cross-referencing and permits users to navigate the document.

I/O   Input and output. I/O can be input and output from either a computer program, a port, or a peripheral device.

Internet   In general, the Internet is the conglomeration of computer networks now connected to the international switched-packet telephone system supporting TCP/IP. Less generally, any computer network that supports TCP/IP and is interconnected.

interpreter A command interpreter or shell. This is a program that passes your instructions to the operating system. (It also reports back from the operating system when required.) An interpreter is also any program that interprets special data (for example, a PostScript interpreter or even a BASIC interpreter.)

IP Internet Protocol. The protocol responsible for transferring data across the Internet.

ispell An interactive spell-checker common to many UNIX platforms. Use ispell to correct simple spelling errors in your text files.

job Any process you've started. UNIX keeps track of all jobs so that you can track their progress or even kill them.

job control A feature of UNIX that allows you to start and stop jobs interactively.

job number A number assigned to a particular job. (UNIX identifies and tracks jobs by number.)

kill A UNIX program for killing processes. This is useful for eliminating runaway, stagnant processes. (To kill such a process, enter the command kill followed by the process number. To get a list of processes, issue the ps command.)

Korn shell (ksh) A UNIX command interpreter written by David Korn, from Bell Labs. (ksh is used on several UNIX platforms, most notably AIX.)

LAN Local area network. This is generally a small Ethernet network of computers wired together. Typically, LANs are used in small business or academic environments, where the network does not expand beyond several adjacent rooms. (However, in a corporate environment, a LAN can be quite large.)

less A UNIX utility used to display a file one page at a time. less is very much like more, but it allows you to scroll backwards.

link A pointer to a file. You can set multiple links to the same file. For example, suppose you had a file named addresses.txt with addresses in it. You could create links to addresses.txt using different names, including addresses, address, contacts, and so forth. Other users could reach the file using any of these names.

Linux A free UNIX clone that runs on widely disparate architecture, including *x86* (Intel), Alpha, Sparc, and PowerPC processors. Linux is becoming increasingly popular as a Web server platform.

lp A UNIX command used to send files to the printer. lp has endless command-line options. Check the lp man page for details.

lpr A UNIX command used to send files to the printer. See the lpr or lp man pages for details.

ls A UNIX program that lists directory contents.

MachTen Linux for the Macintosh. (See *Linux*.)

373

mail   The standard UNIX mail program.

man page   A manual page. Man pages are help files that describe how to use UNIX commands. You can obtain man pages by issuing the man command. For example, to obtain the man page on the command ls, issue the command **man ls**.

mkdir   A UNIX command that creates directories. For example, to create a directory called /home/mydirectory, issue the command **mkdir /home/mydirectory**. (See the mkdir man page for more information.)

more   A UNIX program that displays file contents one screen at a time. To use more, issue the more command plus the file you want to view. For example, to view the contents of my_address_list.txt, issue the command **more my_address_list.txt**. (See the more man page for details. Also, compare with *less*.)

Motif   A commercial windowing system and set of programming libraries used to create windowed applications in X. (See *mwm*.)

mount   A UNIX command used to access file systems by mounting them. (You can also use mount without arguments to report currently mounted file systems. See the mount man page for details.)

multitasking   In the general sense, multitasking is the process of performing multiple tasks simultaneously. (For example, reading this book and eating dinner.) In computer terminology, multitasking is the process of running multiple programs or processes simultaneously.

multiuser   An operating system is "multiuser" if many users can work on the same computer simultaneously.

mv   A UNIX command used to move files from one directory to another. To move a file using mv, issue the mv command plus the destination directory. For example: **mv myfile /home/bwagner/myfile**. (See the mv man page for more details.)

mvdir   A UNIX command used to move directories. To move a directory using mvdir, issue the mvdir command plus the destination directory. For example: **mv /mydirectory /home/bwagner/mydirectory**. (See the mvdir man page for more details.)

mwm   The Motif Window Manager. mwm is a window manager for UNIX. It has a very slick look and feel. You can create, size, move, hide, and destroy Motif windows using your mouse. mwm was created with Motif, a set of programming libraries that produce clean, attractive window interfaces.

news   This generally refers to USENET news.

NFS   Network File System. A system that allows you to transparently import files from remote hosts. These files appear and act as though they were installed on your local machine.

NIS   Network Information System. A system developed by Sun Microsystems that allows Internet hosts to transfer information after authenticating themselves with a single password. NIS was once called the *Yellow Pages system*.

OpenLook   A windowing system created by Sun Microsystems.

OSF/1   A version of UNIX created by the Open Software Foundation but now maintained by the OpenGroup. You can find the OpenGroup at `http://www.opengroup.org`.

passwd   A file located in the /etc directory that stores usernames and other user information (including, on occasion, users' encrypted passwords.)

path   The full directory path to a particular file or directory. For example, /etc: /etc/passwd is a path to the file passwd. (Also, the path variable stores all directories that UNIX will search when looking for a file.)

Perl   The Practical Extraction and Report Language. Perl is an extremely powerful text-scanning and processing language. It's often used to extract meaningful reports from mountains of plain-text data. Perl is like a combination of the shell languages, awk, and sed on steroids.

permissions   Controls applied to files and against users. For example, you can specify whether users can read, write, open, or execute files. These permissions appear on a standard ls -l directory listing on the far-left column:

```
-rw-r--r--   1 bwagner   200        66 Jun 28 23:25 cig.c
```

pico   A freely available text editor for UNIX. (pico is more commonly seen on Linux systems. However, it's available for all UNIX flavors.) pico is easy to use and has a user-friendly interface.

pine   A mail client for UNIX created at the University of Washington. pine is most often seen on Linux systems but is available for all UNIX flavors. pine is popular because it has a user-friendly interface. (Incidentally, pine stands for "pine is not elm." elm is another popular UNIX mail program.)

POSIX   Portable Operating System Interface. POSIX is a programming standard. Applications that are POSIX compliant are easily portable to platforms other than the ones on which they were originally compiled. The POSIX standard promotes development of programs that can run on many different operating systems, not just one.

PostScript   An interpreted language used to communicate with printers. Also, PostScript is a file format used to store text and graphics files. (See *Encapsulated PostScript*.)

Process   A program or job that is currently running.

prompt   In general, the $, #, >, or % symbol, which signals that UNIX is ready to accept commands. Also, any signal from UNIX that it's waiting for your input.

ps   A UNIX command for listing current processes. To list all your current processes, issue the command **ps**. To list all processes currently running on your machine, issue the command **ps -A**.

pwd   A UNIX program that displays the working directory (the directory you're now in). To discover the working directory, issue the pwd command, like this: **pwd.**

queue   A list of jobs waiting to be printed. The queue keeps track of those jobs and the order in which they were presented.

quote   Any quotation symbol, including the following: `, ', ". These are used for various purposes but most often to store values.

read-only   This refers to an attribute. When a file system is "read-only," users can read it but cannot write to it.

redirection   The process of sending input or output to another file or process. This is done with any of a series of characters, including >, >>, <, <<, and ¦. For example, suppose you want to store a list of your directory's contents in the file mydirectory. You could issue the following command: **ls -l > mydirectory**. This command lists your directory contents and redirects the results to the file mydirectory.

rlogin   A UNIX program that allows you to connect your terminal to remote hosts. rlogin is much like telnet, except that rlogin allows you to dispense with entering your password each time you log in.

rm   A UNIX program that removes files. To remove a file, issue the rm command plus the file you're removing (for example: **rm thisfile.txt**).

rmdir   A UNIX program that removes directories. To remove a directory, issue the rmdir command plus the directory you're removing (for example: **rm /thisdirectory**).

root   The super-user or all-powerful administrative account on UNIX systems.

router   A computerized device that routes data over networks, especially the Internet.

SCSI   Small Computer Systems Interface. SCSI is a data transport system used by many hard disks, floppy drives, and CD-ROMs. SCSI drives are extremely fast and can be daisy-chained together (in other words, they can be strung together using cable). Almost all UNIX workstations use SCSI.

sed   The stream editor. sed is an extremely powerful text-editing tool. Using sed scripts, you can automate text editing.

sendmail   A mail transport system common to all UNIX distributions. sendmail is based on the Simple Mail Transport Protocol (SMTP).

shar   A UNIX program that creates shell archives. *Shell archives* are strings of files packed together for easy transport over the network. These can be unpacked by /bin/sh and expanded back to their original form.

shell   A command interpreter or program that passes your instructions to the operating system. (It also reports back from the operating system when required.)

shell script   A program written in plain text that can be executed by a shell.

Solaris   A version of UNIX from Sun Microsystems, Inc. (Solaris was preceded by SunOS.)

sort   A UNIX utility for sorting, merging, or sequencing text file contents.

source code   Raw, uncompiled program code that, when compiled, will constitute an application or program.

standard error (`stderr`)   Error output from programs. This is usually printed to your terminal screen. However, you can redirect this output elsewhere if you choose.

standard input (`stdin`)   Your commands are standard input. UNIX reads commands (which are expressed in text) from your terminal and keyboard.

standard output (`STDOUT`)   Output from computer programs. This output is usually printed to your terminal. For example, when you issue the `ls` command, UNIX responds with standard output of which files exist in your directory. This list of files is standard output.

subdirectory   Any directory below `/` or any directory below the working directory.

super-user   (See *root*.)

tail   A UNIX program that, by default, displays the last ten lines of the specified file. You can manipulate output from `tail` by specifying a number of lines. For example, to view the last 30 lines of a file, issue the following command: **`tail -30 myfile`**.

tar   A UNIX program that creates tape archives of your directories and files.

tcsh   A shell that resembles `csh`. `tcsh` has some advanced features, including command-line completion.

telnet   A protocol and an application that allows you to log in and control your system from remote locations. During a `telnet` session, your machine responds precisely as it would if you were actually working on its console.

UNIXWare   A version of UNIX that has been owned by both Novell and SCO.

uucp   UNIX-to-UNIX copy. A program often used to transport news and mail across the Internet. (See the `uucp` man page for more details.)

uuencode   A file format commonly used to transport binary files over email. (Email is plain text, binary files are not. Therefore, uuencode is used to convert binary files to text suitable for transport via email.)

vi   A text editor that comes with most UNIX distributions. `vi` is controlled mainly through control keys and is not particularly user friendly. (`pico` might be a better choice until you get more UNIX experience.)

working directory   The directory you're currently in. (You can determine your working directory using the command pwd.)

workstation   A computer system designed specifically to run UNIX.

WWW   The World Wide Web. A worldwide network of computers that are connected to the Internet and support HTTP. (See *HTTP*.)

X   A windowing system (and also a networking protocol) developed by the Massachusetts Institute of Technology. X is platform independent and provides high-speed network access through the client/server model.

Xterm   A terminal window that functions as an X server.

XENIX   A name referring to several versions of UNIX, including ones owned by Microsoft, Santa Cruz Operation, and Trusted Information Systems.

xman   A program for viewing man pages in X. To start xman, open a terminal window and issue the following command: xman &.

Index

Symbols

! (filename metacharacter), 59-60
! command, 286
$ (dollar sign), grep utility metacharacters, 86
$ prompt, 40
$p command, 97
% prompt, 40
[] (brackets), grep utility metacharacters, 84-87
^ (caret), grep utility metacharacters, 84-85, 88
| (pipe), grep utility metacharacters, 85
* (asterisk)
    filename metacharacter, 58-59
    grep utility metacharacters, 84
    using with dangerous commands, 317
    wildcard, 79-80
+/ command, 100
+? command, 100
+n command, 100
-k option (man command), 202-203
. (period), grep utility metacharacters, 84
. (period) command, 97
.+Xp command, 97

.-Xp command, 97
/ directory, 68
/etc/printcap file, 121-122
/etc/resolv.conf file, 215
/etc/termcap file, 320
3270 (IBM mainframe terminals), 190
< (redirection character), 64
<< (redirection character), 64
? (filename metacharacter), 59
? command, 286

A

a command, 97, 100
A Shell, 54
A/UX
    online resources, 357-358
    UNIX versions, 20
addressing email, 225-226
    hostnames, 225
    usernames, 225
AfterStep window manager, 149
AIX
    online resources, 358
    UNIX versions, 20
aliases, X windowing system fonts, 171-173
Alpha (workstation), 13

Amaya Web browser, 241, 247-249
    Web site, 249
Amiga Window Manager (amiwm), 149
AND (conditional command structure), 62
anonymous FTP servers, logging in, 281
ANSI (American National Standards Institute), 19
API (application program interface), 248
Apple Web site, 20
applets, 316
applications
    client applications, 143
    commercial applications, 16
    launching inside Xterm windows, 175
    Microsoft applications, running on UNIX, 143
    running inside Xterm windows, 174-177
        basic command-line options, 176-177
    server applications, 143
    StarOffice office suite, 190-196
        export feature, 195
        integration, 195
        objectbars, 195
        StarCalc, 191

D

X

Y-Z